SCOTT FORESMAN ENGLISH
SECOND EDITION

ON YOUR MARK 1

INTRODUCTORY

D0341966

Karen Davy

Longman

On Your Mark 1, Second Edition

Pearson Education, 10 Bank Street, White Plains, NY 10606

Editorial directors: Allen Ascher and Louise Jennewine
Acquisitions editor: Bill Preston
Director of design and production: Rhea Banker
Senior development editor: Marilyn Hochman
Production manager: Alana Zdinak
Production supervisor: Liza Pleva
Managing editor: Linda Moser
Senior production editor: Virginia Bernard
Senior manufacturing manager: Patrice Fraccio
Manufacturing supervisor: Edith Pullman
Photo research: Quarasan
Cover design: Charles Yuen
Text design and composition: Quarasan
Photo and illustration credits: See p. vi.

Library of Congress Cataloging-in-Publication Data
Davy, Karen
    On your mark 1: introductory / Karen Davy.—2nd ed.
        p. cm.—(Scott Foresman English)
    Includes index.
    ISBN 0-201-47174-4
    1. English language textbooks for foreign speakers. I. Title. II. Series.

PE1128.D356 2000
428.2′4—dc21

99-33870
CIP

3 4 5 6 7 8 9 10—WC—04 03 02 01

CONTENTS

SUMMARY OF SKILLS

Theme	Vocabulary and Grammar	Listening and Speaking	Reading and Writing
Unit 1 **What's Your Name?** Page 1	➡ Learn new words. *What's/It's*	**Listening:** Identifying Classroom Objects **Speaking:** Asking for and Giving Personal Information ➡ Ask for a spelling.	**Reading:** First and Last Names **Writing:** First and Last Names ➡ Use capital letters.
Unit 2 **Where Is It?** Page 11	➡ Learn new words. The Verb *Be*: Singular/Plural; Singular and Plural Nouns; *In, On, Under*	**Listening:** Using Details about Locations **Speaking:** Making Introductions ➡ Check Information.	**Reading:** An ID Card **Writing:** Filling Out an ID Card ➡ Use capital letters.
Unit 3 **At School** Page 21	➡ Learn new words. The Verb *Be*: *Who/He, She, They*; The Verb *Be*: *Where/I, You, He, She, They*	**Listening:** Identifying Phone Numbers and Addresses **Speaking:** Asking for and Giving Personal Information ➡ Check Information.	**Reading:** A Narrative about Personal Information **Writing:** Filling Out an ID Card; A Narrative about Oneself ➡ Use punctuation marks.

Review (Units 1–3)

Theme	Vocabulary and Grammar	Listening and Speaking	Reading and Writing
Unit 4 **At Home** Page 33	➡ Learn new words. Subject Pronouns/ Possessive Adjectives; The Verb *Be*: Yes/No Questions	**Listening:** Understanding Family Words **Speaking:** Asking for and Giving Information about Families ➡ Check Information.	**Reading:** A Narrative about a Family **Writing:** Filling Out a Family's Information Card; A Narrative about Oneself and One's Family ➡ Use punctuation marks.
Unit 5 **What Time Do You Have Lunch?** Page 43	➡ Learn new words. Simple Present Tense: *Do, Go,* and *Have*	**Listening:** Identifying Time on Digital and Analog Clocks **Speaking:** Asking for and Giving Information about Schedules ➡ Ask for information. Give information.	**Reading:** A Narrative about a Class Schedule **Writing:** A Class Schedule; A Narrative about a Class Schedule ➡ Spell carefully.
Unit 6 **What Do You Do on the Weekend?** Page 53	➡ Learn new words. Simple Present Tense Simple Present Tense with Time Expressions	**Listening:** Identifying Days of the Week **Speaking:** Asking for and Giving Information about Weekly Schedules ➡ Make a suggestion.	**Reading:** A Narrative about a Weekly Schedule **Writing:** A Weekly Schedule; A Narrative about a Weekly Schedule ➡ Use days of the week or times of the day in your sentences.

Review (Units 4–6)

Theme	Vocabulary and Grammar	Listening and Speaking	Reading and Writing
Unit 7 **What's the Matter?** Page 65	➡ Learn new words. *Can/Can't*; *Can/Can't*: Yes/No Questions and Short Answers	**Listening:** Understanding Details about Feelings and Health Problems **Speaking:** Asking for and Giving Information about Health Problems ➡ Correct yourself.	**Reading:** A Narrative about a Visit to a Doctor's Office **Writing:** A Medical Form ➡ Always print clearly when you fill out forms. Don't write in script.
Unit 8 **What Would You Like?** Page 75	➡ Learn new words. *A/An* or *Some*; Simple Present Tense: Yes/No Questions and Short Answers	**Listening:** Identifying Items on an Order Form **Speaking:** Placing and Taking a Food Order ➡ Be polite.	**Reading:** A Fast-Food Menu **Writing:** Filling Out a Food Order Form ➡ Use a period (.) in prices.
Unit 9 **Is the Library Near Here?** Page 85	➡ Learn new words. *And* and *Or*; Imperatives	**Listening:** Following Directions **Speaking:** Asking for and Giving Directions ➡ Check Information.	**Reading:** Following Directions **Writing:** Drawing a Map; Directions from Home to School ➡ Use capital letters.

Review (Units 7–9)

Theme	Vocabulary and Grammar	Listening and Speaking	Reading and Writing
Unit 10 **What Do They Do?** Page 97	➡ Learn new words. Verb + Infinitive; *Why/Because*	**Listening:** Identifying People's Occupations **Speaking:** Asking for and Giving Information about People's Occupations ➡ Show interest.	**Reading:** A Narrative about Occupations **Writing:** Filling out a Chart about Occupations; A Narrative about Occupations ➡ Join sentences. Use *and*, *but*, and *because*.
Unit 11 **What Are You Doing?** Page 107	➡ Learn new words. Present Progressive Tense: Information Questions; Present Progressive Tense: Yes/No Questions	**Listening:** Identifying Free-time Activities **Speaking:** Describing People's Free-time Activities ➡ Check information.	**Reading:** A Letter to a Friend **Writing:** A Letter to a Friend ➡ Start a letter with a greeting. End a letter with a closing.
Unit 12 **This Jacket Is Too Big!** Page 117	➡ Learn new words. Demonstrative Adjectives; Adjectives	**Listening:** Identifying People's Clothes **Speaking:** Dramatizing a Shopping Experience ➡ Don't just say *yes* or *no*. Give more information.	**Reading:** A Catalogue Page **Writing:** A Catalogue Order Form ➡ Always check your writing.

Review (Units 10–12)

CREDITS

Hello and *Goodbye*

  1 Listen and repeat.

a.

Hello. I'm Yoshi.

Hi. I'm Ted.

b.

Goodbye.

Goodbye.

Things to Say

Things to Do

  3 Listen and repeat.

a. Sit down.

b. Stand up.

c. Open your book.

d. Close your book.

e. Look at the picture.

f. Raise your hand.

g. Work with a partner.

h. Write on the board.

i. Repeat.

Things to Know

4 Listen and repeat.

a. a picture

b. a board

c. a window

d. a desk

e. a book

f. a page

g. a door

h. a pen

i. a pencil

5 Work with a partner. Ask and answer questions.

Example:

a. What's this?

b. It's a picture.

WHAT'S YOUR NAME?

1. Hi. I'm Ted. What's your name?

Laura.

2. It's nice to meet you.

Nice to meet you, too.

3. Good morning.

Good morning, Mrs. Cook.

4. I'm Mrs. Cook. What's your name?

Laura Garza.

5. Hi, Laura. Where are you from?

I'm from Mexico.

GETTING STARTED

Warm Up

 1 Listen.

 2 Listen and repeat.

3 Work with a partner. Introduce yourself.

A: Hi. I'm _____. What's your name?

B: _____.

A: It's nice to meet you.

B: Nice to meet you, too.

Building Vocabulary

The Classroom

1 Listen and repeat.

a. a letter

b. a word

c. a book bag

d. a sentence

e. a question

f. chalk

g. an eraser

h. a notebook

i. paper

j. a map

k. a pen

l. a pencil

2 Work with a partner. Look at the picture. Ask and answer questions.

Example:

A: What's this?

B: It's a notebook.

3 **Vocabulary Check** Write the words.

a book bag	a letter	paper	a question
chalk	a map	a pen	a sentence
an eraser	a notebook	a pencil	a word

Example:

a question

a. _____

b. _____

c. _____

d. _____

e. _____

f. _____

g. _____

h. _____

i. _____

j. _____

k. _____

 **Learn new words.**

Write new words in a notebook. Draw pictures. Write sentences.

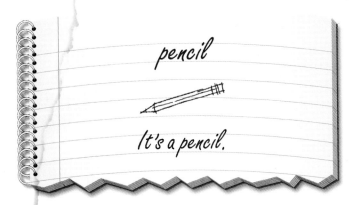

pencil

It's a pencil.

Numbers (0–10)

 4 Listen and repeat. Practice with a partner.

0	1	2	3	4	5	6	7	8	9	10
zero	one	two	three	four	five	six	seven	eight	nine	ten

 5 **Vocabulary Check** Listen. Circle the number.

Example:

8   (2)   9

a. 9   3   5   **f.** 7   6   0

b. 8   4   1   **g.** 8   2   3

c. 1   7   9   **h.** 6   9   8

d. 5   4   6   **i.** 4   2   5

e. 0   7   10

6 Work with a partner. Say the numbers.

Example:

2 + 3 =   Two plus three is five.

a. 3 + 1 =   **g.** 7 + 3 =

b. 5 + 2 =   **h.** 8 + 1 =

c. 4 + 4 =   **i.** 2 + 4 =

d. 6 + 3 =   **j.** 4 + 6 =

e. 1 + 2 =   **k.** 6 + 2 =

f. 9 + 0 =   **l.** 4 + 5 =

7 Write the numbers.

Example:

two __2__

   a. four   _____   **f.** seven   _____
   b. five   _____   **g.** nine   _____
   c. six   _____   **h.** one   _____
   d. ten   _____   **i.** eight   _____
   e. three   _____   **j.** zero   _____

8 Look at the picture. Count. Write the numbers.

Example:

__1__ teacher

   a. _____ windows   **d.** _____ books   **f.** _____ students
   b. _____ doors   **e.** _____ pictures   **g.** _____ pencils
   c. _____ desks

9 Count. Write the numbers.

   a. your books   _____   **d.** your notebooks   _____
   b. your pens   _____   **e.** your erasers   _____
   c. your pencils   _____

The Alphabet

10 Listen and repeat.

a b c d e f g h i j k l m n o p q r s t u v w x y z
A B C D E F G H I J K L M N O P Q R S T U V W X Y Z

11 Listen and repeat.

1. b	c	d	**4.** a	g	j	**7.** i	y			
2. e	g	p	**5.** l	m	n	**8.** q	u	w		
3. b	o	p	**6.** f	s	x	**9.** r	l			

12 **Vocabulary Check** Listen. Circle the letter.

Example:

g   h   (j)

1. b	m	r	**4.** l	v	w	**7.** b	f	k
2. a	o	u	**5.** d	t	z	**8.** c	k	w
3. c	f	k	**6.** i	o	u	**9.** g	q	y

Countries

13 Listen. Write the country.

Korea	Egypt	the United States	Mexico
Guatemala	Brazil	the Dominican Republic	

Example:

_____Korea_____

a. _____   b. _____

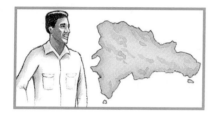 

c. _____   d. _____

e. _____   f. _____

GRAMMAR

What's/It's

 1 Listen.

Questions		Answers
What's this?		**It's** a book bag.
		It's an ID card.
		It's chalk.
What's your name?		Laura Garza.

2 Look at the pictures. Write the words. Practice with a partner.

1. A: ____What's____ this?
B: It's ____a____ notebook.

2. A: _____ your name?
B: Carol Brown.

3. A: _____ this?
B: It's _____ eraser.

4. A: What's _____?
B: _____ paper.

LISTENING and SPEAKING

 1 Listen. Circle the picture.

Example:

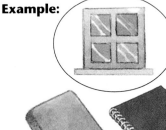

a.

b.

c.

d.

e.

f.

2 Listen and repeat.

STRATEGY **Ask for a spelling.**

Example:

A: What's your name?

B: Victor.

A: How do you spell that?

B: V-I-C-T-O-R.

3 Work with a partner. Practice the conversation in Exercise 2. Use your name and country.

READING and WRITING

1 Work with a partner. Spell Laura's first name.
Spell Laura's last name.

2 Write your name.

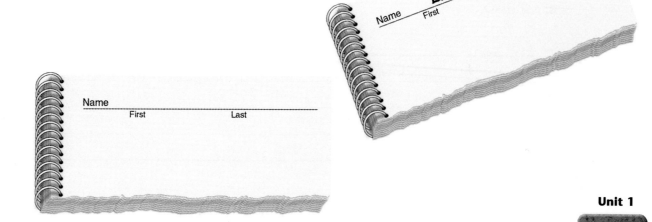

GY ▶ **Use capital letters.**

capital letters: A B C D E F G H I J
                  K L M N O P Q R S T
                  U V W X Y Z

small letters: a b c d e f g h i j
                k l m n o p q r s t
                u v w x y z

Use a capital letter:

- names: Laura Garza
- countries: Mexico
- first word of a sentence: It's an eraser.

☑ ③ **Writing Check** Use capital letters.

Example:

my name is laura. *My name is Laura.*

a. what's your name?

_____

b. i'm from the united states.

_____

c. it's a notebook.

_____

d. my name is carol brown.

_____

e. how do you spell that?

_____

④ Work with a partner. Check your answers in Exercise 3.

⑤ Ask three classmates their first names. Ask them to spell their names. Write the names.

Example:

A: What's your first name?

B: Ted.

A: How do you spell that?

B: T–E–D.

  Ted

First Names
Classmate 1:
Classmate 2:
Classmate 3:

GETTING STARTED

Warm Up

 1 Listen.

 2 Listen and repeat.

 3 Work with a partner. Ask and answer the questions.

Example:

A: Where's his homework?

B: It's in his book bag.

a. Where's his book bag?

b. Where are his books?

Building Vocabulary

The Classroom

1 Look at the picture. Listen and repeat.

d. a locker

c. a book bag

b. a table

a. a chair

e. a wastebasket

2 Work with a partner. Ask and answer questions.

Example:

A: What's this?

B: It's a chair.

3 Look at the picture. Listen and repeat.

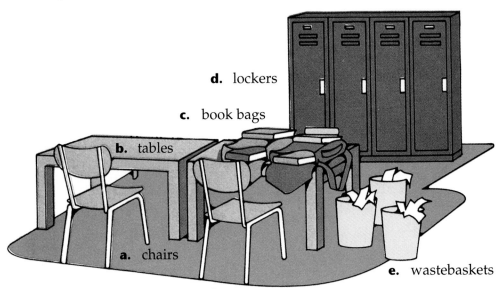

d. lockers

c. book bags

b. tables

a. chairs

e. wastebaskets

4 Work with a partner. Ask and answer questions.

Example:

A: What are these?

B: They're chairs.

People

 5 Listen and repeat. Practice with a partner.

a. She's a girl.

b. He's a boy.

c. He's a man.

d. She's a woman.

e. They're girls.

f. They're boys.

g. They're men.

h. They're women.

6 **Vocabulary Check** Write the words.

a book bag	a girl	a table
a boy	a locker	a wastebasket
a chair	a man	a woman

a. _____   b. _____   c. _____

d. _____   e. _____   f. _____

g. _____   h. _____   i. _____

STRATEGY **Learn new words.**

Write new words in alphabetical (ABC) order.

book bag
This is a book bag.

boy
He's a boy.

chair
This is a chair.

Unit 2

14

Numbers (11–20)

7 Listen and repeat.
Practice with a partner.

11	12	13	14	15
eleven	twelve	thirteen	fourteen	fifteen
16	17	18	19	20
sixteen	seventeen	eighteen	nineteen	twenty

8 **Vocabulary Check** Listen. Circle the number.

Example:

16 ⟨17⟩ 19

a. 3   13   14   **d.** 16   18   19   **g.** 14   15   17
b. 15   18   19   **e.** 10   12   20   **h.** 13   16   17
c. 10   12   20   **f.** 11   13   17   **i.** 10   11   13

9 Work with a partner. Say the numbers.

Example:

13 – 2 =   Thirteen minus two is eleven.

a. 17 – 3 =   **f.** 16 – 5 =
b. 19 – 13 =   **g.** 14 – 2 =
c. 15 – 4 =   **h.** 20 – 11 =
d. 20 – 7 =   **i.** 19 – 5 =
e. 18 – 6 =   **j.** 17 – 2 =

10 Look at the picture. Count. Write the numbers.

a. _11_ book bags   **c.** ____ lockers   **e.** ____ pencils
b. ____ books   **d.** ____ notebooks   **f.** ____ pens

GRAMMAR

The Verb *Be*: Singular/Plural

 1 Listen.

	Questions	Answers	Contractions
Singular	What**'s** this?	It**'s** a pen.	What + is = What's
			It + is = It's
Plural	What **are** these?	They**'re** books.	They + are = They're

Singular and Plural Nouns

2 Listen.

	Singular	Plural
Regular	one book	two book**s**
	a table	three table**s**
Irregular	a man	three **men**
	one woman	two **women**

3 Look at the pictures. Circle the correct questions.

Example:

What's this?   (What are these?)

a. What's this?   What are these?   **b.** What's this?   What are these?

c. What's this?   What are these?   **d.** What's this?   What are these?

4 Work with a partner. Ask and answer the questions in Exercise 3.

Example:

A: What are these?

B: They're erasers.

In, On, Under

 5 Listen.

Questions	Answers	Contraction
Where's the pen?	It's **in** the notebook.	Where is = Where's
Where's the notebook?	It's **on** the chair.	
Where are the books?	They're **under** the chair.	

6 Look at the picture. Write the words. Practice with a partner.

Example:

The notebook is _____*on*_____ the table.

a. The book bag is _____ the table.

b. The pencils are _____ the table.

c. The pen is _____ the notebook.

d. The wastebasket is _____ the table.

e. The paper is _____ the wastebasket.

f. The book is _____ the book bag.

g. The paper is _____ the notebook.

7 Work with a partner. Check your answers in Exercise 6.

Example:

A: Where's the notebook?

B: It's on the table.

8 Work with a partner. Ask and answer questions about the picture.

Example:

the notebook

> **A:** Where's the notebook?
>
> **B:** It's on the table.

a. the pencil   **d.** the girl (She's ...)

b. the books   **e.** the paper

c. the book bag   **f.** the man (He's ...)

9 Work with a partner. Ask and answer questions about your things.

a. Where's your pen?   **d.** Where's your ... ?

b. Where's your notebook?   **e.** Where are your ... ?

c. Where are your books?

LISTENING and SPEAKING

1 Listen. Circle the picture.

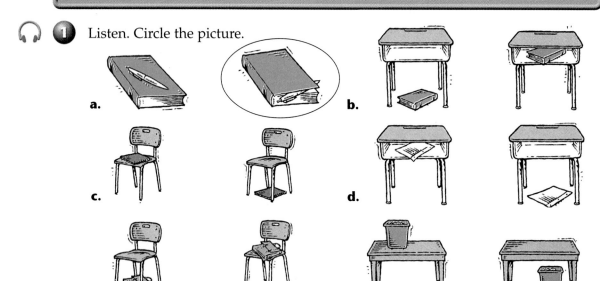

a.   b.

c.   d.

e.   f.

2 Listen and repeat.

STRATEGY   **Check information.**

> **A:** I'm Cam.
> **B:** I'm sorry. Is it Kim?
> **A:** No. It's *Cam.*
> **B:** Oh. Hi, Cam.

3 Work in groups of three. Practice the conversation in Exercise 2. Use your names and countries. Take turns.

READING and WRITING

1 Work with a partner. Read the ID cards. Ask and answer the questions.

a. What's his first name?
b. How do you spell that?
c. What's his last name?
d. How do you spell that?
e. What's his address?
f. What's her first name?
g. How do you spell that?
h. What's her last name?
i. How do you spell that?
j. What's her address?

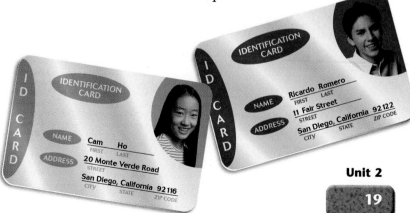

Unit 2

19

Use capital letters.

Use a capital letter:

- first names: **Cam**
- last names: **Ho**
- streets: **Fair Street**
- cities: **San Diego**
- states: **California**

2 **Writing Check** Write capital letters.

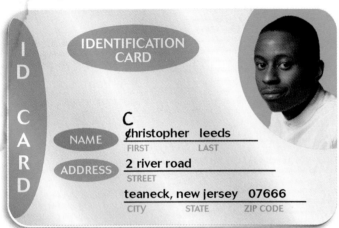

3 Work with a partner. Check your answers in Exercise 2.

4 Fill in your ID card.

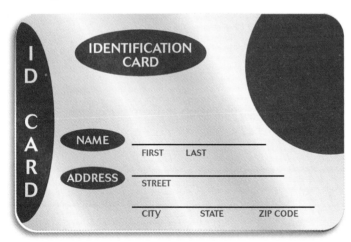

5 Work with a partner. Ask the questions. Write the answers.

A: What's your first name?

B: _____ .

A: What's your last name?

B: _____ .

My partner's name is _____ .

Unit 3

GETTING STARTED

Warm Up

 1 Listen.

 2 Listen and repeat.

3 Work with a partner. Ask and answer the questions.

Example:

A: What's the teacher's name?

B: It's Mrs. Chen.

a. What's the student's name?
b. Who's Ms. Halsted?
c. Who's Mr. Mendoza?

Building Vocabulary
Places at School

 1 Listen and repeat.

a. the library

b. the cafeteria

c. the gym

d. the principal's office

e. an English class

f. a restroom

2 Work with a partner. Ask and answer questions.

    Example:

    A: What's this?

    B: It's the library.

People at School

 3 Listen and repeat.

a. This is Mrs. Gold.
She's the cashier at Parker School.

b. This is Mr. Mendoza.
He's the librarian at Parker School.

c. This is Mr. Nelson.
He's a PE teacher.

d. This is Ms. Halsted.
She's the principal.

e. This is Mrs. Chen.
She's an English teacher.

f. This is Mario.
He's a student.

 4 Work with a partner. Ask and answer questions.

Example:

A: Who's this?

B: It's Mrs. Gold. She's the cashier at Parker School.

5 **Vocabulary Check** Write the words.

the cafeteria	the gym	the principal's office
an English class	the library	a restroom

a. _____ b. _____ c. _____

d. _____ e. _____ f. _____

6 Complete the sentences.

the cashier	the librarian	the principal	a student	a teacher

a. Mario is _____ at Parker School. **b.** Ms. Halsted is _____ at Parker School.

c. Mrs. Gold is _____. **d.** Mrs. Chen is _____.

e. Mr. Mendoza is _____.

Learn new words.

Write new words in word groups.

School

People	Places
cashier	cafeteria
librarian	classroom
principal	gym
student	library
teacher	restroom

Numbers (20–100)

  7 Listen and repeat. Practice with a partner.

20	21	22	23	24
twenty	twenty-one	twenty-two	twenty-three	twenty-four
25	26	27	28	29
twenty-five	twenty-six	twenty-seven	twenty-eight	twenty-nine

30	40	50	60	70	80	90	100
thirty	forty	fifty	sixty	seventy	eighty	ninety	one hundred

8 **Vocabulary Check** Listen. Circle the number.

Example:

20 ⟨30⟩ 80

a. 19 90 99	**d.** 45 55 65	**g.** 33 38 83
b. 60 70 80	**e.** 16 60 66	**h.** 17 70 71
c. 14 40 50	**f.** 67 76 77	**i.** 22 25 52

9 Work with a partner. Say the numbers.

Example:

$10 \times 2 =$ Ten times two is twenty.

a. $10 \times 6 =$	**d.** $10 \times 9 =$	**g.** $7 \times 4 =$
b. $11 \times 8 =$	**e.** $10 \times 10 =$	**h.** $9 \times 6 =$
c. $6 \times 5 =$	**f.** $8 \times 5 =$	**i.** $9 \times 8 =$

10 Write the numbers.

Example:

fifty _50_

a. sixty _____	**e.** one hundred _____
b. thirty _____	**f.** seventy _____
c. eighty _____	**g.** ninety _____
d. twenty _____	**h.** forty _____

Addresses and Phone Numbers

  Listen and repeat.

YOUR AREA CODE IS 727

Lee Michael	7202 Oak Moss Road	555-2678
Leon Anne	251 Shade Avenue	555-0901
Love Greg	2026 New England Street	555-4263
Loveless Tim	3705 Westport Lane	555-8876
Low Judy	414 Post Road	555-4454
Lucas Teresa	9821 Prado Drive	555-8821

12 Work with a partner. Ask and answer questions.

Examples:

A: What's Michael Lee's address?

B: It's seventy-two-oh-two Oak Moss Road.

A: And what's his phone number?

B: It's area code seven-two-seven five-five-five two-six-seven-eight.

A: What's Anne Leon's address?

B: It's two-fifty-one Shade Avenue.

A: And what's her phone number?

B: It's area code seven-two-seven five-five-five oh-nine-oh-one.

GRAMMAR

The Verb *Be: Who/He, She, They*

  Listen.

	Questions	Answers
Singular	Who**'s** he?	He**'s** Mr. Carr.
		He**'s** a librarian.
	Who**'s** she?	She**'s** Ms. Edwards.
		She**'s** a cashier.
Plural	Who **are** they?	They**'re** Ms. Lang and Mr. Sánchez.
		They**'re** teachers.
Contractions		
Who + is = Who's		She + is = She's
He + is = He's		They + are = They're

2 Look at the pictures. Write the words. Practice with a partner.

1. **A:** Who's _____*he*_____?
   B: _____*He's*_____ Mario.
       _____*He's*_____ a student at
   Parker School.

2. **A:** Who's _____ ?
   B: _____ Ms. Halsted.
       _____ the principal
   at Parker School.

3. **A:** Who _____ they?
   B: _____ Gaby and
   Carmen. _____
   students.

4. **A:** Who's _____ ?
   B: _____ Mrs. Gold.
       _____ the cashier.

5. **A:** Who are _____?
   B: _____ Mrs. Chen
   and Mr. Nelson.
   _____ teachers.

6. **A:** Who's _____?
   B: _____ Mr. Mendoza.
       _____ the librarian.

The Verb Be: Where/I, You, He, She, They

 3 Listen.

Questions	Answers
Where **am** I?	You'**re** in English class.
Where **are** you?	I'**m** in the gym.
Where **is** he?	He'**s** in the cafeteria.
Where **is** she?	She'**s** in the library.
Where **are** they?	They'**re** in the principal's office.

Contractions

You + are = You're	I + am = I'm

4 Write the correct answer. Practice with a partner.

1. **A:** Where _____is_____ (is/are) Mr. Miller?

   B: He 's_____ ('s/'re) in the library.

2. **A:** Where _____ (am/are) you?

   B: I _____ ('m/'s) in the principal's office.

3. **A:** Where _____ (is/are) David and Tina?

   B: They _____ ('s/'re) in the gym.

4. **A:** Where _____ (is/are) Debbie?

   B: She _____ ('m/'s) in the cafeteria.

LISTENING and SPEAKING

 1 Listen. Circle the phone number.

a. 555-5404	555-4505
b. 861-3670	816-3607
c. 922-1413	922-4030
d. (612) 555-1778	(612) 555-1779
e. (167) 555-0136	(176) 555-0136

 2 Listen. Fill in the numbers.

_____ Washington Avenue
Miami Beach, Florida 3 __ 14 __
Telephone: (305) 555-__9____

3 Listen and repeat.

STRATEGY **Check information.**

> **A:** What's your address?
> **B:** It's 6230 Beach Drive.
>
> **A:** Sixty-two thirteen or sixty-two thirty?
> **B:** Sixty-two *thirty*.

4 Work with a partner. Practice the conversation in Exercise 3. Use your names, addresses, and phone numbers.

5 Work in groups of four. Introduce your partner. Tell his or her address and phone number.

This is _____.

His/Her address is _____.

His/Her phone number is _____.

READING and WRITING

1 Read about Sara.

My name is Sara Brown. I'm a student at Parker School. My student number is 389-38-9983.

My address is 6230 Beach Drive, Miami, Florida 33156.

My phone number is (305) 555-2536.

Unit 3

29

2 Fill in Sara's student ID card.

STRATEGY **Use punctuation marks.**

Write a question mark **(?)**:
- questions: What's your name?

Write a period **(.)**:
- titles: Mr. Mendoza, Mrs. Chen, Ms. Halsted
- statements: My name is Mario.

 3 **Writing Check** Write the sentences. Use capital letters and punctuation marks.

a. mary is a student
   Mary is a student.

b. what's her address
   _____

c. her address is 458 main street, denver, colorado
   _____

d. what's your teacher's last name
   _____

e. where are mrs garcía and mr thomas
   _____

4 Work with a partner. Check your answers in Exercise 3.

5 Fill in your student ID card.

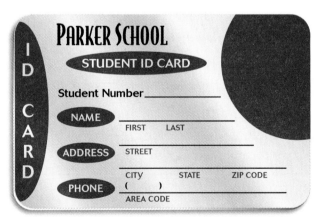

6 On your paper, write about yourself. Write sentences like Sara's in Exercise 1 on page 29.

1 Complete the conversation. Use the sentences in the box.

What's your phone number?	How do you spell your last name?
Where are you from?	How do you spell your first name?
What's your address?	What's your name?

MRS. CHEN: Hi. **(1.)** _What's your name?_

ELENA: My name is Elena Blanco.

MRS. CHEN: **(2.)** _____

ELENA: I'm from Mexico.

MRS. CHEN: **(3.)** _____

ELENA: E–L–E–N–A.

MRS. CHEN: **(4.)** _____

ELENA: It's B–L–A–N–C–O.

MRS. CHEN: **(5.)** _____

ELENA: 769 Center Street.

MRS. CHEN: **(6.)** _____

ELENA: It's 354-2901.

2 Match the questions with the answers. Write the letters.

1. What's this? ___e___ **a.** Fine, thanks.

2. Who's this? ____ **b.** It's under my desk.

3. What are these? ____ **c.** They're pens.

4. How are you? ____ **d.** I'm Danny Block.

5. Where's your notebook? ____ **e.** It's an ID card.

6. Who are you? ____ **f.** It's Ms. Jackson.

3 Complete the conversations with the correct form of *be*: am/'m, are/'re, or is/'s. Use contractions when possible.

1. **A:** Where _are_ you from?

 B: I ____ from Australia.

2. **A:** Who ____ she?

 B: She ____ the librarian, Ms. Webster.

3. **A:** Where ____ you and José?

 B: We ____ in the gym.

4. **A:** Who ____ they?

 B: They ____ the new students. They ____ from Mexico.

5. **A:** Where ____ your English book?

 B: It ____ in my locker.

4 Follow the instructions.

Example:

Draw a wastebasket.
Draw a piece of paper IN the wastebasket.

a. Write your first name.
Write your last name UNDER your first name.

b. Draw a table.
Draw a pencil ON the table.

c. Write the letter O.
Write the number six IN the letter.

5 Cross out the word that's different.

a. six	four	~~one~~	twelve
b. word	sentence	board	question
c. cafeteria	restroom	office	student
d. chair	map	desk	table
e. librarian	cashier	gym	principal
f. fifteen	nineteen	eighteen	thirteen
g. pencil	chalk	eraser	pen

GETTING STARTED

Warm Up

1 Listen.

2 Listen and repeat.

3 Work with a partner. Ask and answer the questions.

Example:

A: What's the boy's name?

B: His name is Teng.

a. How old is Teng?

b. What's Teng's sister's name?

c. How old is she?

Building Vocabulary
The Family

 **1** Listen and repeat.

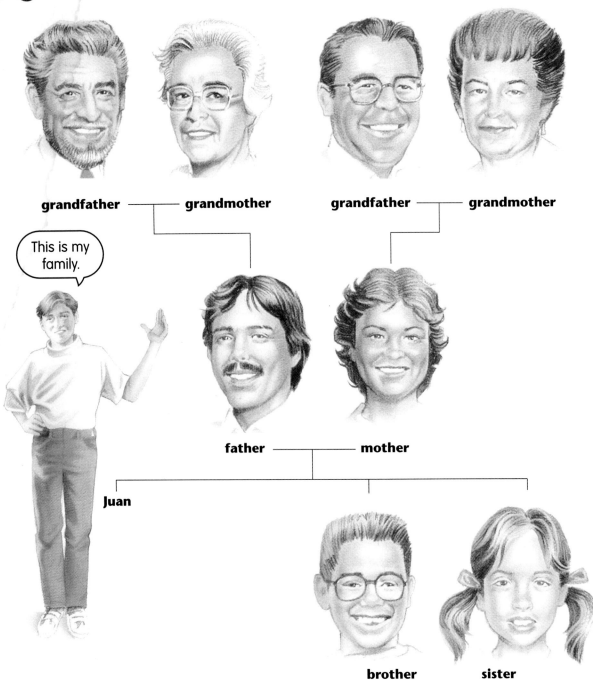

grandfather —— grandmother   grandfather —— grandmother

This is my family.

father —— mother

Juan

brother   sister

2 Work with a partner. Ask and answer questions about Juan's family.

Example:

A: Who's he?

B: He's his grandfather.

🎧 ③ Listen and repeat.

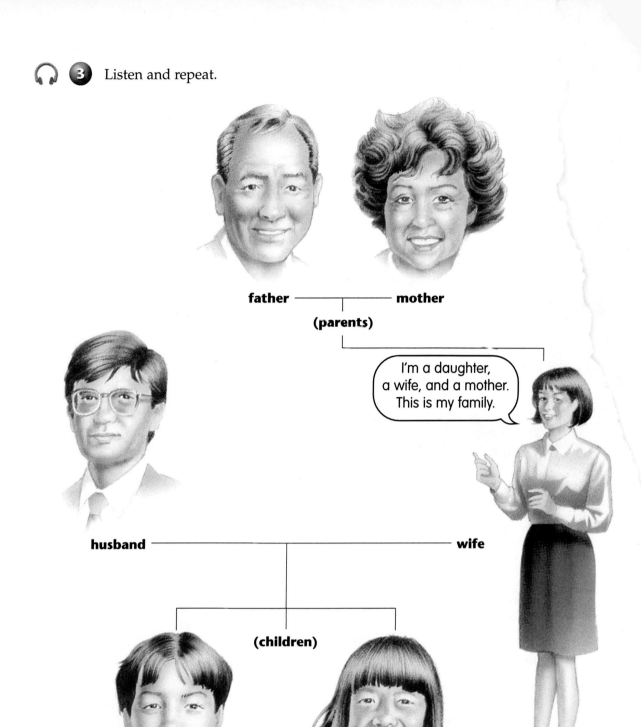

father ———————— mother

(parents)

I'm a daughter, a wife, and a mother. This is my family.

husband ———————————————— wife

(children)

son   daughter

Kim

④ Work with a partner. Ask and answer questions about Kim's family.

Example:

A: Who are they?

B: They're her parents.

Learn new words.

Write new words in pairs.

Family

grandfather – grandmother
father – mother
brother – sister
husband – wife
son – daughter

Places at Home

 **5** Listen and repeat.

a. the bedroom

b. the bathroom

c. the living room

d. the dining room

e. the kitchen

f. the garage

g. the yard

6 Work with a partner. Ask and answer questions.

Example:

A: What's this?

B: It's the bedroom.

Unit 4

 36

7 **Vocabulary Check** Write the words.

brother	father	mother	son
daughter	husband	sister	wife

I'm her son.
She's my ___*mother*___.

I'm her father.
She's my _____.

a. Barbara   Tom

b. Marcy   Edward

I'm her daughter.
She's my _____.

I'm her husband.
She's my _____.

c. Marcy   Barbara

d. Edward   Barbara

I'm her brother.
She's my _____.

He's my father.
I'm his _____.

e. Tom   Marcy

f. Tom   Edward

8 Look at Exercise 7. Write the names.

	Name
a. Her brother's name is Tom.	*Marcy*
b. Her children's names are Marcy and Tom.	_____
c. His father's name is Edward.	_____
d. His parents' names are Edward and Barbara.	_____

GRAMMAR

Subject Pronouns/Possessive Adjectives

1 Listen.

Subject Pronouns	Possessive Adjectives
I'm Tara.	**My** name is Tara.
You're Paul.	**Your** name is Paul.
He's my father.	**His** name is John.
She's my mother.	**Her** name is Nancy.
It's my cat.	**Its** name is Fritz.
We're brother and sister.	**Our** last name is Lipton.
They're my parents.	**Their** last name is Lipton, too.

2 Write the correct words. Practice with a partner.

Example:

(I/My) ___I___ 'm a student. **(I/My)** ___My___ name is Marcos.

a. **(I/My)** _____ sister's name is Jenny. **(She/Her)** _____'s a student, too.

b. Jenny and **(I/my)** _____ are students at Metro High School.
(We/Our) _____'re in Mr. Filippi's English class.

c. **(We/Our)** _____ parents are teachers. The name of
(they/their) _____ school is Parker School.

d. Parker School is in Miami Beach. **(It/Its)** _____'s on Washington Avenue.

e. The PE teacher at Parker School is Mr. Nelson. **(He/His)** _____
son, Brian, is a student at Parker School. Brian is in
(he/his) _____ father's PE class.

The Verb *Be*: Yes/No Questions

 3 Listen.

Questions	Answers
Are you a student?	Yes, I **am**. No, I**'m not**. I'm a teacher.
Is your father a teacher?	Yes, he **is**. No, he **isn't**. He**'s** a principal.
Is your mother a librarian?	Yes, she **is**. No, she **isn't**. She**'s** a teacher.
Is your last name Gómez?	Yes, it **is**. No, it **isn't**. It**'s** González.
Are you and your sister in my class?	Yes, we **are**. No, we **aren't**. We**'re** in Mr. Filippi's class.
Are your parents teachers?	Yes, they **are**. No, they **aren't**. They**'re** librarians.

Contractions

is + not = isn't	we + are = we're	are + not = aren't

4 Complete the questions with **am, are,** or **is.** Look at the pictures. Answer the questions. Practice with a partner.

Example:

A: ___Are___ you in the living room?

B: _No, I'm not. I'm in the kitchen._

1. A: _____ your father in the garage?
   B: _____
      _____

2. A: _____ your mother in the kitchen?
   B: _____
      _____

3. A: _____ the cat in the yard?
   B: _____
      _____

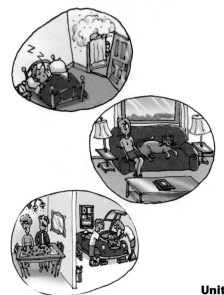

4. A: _____ your sister in the living room?
   B: _____
      _____

5. A: _____ your grandparents in the yard?
   B: _____
      _____

6. A: _____ your brothers in the garage?
   B: _____
      _____

LISTENING and SPEAKING

  1 Listen. Circle the family word.

a. Dolores is Jeff's _____.	grandmother	(mother)	daughter	sister
b. Tim is Jeff's _____.	grandfather	father	son	brother
c. Emma is his _____.	grandmother	mother	daughter	sister
d. George is his _____.	grandfather	father	son	brother
e. Kelsey is his _____.	grandmother	mother	daughter	sister

  2 Listen and repeat.

a. Tell me about your family, Carlos. / OK.

b. Who are they? / They're my parents.

c. Your parents? / Yes. My mother's name is Luisa, and my father's name is David.

d. Is she your sister? / Yes, she is. Her name is Connie. She's 15.

e. And how old are you? / I'm 21.

STRATEGY ▶ **Check information.**

> **A:** Who are they?
> **B:** They're my parents.
> **A:** Your parents?
> **B:** Yes.

3 Bring in a photo of your family or draw a picture of them.

4 Work with a partner. Practice the conversation in Exercise 2. Show your photo or picture from Exercise 3. Talk about your family. Take turns.

1 Read about Carla and her family.

Carla Willis is 16 years old. Her father's name is Elliot. He is 38 years old. Her mother's name is Sharon. She is 37. Her brother's name is Paul, and her sister's name is Ellen. Paul is 14, and Ellen is 10. The Willis family is from Georgia. Their address is 6996 Oak Street, Atlanta, Georgia, 30907. Their phone number is (404) 555-2036.

2 Fill in the Willis family's card.

CITY RECREATIONAL CENTER
Family Information Card

The ___Willis___ Family

Father's Name: _____ Age: _____

Mother's Name: _____ Age: _____

Children: _____ Age: _____

_____ Age: _____

_____ Age: _____

_____ Age: _____

Address: _____

_____

Phone: _____

STRATEGY **Use punctuation marks.**

Use an apostrophe ('):
- contractions: what's, he's, I'm, we're, aren't, isn't
- possessives: Carla's family, her brother's name

Use a comma (,):
- short answers after *Yes* and *No:*   Yes, I am. No, you aren't.
- lists with *and:*   Sally is a mother, a daughter, and a sister.
  My sisters are Gina, Alicia, and Laura.
- addresses: Atlanta, Georgia

3 **Writing Check** Write the sentences. Use capital letters and punctuation marks correctly.

a. whos this

Who's this?

b. its my family

_____

c. were from chile

_____

d. my sisters name is lydia

_____

e. my three brothers are miguel papo and harry

_____

4 Work with a partner. Check your answers in Exercise 3.

5 Fill in your family's card.

CITY RECREATIONAL CENTER
Family Information Card

The _____ Family

Father's Name: _____ Age: _____

Mother's Name: _____ Age: _____

Children: _____ Age: _____

_____ Age: _____

_____ Age: _____

_____ Age: _____

Address: _____

_____

Phone: _____

6 Look at your family's card. Write about yourself and your family.

_I am_ _____

_____

_____

_____

_____

_____

WHAT TIME DO YOU HAVE LUNCH?

Unit 5

Do you have your class schedule, Junko?

Yes.

What time do you have science?

1.

Class Schedule

Sara Kemp

Time	Class	Room
9:00	Science	103
10:00	English	304
11:00	Physical Education	Gym
12:00	Lunch	Cafeteria
1:00	Computer	10
2:00	Math	202

2.

Let's see. I have science at ten.

Too bad! I have it at nine! When do you have social studies?

At nine. When do you have math class?

Class Schedule

Junko Yamamoto

Time	Class	Room
9:00	Social Studies	103
10:00	Science	304
11:00	Computer	10
12:00	Lunch	Cafeteria
1:00	English	304
2:00	Math	202

At two.

Great! I have math then, too.

3.

4.

GETTING STARTED

Warm Up

  1 Listen.

  2 Listen and repeat.

 3 Work with a partner. Ask and answer the questions.

Example:

A: What time does Sara have science class?

B: At nine o'clock.

a. What time does Sara have computer class?

b. What time does Junko have science class?

c. What time does Junko have English class?

Building Vocabulary

School Days

 1 Listen and repeat.

a. They're in social studies class.

b. They're in the cafeteria.

c. They're in PE class.

d. They're in math class.

e. They're in computer class.

f. They're in science class.

2 Work with a partner. Ask and answer questions.

Example:

A: Where are they?

B: They're in social studies class.

Telling Time

 3 Listen and repeat.

a. It's nine o'clock.

b. It's nine-oh-five.
It's five after nine.

c. It's nine ten.
It's ten after nine.

d. It's nine fifteen.
It's a quarter after nine.

e. It's nine twenty.
It's twenty after nine.

f. It's nine twenty-five.
It's twenty-five after nine.

g. It's nine thirty.

h. It's nine thirty-five.
It's twenty-five to ten.

i. It's nine forty.
It's twenty to ten.

j. It's nine forty-five.
It's a quarter to ten.

k. It's nine fifty.
It's ten to ten.

l. It's nine fifty-five.
It's five to ten.

4 Work with a partner. Ask and answer questions about the clocks.

Example:

A: What time is it?

B: It's nine o'clock.

STRATEGY **Learn new words.**

Write two sentences with the same meaning.

What time is it?

It's six fifteen.
It's a quarter after six.

Daily Routines

  5 Listen and repeat.

a. I get up at 6:30.

b. I have breakfast at 7:00.

c. I go to school at 7:30.

d. I have lunch at 11:20.

e. I go home at 3:10.

f. I do homework at 5:00.

g. I have dinner at 6:15.

h. I go to bed at 10:00.

6 Work with a partner. Ask and answer questions about your daily routines.

Example:

A: I get up at 7:00. How about you?

B: I get up at 6:45.

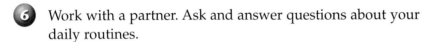

7 **Vocabulary Check** Write the words.

computer   English   math   PE   science   social studies

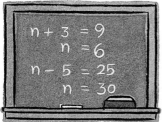

a. _math class_

b. _____

c. _____

d. _____

e. _____

f. _____

8 Circle the time.

a. It's eight twenty.
(It's eight thirty.)

b. It's a quarter to four.
It's a quarter after
three.

c. It's four fifty.
It's four ten.

d. It's nine forty.
It's nine-oh-four.

e. It's twenty-five to
eleven.
It's twenty-five to
twelve.

f. It's a quarter to
twelve.
It's a quarter after
twelve.

GRAMMAR

Simple Present Tense: *Do, Go,* and *Have*

1 Listen.

	Information Questions	Answers
Do	When **do** you **do** your homework?	I **do** my homework after school.
	Where **does** she **do** her homework?	She **does** her homework at home.
	What time **do** they **do** their homework?	They **do** their homework at 5:00.
Go	What time **do** you **go** to school?	I **go** to school at 8:00.
	Where **does** he **go** to school?	He **goes** to Parker School.
	When **do** they **go** home?	They **go** home at 4:00.
Have	What time **do** you **have** lunch?	I **have** lunch at 12:15.
	Where **does** she **have** lunch?	She **has** lunch in the cafeteria.
	When **do** they **have** English?	They **have** English at 1:30.

2 Write the correct words. Practice with a partner.

1. **A:** What time (do/does) _____*does*_____ Ellen have PE?

   B: She (have/has) _____ PE at 10:00.

2. **A:** When (do/does) _____ Yoshi have social studies?

   B: He (have/has) _____ social studies at 11:00.

3. **A:** Where (do/does) _____ you go to school?

   B: My sister and I (go/goes) _____ to Robinson School.

4. **A:** Where (do/does) _____ Sally and Rudy do their homework?

   B: They (do/does) _____ their homework in the library.

5. **A:** What time (do/does) _____ your math teacher go home?

   B: He (go/goes) _____ home at 2:00.

3 Write sentences about these people.
Then write sentences about yourself.

Example:

8:15   *go to school*

She _goes to school at 8:15._

I _go to school at 7:30._

a. 10:30   *have English class*

They _____

I _____

b. 11:50   *have lunch*

He _____

I _____

c. 4:00   *do her homework*

She _____

I _____

d. 11:00   *go to bed*

He _____

I _____

1 Listen. Circle the clock.

Example:

a.

b. c.

d. e.

 2 Listen and repeat.

What time do you have lunch, Joan?

I have lunch at 11:45. How about you?

I have lunch at 12:30.

Oh, and when do you go home?

At 3:30. How about you?

Where do you do your homework?

I go home at 5:00 or 5:30.

I do my homework in the library.

I do my homework at home.

And what time do you go to bed?

I go to bed at 10:00 or 10:30.

STRATEGY **Ask for information. Give information.**

A: What time do you have lunch?

B: I have lunch at 11:45. How about you?

A: I have lunch at 12:30.

3 Work with a partner. Practice the conversation in Exercise 2. Talk about your daily routines.

4 Work in groups of three. Introduce your partner. Tell about his or her daily routine.

This is _____.

He/She has _____ at _____ .

He/She _____ .

READING and WRITING

1 Read about Nabil's schedule. Read and answer the questions with a partner.

> My name is Nabil Jabba. I go to Parker School. I have six classes. At 8:30, I have computer class. I have math class at 9:15 and English at 10:00. At 10:45, I have science. I have lunch at 11:45. I have social studies class at 1:00. I have PE at 1:45.

a. Where does Nabil go to school?
b. What time does Nabil have math class?
c. What time does he have science class?
d. What's his first class?
e. What's his last class?
f. What class does he have at 1:00?

STRATEGY **Spell carefully.**

Some words sound the same or almost the same. Their spellings and meanings are different.

- you're   your
- he's   his
- we're   where
- they're   their
- to   two

2 Writing Check Complete the sentences. Write the correct words. Use capital letters correctly.

1. **A:** (We're/Where) _____Where_____ are you from?

    B: (We're/Where) _____ from San Salvador.

2. **A:** Is (you're/your) _____ name Cristina?

    B: Yes, it is. And (you're/your) _____ Alice?

3. **A:** What time do you go (to/two) _____ school?

    B: At (to/two) _____ o'clock.

4. **A:** Is (he's/his) _____ father here?

    B: Yes, (he's/his) _____ over there.

5. **A:** (They're/Their) _____ in the gym.

    B: Yes. And (they're/their) _____ PE teacher is there, too.

3 Work with a partner. Check your answers in Exercise 2.

4 Fill in your class schedule.

Class Schedule

Name: _____

        Last   **First**

Time   Class

_____   _____

_____   _____

_____   _____

_____   _____

_____   _____

_____   _____

_____   _____

5 Look at your class schedule. Write about your daily routine.

_____I get up at_____

_____

_____

_____

_____

_____

_____

WHAT DO YOU DO ON THE WEEKEND?

1. Hey, Emma. Let's go to the movies after school this week.

OK. Let's go on Tuesday.

2. Sorry. I have band practice every Tuesday.

Well, how about Wednesday?

September

3 Monday
library
4 Tuesday
band practice
5 Wednesday
soccer
6 Thursday
basketball practice
7 Friday

3. I always play soccer in the park on Wednesday.

Then how about Thursday?

4. On Thursday, I have basketball practice.

You're busy, Shu Li! What do you do on the weekend?

Oh, I always do a lot of homework on the weekend, but I never do homework on Friday.

5. So you're free on Friday. Great! Let's go to the movies on Friday.

GETTING STARTED

Warm Up

🎧 **1** Listen.

🎧 **2** Listen and repeat.

3 Work with a partner. Ask and answer the questions.

Example:

A: When does Shu Li have band practice?

B: On Tuesday.

a. When does Shu Li have basketball practice?
b. When does she play soccer?
c. When is she free?

Building Vocabulary
Activities

1 Listen and repeat.

a. He has art class at 10:00.

b. They have music class at 1:00.

c. He has band practice at 3:00.

d. They have soccer practice at 3:00.

e. After school, they play basketball in the gym.

f. After school, he plays baseball in the park.

g. On the weekend, he goes to the shopping mall.

h. On the weekend, they go to the movies.

2 Work with a partner. Ask and answer questions.

Examples:

A: What does he do at 10:00?

B: He has art class.

A: What do they do after school?

B: They _____.

Days of the Week

 3 Listen and repeat.

Sunday	Monday	Tuesday	Wednesday	Thursday	Friday	Saturday

4 Work with a partner. Ask and answer the questions.

Examples:

A: What day comes before Tuesday?   **A:** What day comes after Monday?

B: Monday comes before Tuesday.   **B:** Tuesday comes after Monday.

a. What day comes before Friday?   **d.** What day comes after Saturday?

b. What day comes before Saturday?   **e.** What day comes after Friday?

c. What day comes after Tuesday?   **f.** What day comes before Monday?

Times of the Day

 5 Listen and repeat.

morning

afternoon

evening

night

 Learn new words.

Write the short forms of words.

Days of the Week	Short Forms
Monday	Mon.
Tuesday	Tues.
Wednesday	Wed.
Thursday	Thurs.
Friday	Fri.
Saturday	Sat.
Sunday	Sun.

6 **Vocabulary Check** Write sentences.

in art class	at band practice	at baseball practice	at basketball practice
at the movies	in music class	at the shopping mall	at soccer practice

a. *They're at the movies.*

b. _____

c. _____

d. _____

e. _____

f. _____

g. _____

h. _____

7 Write the words.

a. M<u>onday</u>, T_____, W_____,
T_____, and F_____ are weekdays.

b. S_____ and S_____ are the weekend.

8 Work with a partner. Look at Pedro's schedule. Ask and answer questions.

Example:

A: What does Pedro do on Monday morning?

B: He has soccer practice.

Monday	
morning	have soccer practice
afternoon	
night	do homework

Tuesday	
morning	go to English class
afternoon	have lunch with Connie
night	go to the library

Wednesday	
morning	do homework
afternoon	play basketball in the park
night	

Thursday	
morning	go to English class
afternoon	have lunch with Sally
night	go to the movies

Friday	
morning	do homework
afternoon	have soccer practice
night	go to the mall

Simple Present Tense

  **1** Listen.

I **work** at the mall after school.

We **eat** breakfast before school.

You **read** the newspaper on Saturday.

You **listen** to music after school.

He **studies** every day.

They **write** letters on Sunday.

She **watches** TV every weekend.

2 Write the correct words. Practice with a partner.

   a. Lucia and I **(play/plays)** _____play_____ soccer every Saturday.

   b. Lucia's brother Alex **(play/plays)** _____ basketball on Monday and Wednesday.

   c. We **(eat/eats)** _____ lunch in the cafeteria every day.

   d. Lucia **(study/studies)** _____ art after school on Tuesday.

   e. You **(listen/listens)** _____ to music every day.

   f. Alex and Lucia **(write/writes)** _____ letters on Sunday afternoon.

   g. Their parents **(watch/watches)** _____ TV on Sunday night.

   h. I **(study/studies)** _____ on Sunday night.

Simple Present Tense with Time Expressions

🎧 **3** Listen.

> **In**
>
> I go to school **in the morning.**   I do homework **in the evening.**
>
> I go home **in the afternoon.**
>
> **At**
>
> He has band practice **at 3:00.**   He has basketball practice **at night.**
>
> **On**
>
> We have English class **on Monday and Friday afternoons.**
>
> We do homework **on the weekend.**
>
> **Always/Never**
>
> They **always** play baseball in the park.   They **never** play baseball in the street.

4 Complete the conversations. Write *at*, *in*, or *on*. Practice with a partner.

1. A: What do you do ___on___ Friday?

   B: _____ the morning, I have English class. _____ the afternoon, I work. _____ the evening, I eat dinner with my family.

2. A: What do you do _____ night?

   B: _____ weekdays, I do homework. _____ the weekend, I go to the movies or watch TV.

3. A: What time do you get up _____ the weekend?

   B: _____ Saturday, I get up _____ 8:00. I have soccer practice _____ 9:00. _____ Sunday, I get up at 10:00.

5 Complete the sentences about yourself. Write *always* or *never*.

a. I _____ study in the library.

b. I _____ play soccer in the park.

c. I _____ go to the movies on the weekend.

d. My classmates and I _____ have math class in the morning.

e. Our English teacher _____ writes new words on the board.

f. I _____ do homework in the morning.

LISTENING and SPEAKING

 1 Listen. Circle the days.

Example:

| (Mon.) | Tues. | (Wed.) | Thurs. | Fri. | Sat. | Sun. |

a. Mon.   Tues.   Wed.   Thurs.   Fri.   Sat.   Sun.

b. Mon.   Tues.   Wed.   Thurs.   Fri.   Sat.   Sun.

c. Mon.   Tues.   Wed.   Thurs.   Fri.   Sat.   Sun.

d. Mon.   Tues.   Wed.   Thurs.   Fri.   Sat.   Sun.

e. Mon.   Tues.   Wed.   Thurs.   Fri.   Sat.   Sun.

 2 Listen and repeat.

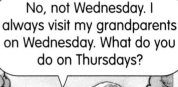

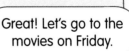

STRATEGY **Make a suggestion.**

A: Let's go to the movies this week.

B: OK. How about Tuesday?

3 Work with a partner. Practice the conversation in Exercise 2. Make a suggestion, and talk about your weekly schedule.

Unit 6

60

READING and WRITING

 Read about Ayo's busy week. Answer the questions with a partner.

My name is Ayo Sinaba. I have a busy schedule. On Monday, I have band practice. I play soccer on Tuesday and Thursday. I study art on Wednesday. On Friday, I have baseball practice. On Saturday morning, I play baseball in the park. In the afternoon, I go to the movies. I do homework and write letters on Sunday.

a. What's Ayo's last name?
b. What does he do on Monday?
c. When does he play soccer?
d. What does he study on Wednesday?
e. What does he do on Friday?
f. Where does he go on Saturday morning?
g. What does he do on Saturday afternoon?
h. What does he do on Sunday?

STRATEGY ▶ **Use days of the week or times of the day in your sentences.**

Use them at the beginning. Note the comma.

> On Monday, I have band practice.
> At 6:00, I have dinner.

Use them at the end.

> I play baseball on Tuesday.
> I have dinner at 6:00.

  Writing Check Write the sentences in a different way. Use capital letters and punctuation correctly.

a. I always go to the mall on the weekend.
   On the weekend, I always go to the mall.
   _____

b. My brother and I play baseball on Sunday morning.
   _____
   _____

c. On weekdays, we go to school.
   _____
   _____

d. My mother has English class on Monday, Wednesday, and Friday.
   _____
   _____

e. My family watches television in the evening.
   _____
   _____

Unit 6

61

3 Work with a partner. Check your answers in Exercise 2.

4 Write the days of the week. Then fill in your schedule for the week.

5 Write about your weekly routine.

On Monday, I _____

_____

_____

_____

_____

_____

_____

_____

_____

_____

1 Complete the conversation with the correct form of *be*: *'m/am*, *'re/are*, or *'s/is*. Use contractions when possible. Use capital letters correctly.

JUAN: Hi. (1.) _Are_ you Mandy?
MANDY: Yes, I (2.) ____.
JUAN: (3.) ____ your last name Scott, Mandy?
MANDY: Yes, it (4.) ____.
JUAN: (5.) ____ your parents teachers here?
MANDY: Yes, they (6.) ____. My mother (7.) ____ the PE teacher, and my father (8.) ____ a science teacher.
JUAN: (9.) ____ your brother and sister at this school, too?
MANDY: No, they (10.) ____ not. They (11.) ____ students at Washington School.

2 Write sentences with the same meanings.

a. I'm Rachel. — *My name is Rachel.*
b. They're Al and Matt. — _____
c. _____ — Her name is Sarah.
d. He's Bobby. — _____
e. _____ — Our names are Bruce and Alice.
f. You're Mona. — _____
g. _____ — Its name is Frisky.

3 Complete the story with the correct simple present form of the verbs in parentheses.

My family and I (1. have) _have_ a very busy week. My parents (2. get up) _____ at 6:00. My sister (3. get up) _____ at 6:30, and I (4. get up) _____ at 7:00. We (5. have) _____ breakfast at 7:30. My father (6. go) _____ to work at 8:00. He (7. work) _____ at the mall. My sister and I (8. go) _____ to school at 8:15. My mother (9. work) _____ at home.

After school, my sister (10. go) _____ to band practice, and I (11. play) _____ basketball. We (12. go) _____ home at 4:30. I (13. do) _____ my homework in the living room, and my sister (14. study) _____ in her bedroom. We (15. have) _____ dinner at 6:30. After dinner, my parents (16. watch) _____ TV, my sister (17. listen) _____ to music, and I (18. play) _____ basketball.

4 Complete the questions with *What, What time, When,* or *Where.*

1. **A:** _____When_____ do you have English class?
   B: Monday, Wednesday, and Friday at 2:15.

2. **A:** _____ does your family have dinner?
   B: At 6:00.

3. **A:** _____ do you study?
   B: I always do my homework in the library.

4. **A:** _____ do you do your homework?
   B: I always do my homework after dinner.

5. **A:** _____ do you do after school?
   B: I have band practice.

5 Complete the sentences with *at, in,* or *on.* Use capital letters correctly.

a. At our school, we have PE class **(1.)** _in_ the morning. My class has PE **(2.)** _____ 9:30, and my sister's class has PE **(3.)** _____ 10:15. **(4.)** _____ the afternoon, we play sports in the gym. We go home **(5.)** _____ 4:00. **(6.)** _____ the weekend, we play sports in the park.

b. My father works **(1.)** _____ night. He goes to work **(2.)** _____ Monday, Wednesday, and Friday. **(3.)** _____ Tuesday and Thursday, my mother and father study English. My father has class **(4.)** _____ the morning, and my mother has class **(5.)** _____ the afternoon.

6 Answer the questions. Write sentences.

a. What do you do BEFORE school?

_____

_____

b. What do you do AFTER school?

_____

_____

c. What do you ALWAYS do on the weekend?

_____

_____

GETTING STARTED

Warm Up

 1 Listen.

 2 Listen and repeat.

 3 Work with a partner. Ask and answer the questions.

    a. How does Kenji feel?

    b. What does Dr. Martin look at?

    c. What's Kenji's temperature?

    d. Where can Kenji get the medicine?

Building Vocabulary
Feelings

 1 Listen and repeat.

Dean

Tom

Althea

a. great

b. terrible

c. happy

Lily

Patty

Darryl

d. sad

e. sick

f. hungry

Nell

Chen

g. thirsty

h. tired

2 Work with a partner. Ask and answer questions.

Example:

A: How does Dean feel?

B: He feels great.

Unit 7

66

Parts of the Body

  Listen and repeat.

a. finger
b. hand
c. right arm
d. left arm
e. throat
f. head
g. back
h. leg
i. stomach
j. toe
k. foot

 Work with a partner. Pretend you don't feel well. Take turns asking, "What's the matter?" and answering.

Examples:

A: What's the matter?
B: My throat hurts.

A: What's the matter?
B: My left leg hurts.

Health Problems

5 Listen and repeat.

I have a   **headache.**
                stomachache.
                backache.

I have a   **sore throat.**
                sore finger.
                sore foot.
                sore arm.
                sore toe.

6 Work with a partner. Pretend a part of your body hurts.
Your partner guesses your problem.

Examples:

A: You have a sore finger.

B: That's right.

A: You have a
    stomachache.

B: No. I have
    a backache.

STRATEGY **Learn new words.**

Write compound words. A compound word is made from two or more
words.

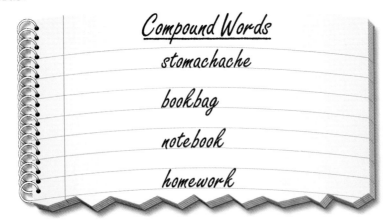

Compound Words

stomachache

bookbag

notebook

homework

Vocabulary Check Write the words.

arm	finger	hand	left leg	stomach	toe
back	foot	head	right leg	throat	

a. _____
b. _____
c. _____
d. _____
e. _____
f. _____
g. _____
h. _____
i. _____
j. _____
k. _____

a.	*throat*	**e.**	_____	**i.**	_____
b.	_____	**f.**	_____	**j.**	_____
c.	_____	**g.**	_____	**k.**	_____
d.	_____	**h.**	_____		

8 Write the word or words that mean the same. Use *sore* or *-ache*.

Example:

My throat hurts. = I have a ___sore throat___ .

a. Rodolfo's stomach hurts. = He has a _____ .
b. Keiko's head hurts. = She has a _____ .
c. Fred's arm hurts. = He has a _____ .
d. Kareen's back hurts. = He has a _____ .
e. Jane's foot hurts. = She has a _____ .
f. Kim's toe hurts. = She has a _____ .

9 Write sentences about the people.
Use the words in the box.

great	hungry	sick	thirsty
happy	sad	terrible	tired

a. *She feels terrible.*

b. _____

c. _____

d. _____

e. _____

f. _____

g. _____

h. _____

GRAMMAR

Can/Can't

1 Listen.

I **can walk** on my hands.

She **can cook**.

They **can swim**.

I **can't speak** Spanish.

Buenos días. ?

He **can't drive**.

We **can't sing**.

Contraction

cannot = **can't**

2 Look at the pictures. Complete the sentences. Use *can* or *can't* with the words.

a. run
   She ___*can't run*___.

b. play basketball
   They _____.

c. ride a bike
   He _____.

d. swim
   He _____.

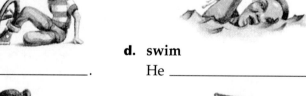

e. read
   She _____.

f. write
   She _____.

Unit 7

71

Can/Can't: Yes/No Questions and Short Answers

3 Listen.

Questions	Answers
Can you **speak** English?	Yes, I **can**.
	No, I **can't**.
Can she **play** the guitar?	Yes, she **can**.
	No, she **can't**.

4 What can you do? Write a check (✓) on the line.
Write another activity you can do.

		I can …	My partner can …
a.	speak Spanish	_____	_____
b.	play the guitar	_____	_____
c.	ride a bike	_____	_____
d.	swim	_____	_____
e.	use a computer	_____	_____
f.	say the English alphabet	_____	_____
g.	cook	_____	_____
h.	drive	_____	_____
i.	_____	_____	_____

5 Work with a partner. What can your partner do?
Ask questions from Exercise 4 and write a check (✓) on the line.

Examples:

A: Can you speak Spanish?

B: No, I can't.

A: Can you play the guitar?

A: Yes, I can.

6 Tell the class about your partner.

Example:

_____ can't speak Spanish.

He/She can play the guitar.

LISTENING and SPEAKING

1 Listen. Circle the correct word.

a. Sam is _____.	hungry	thirsty
b. Maria has a _____.	headache	stomachache
c. Grace is _____.	sad	sick
d. Ed is _____.	sick	tired
e. Bob feels _____.	terrible	great
f. Barbara has a _____.	sore throat	sore toe

2 Listen and repeat.

STRATEGY **Correct yourself.**

A: What's the matter?

B: I have a throatache.

A: A throatache?

B: Oh, I'm sorry. I mean a sore throat.

3 Work with a partner. Practice the conversation in Exercise 2.

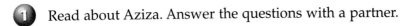

READING and WRITING

1 Read about Aziza. Answer the questions with a partner.

Aziza Hassad can't go to school today because she has a stomachache. She's at the doctor's office. The nurse is filling out a medical form for her. Aziza lives in Detroit, Michigan. Her ZIP Code is 48210. Her street address is 364 Lincoln Street. Her phone number is (313) 555-8902. Her father's name is Ali Hassad, and her mother's name is Huda Hassad.

a. Is Aziza in school today?

b. Where is she?

c. Who is with her?

d. What's the matter with Aziza?

2 Fill out the medical form about Aziza.

MEDICAL FORM

Name: _____
         Last   First

Address: _____
         Street

_____
         City   State   ZIP Code

Phone: (_____) _____
      Area Code

Father's Name: _____ Mother's Name: _____

Reason for seeing the doctor: _____

STRATEGY **Always print clearly when you fill out forms. Don't write in script.**

Name: *Hassad*   *Aziza*
      Last   First

Name: ~~Hassad~~   ~~Aziza~~
      Last   First

3 **Writing Check** Fill out the medical form about yourself. Print clearly.

4 Work with a partner. Check your form.

5 On your paper, write about yourself. Use the information in your medical form.

MEDICAL FORM

Name: _____
         Last   First

Address: _____
         Street

_____
         City   State   ZIP Code

Phone: (_____) _____
      Area Code

Father's Name: _____ Mother's Name: _____

Reason for seeing the doctor: _____

WHAT WOULD YOU LIKE?

Unit 8

Hi. Can I help you?

Yes. I'd like a chicken sandwich and a small order of fries, please.

hamburger	$1.99
cheeseburger	2.29
chicken sandwich	1.89
french fries large	1.15
small	.95
carton of milk	.55
bottle of apple juice	.55

Would you like anything to drink?

A carton of milk, please.

OK. That's $3.39.

1.

2.

And what would you like?

I'd like a cheeseburger and a large order of fries.

Would you like anything to drink?

No, thanks.

That will be $3.44.

3.

4.

GETTING STARTED

Warm Up

 1 Listen.

 2 Listen and repeat.

3 Work with a partner. Ask and answer the questions.
 a. What would the girl like to eat?
 b. What would she like to drink?
 c. What would the boy like?

Unit 8

75

Building Vocabulary

Fast Food

  1 Listen and repeat.

2 Work in groups of three. Ask and answer questions. Take turns.

Examples:

A: What would you like?

B: I'd like a large hot dog.

A: What would you like?

C: I'd like a cheeseburger with fries and a small green salad.

More Fast Food (Amounts)

 3 Listen and repeat.

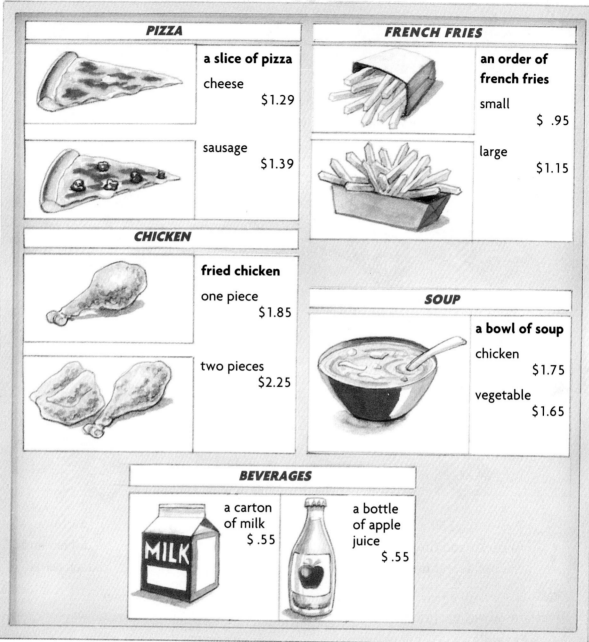

PIZZA

a slice of pizza

cheese
$1.29

sausage
$1.39

FRENCH FRIES

an order of french fries

small
$ .95

large
$1.15

CHICKEN

fried chicken

one piece
$1.85

two pieces
$2.25

SOUP

a bowl of soup

chicken
$1.75

vegetable
$1.65

BEVERAGES

a carton of milk
$ .55

a bottle of apple juice
$ .55

4 Work in groups of three. Order from the menu. Take turns.

Examples:

A: Can I help you?

B: Yes. I want a slice of cheese pizza, please. Oh, and a bottle of apple juice.

A: Can I help you?

C: Yes. I'd like two pieces of fried chicken and a large order of french fries. Oh, and a carton of milk.

Money

 Listen and repeat.

$ .01/1¢	**$ .02/2¢**	**$ .05/5¢**	**$ .10/10¢**	**$ .25/25¢**
one cent	two cents	five cents	ten cents	twenty-five cents

$1.00	**$2.00**	**$5.00**	**$10.00**	**$20.00**
a dollar	two dollars	five dollars	ten dollars	twenty dollars
one dollar				

$1.50	**$2.75**	**$5.16**
a dollar and fifty cents	two dollars and	five dollars and
one dollar and fifty cents	seventy-five cents	sixteen cents

6 Work with a partner. Look at the menu on page 76. Ask and answer
questions about the prices.

Example:

A: How much is a large hot dog?

B: A dollar and fifty-nine cents.

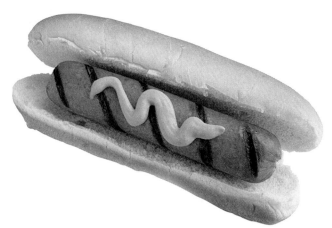

apple juice	french fries	a green salad	pizza	soup
a cheeseburger	fried chicken	a hot dog	a sandwich	

a. _____

b. _____

c. _____

d. _____

e. _____

f. _____

g. _____

h. _____

i. _____

8 Complete the sentences. Write the correct words.

    a. I'd like a **(slice/bowl)** _____bowl_____ of soup.

    b. Would you like a **(carton/piece)** _____ of milk?

    c. We want a **(bottle/bowl)** _____ of apple juice.

    d. Do you want a small **(order/slice)** _____ of pizza?

    e. Would you like a large **(order/bottle)** _____ of french fries?

    f. I'd like two **(pieces/bowls)** _____ of fried chicken.

9 Match the prices with the pictures. Write the numbers.

    a. $3.00 __3__

    b. $5.46 _____

    c. $2.72 _____

    d. $5.33 _____

    e. $2.01 _____

    f. $3.25 _____

    g. $3.10 _____

1.
2.
3.
4.
5.
6.
7.

10 Work with a partner. Look at the menu on page 77. Ask and answer questions about the prices.

Example:

A: How much is a slice of cheese pizza?

B: One dollar and twenty-nine cents.

Look at the menu on page 77.

STRATEGY **Learn new words.**

Add words for things you like.

Drinks
apple juice   my favorite:
milk   orange juice
Pizza
cheese pizza   my favorite:
sausage pizza   vegetable pizza
Soup
chicken soup   my favorite:
vegetable soup   tomato soup

GRAMMAR

A/An or Some

 1 Listen.

> I'd like **a** hot dog.   I'd like **some** hot dogs.
>
> **a** hamburger.   **some** milk.
>
> **a** sandwich.   **some** juice.
>
> **an** apple.   **some** soup.
>
> I'd like **a** cheeseburger and **some** french fries.
>
> **a** slice of pizza and **a** piece of fried chicken.
>
> **an** apple and **some** cheese, please.
>
> **some** fried chicken and **some** juice.

2 Work with a partner.
Make conversations.

Example:

hot dog/milk

A: What would you like?

B: I'd like a hot dog and some milk, please.

a. sandwich/french fries
b. chicken soup/apple
c. slice of pizza/bottle of apple juice
d. piece of fried chicken/order of french fries
e. juice/bowl of vegetable soup
f. pizza/milk

 3 Work with a partner.
Make conversations.

Example:

A: pizza?

A: Would you like some pizza?

B: small salad

B: No, thanks. I'd like a small salad.

1. **A:** fried chicken?   3. **A:** hamburger?
   B: hot dog   **B:** cheeseburger

2. **A:** chicken soup?   4. **A:** juice?
   B: vegetable soup   **B:** apple

Simple Present Tense: Yes/No Questions and Short Answers

4 Listen.

Questions	Answers
Do you **like** salad?	Yes, I **do.**
Do you **like** pizza?	No, I **don't.**
Does he **like** hamburgers?	Yes, he **does.**
Does she **like** hamburgers?	No, she **doesn't.**
Do you and Sue **like** fried chicken?	No, we **don't.**
Do they **like** fried chicken?	Yes, they **do.**
Contractions	
do + not = **don't**	does + not = **doesn't**

5 Match the questions with the answers. Write the numbers.

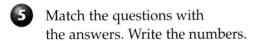

a. _3_ Does Maria have lunch at 12:00?	**1.** Yes, I do.
b. ____ Do you and Tim play baseball?	**2.** No, he doesn't.
c. ____ Does Tim have $5.00?	**3.** Yes, she does.
d. ____ Do you like hamburgers?	**4.** No, they don't.
e. ____ Do Maria and Tim like pizza?	**5.** Yes, we do.

6 Read the questions. Circle your answers. Ask your partner the questions. Circle his or her answers.

Questions	Me	My Partner
a. Do you like hot dogs?	Yes No	Yes No
b. Do you like french fries?	Yes No	Yes No
c. Do you like salad?	Yes No	Yes No
d. Do you like pizza?	Yes No	Yes No
e. Do you like sandwiches?	Yes No	Yes No
f. Do you like fried chicken?	Yes No	Yes No
g. Do you like vegetable soup?	Yes No	Yes No

7 Tell the class about your partner.

Example:

_____ doesn't like hot dogs.

He/She likes french fries.

LISTENING and SPEAKING

1 Listen. Check (✓) the foods and drinks.

a.

ORDER

hamburger
cheeseburger
chicken sandwich
hot dog
french fries
green salad
apple juice
milk

TOTAL _____

b.

ORDER

hamburger
cheeseburger
chicken sandwich
hot dog
french fries
green salad
apple juice
milk

TOTAL _____

c.

ORDER

hamburger
cheeseburger
chicken sandwich
hot dog
french fries
green salad
apple juice
milk

TOTAL _____

2 Listen again. Write the totals.

3 Listen and repeat.

a. Hi. Can I help you?

Yes. I'd like one piece of fried chicken and a small order of fries, please.

b. OK. Anything to drink?

A bottle of apple juice, please.

c. That's $3.35, please.

Here you go.

d. Thank you.

You're welcome.

STRATEGY **Be polite.**

A: That's $3.35, please.
B: Here you go.

A: Thank you.
B: You're welcome.

4 Work with a partner. Practice the conversation in Exercise 3. Use the menu on page 75. You work at the fast-food restaurant. Your partner orders.

READING and WRITING

1 Read the menu.

Menu

hamburger		$1.89
cheeseburger		$2.09
fried chicken		$2.19
cheese pizza	slice	$1.19
	whole	$5.99
cheese sandwich		$2.29

vegetable soup	cup	$1.09
	bowl	$1.89
green salad	small	$1.09
	large	$2.19
french fries	small	$ .99
	large	$1.79
milk		$1.09
apple juice		$1.29

2 Look at the menu in Exercise 1. Write the prices and the totals.

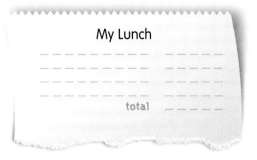

```
1 hamburger              _____
1 bowl of vegetable soup _____
1 large fries            _____
1 apple juice            _____
               total     _____
```

```
1 fried chicken     _____
1 slice of pizza    _____
1 small fries       _____
2 milk              _____
          total     _____
```

STRATEGY **Use a period (.) in prices.**
- $6.32
- $37.95

 3 **Writing Check** Work with a partner. Look again at the menu in Exercise 1. What would you like for lunch? What would your partner like? Fill in the orders.

```
         My Lunch
_____      _____
_____      _____
_____      _____
_____      _____
     total    _____
```

```
     My Partner's Lunch
_____      _____
_____      _____
_____      _____
_____      _____
      total   _____
```

4 Work in groups of four. Check the prices and the totals in Exercise 3.

GETTING STARTED

Warm Up

1 Listen.

2 Listen and repeat.

3 Work with a partner. Ask and answer the questions.

   a. Where are Mrs. Dawson and her son?

   b. Where is Lincoln School?

   c. What building is next to Lincoln School?

Building Vocabulary

Buildings

 1 Listen and repeat.

a. bank   **b.** post office   **c.** supermarket   **d.** hospital

e. police station   **f.** fire station   **g.** clothing store   **h.** drugstore

2 Work with a partner. Ask and answer questions.

Example:

A: Where's the bank?

B: It's next to the post office.

Locations

3 Listen and repeat.

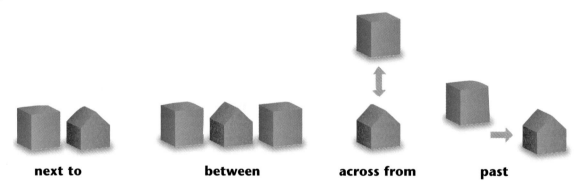

next to   between   across from   past

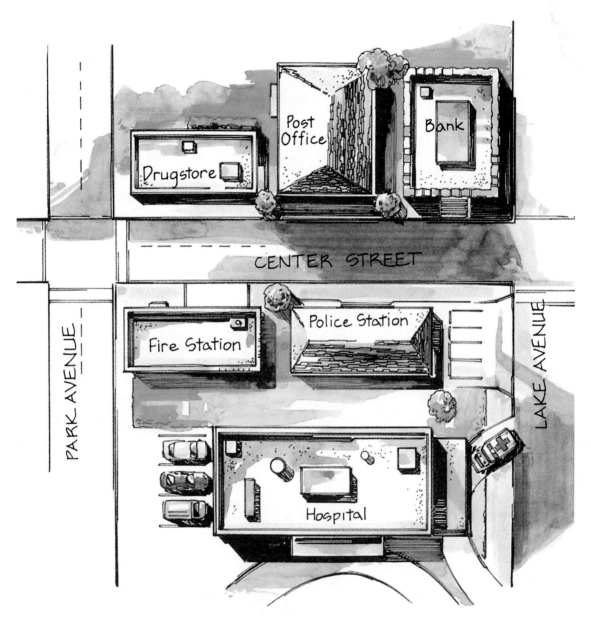

a. The drugstore is on Center Street. It's across from the fire station.

b. The bank is on the corner of Lake Avenue and Center Street. It's past the post office.

c. The fire station is next to the police station.

d. The post office is between the drugstore and the bank.

4 Work with a partner. Ask and answer questions.

Example:

A: Excuse me. Where's the drugstore?

B: It's on Center Street. It's next to the post office.

A: Thank you.

B: You're welcome.

Signs

a. Stop

b. Go

c. No right turn

d. No left turn

e. Do not enter

f. Restrooms

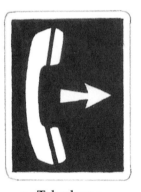

g. Telephone

 Work with a partner. Ask and answer questions.

Example:

A: What does this sign mean?

B: It means "Stop."

7 **Vocabulary Check** Match each person or thing to the place.
Write the words.

| bank | drugstore | fire station | post office |
| clothing store | hospital | police station | supermarket |

a. *fire station*

b. _____

c. _____

d. _____

e. _____

f. _____

g. _____

h. _____

8 Look at the map. Complete the sentences. Use the words in the box.

```
across from    between    next to    past
```

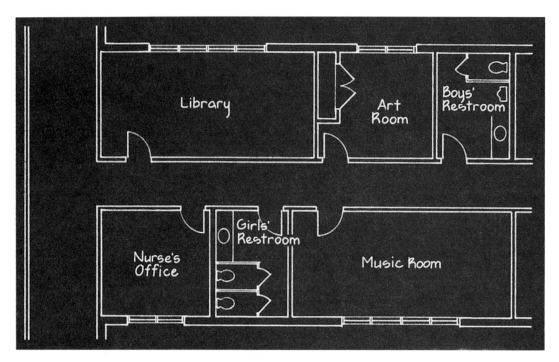

a. The music room is _____past_____ the nurse's office and the girls' restroom.

b. The library is _____ the art room.

c. The art room is _____ the music room.

d. The girls' restroom is _____ the nurse's office and the music room.

e. The boys' restroom is _____ the art room. It's _____ the library and the art room.

9 Write three sentences about the map in Exercise 8. Work with a partner. Your partner guesses the places.

Examples:

A: It's across from the library.

B: Is it the girls' restroom?

A: Yes, it is.

A: It's next to the art room.

B: Is it the library?

A: No, it's not. It's the boys' restroom.

a. _____

b. _____

c. _____

Learn new words.

Some English words look almost the same as words in other languages. They don't always mean the same thing. Make a note.

GRAMMAR

And and *Or*

1 Listen.

I have a pencil. I have an eraser.
I have a pencil **and** an eraser.
Turn right. Walk two blocks.
Turn right **and** walk two blocks.
Do I turn right? Do I turn left?
Do I turn right **or** left?
I don't play basketball after school.
I don't play baseball after school.
I don't play basketball **or** baseball after school. I play soccer.

2 Complete the conversations with *and* or *or*. Practice with a partner.

1. **A:** Where's Randy's Supermarket?
   B: It's on the corner of Clark Street _and_ Fourth Avenue.
2. **A:** Is Nancy's Clothing Store on First Avenue _____ Fourth Avenue?
   B: It's on Fourth Avenue.
3. **A:** What do you have in your book bag?
   B: I have two things. I have a notebook _____ a pen.
4. **A:** Do you go to the gym _____ the cafeteria at 11:30?
   B: I go to the gym at 11:30.
5. **A:** What two classes do you have after lunch?
   B: I have math _____ science.
6. **A:** When do you have art _____ music?
   B: I have art on Tuesdays _____ music on Thursdays.

3 Write a sentence with *and* about yourself. Write a question with *or* for your partner to answer.

   a. _____

   b. _____

Unit 9

91

Imperatives

 4 Listen.

Affirmative	Negative
Turn right.	**Don't turn** left.
Stop.	**Don't go.**
Walk.	**Don't run.**

5 Write the sentences under the signs.

Ride your bike here./Don't ride your bike here.
Turn right here./Don't turn right here.
Turn left here./Don't turn left here.

a. *Don't turn left here.* **b.** _____ **c.** _____

d. _____ **e.** _____ **f.** _____

LISTENING and SPEAKING

  1 Listen. Follow the directions. Draw a line on the map.

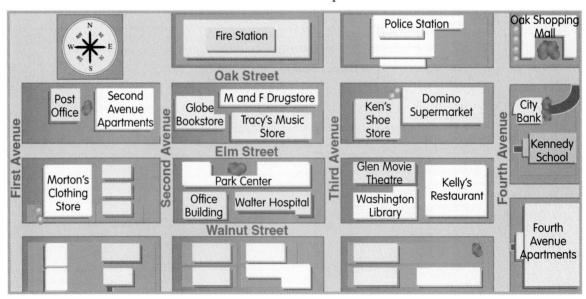

🎧 ② Listen and repeat.

Excuse me. How do I get to Tracy's Music Store?

Turn right and walk one block up Fourth Avenue.

OK. Right and one block up Fourth.

That's right. Turn left on Elm Street and go one block. It's on the corner of Elm and Third.

Corner of Elm and Third. OK. Thanks.

You're welcome.

a.   b.   c.

STRATEGY ▶ **Check information.**

> **A:** How do I get to Tracy's Music Store?
>
> **B:** Turn right and walk one block up Fourth Avenue.
>
> **A:** Right and one block up Fourth.
>
> **B:** That's right. Then …

③ Work with a partner. Practice the conversation in Exercise 2. Use the map in Exercise 1. Ask for and give directions to four places. Take turns.

READING and WRITING

① Read Tom's directions.

> From the school, walk on Elm Street. Go past the Domino Supermarket and a shoe store. Turn left on Third Avenue. Go one block to the hospital. It's on the corner of Third Avenue and Walnut Street. Turn right on Walnut Street. Cross Second Avenue. My house is the second house on the left.

② Follow Tom's directions. Draw a line on the map on page 92. Mark an ✗ on Tom's house.

③ Read each sentence about Tom's directions for the map on page 92. Circle **T** for True or **F** for False.

a.	Tom's directions are from his house to Kennedy School.	T	Ⓕ
b.	Tom goes past the Glen Movie Theater.	T	F
c.	He turns right on Third Avenue.	T	F
d.	He goes past Washington Library.	T	F
e.	The hospital is on the corner of Third Avenue and Oak Street.	T	F
f.	Tom turns left on Walnut Street.	T	F
g.	His house is the third house on the left.	T	F
h.	His house is between First Avenue and Second Avenue.	T	F

Use capital letters.

- names of places: **D**omino **S**upermarket
- names of streets and avenues: **O**ak **S**treet, **T**hird **A**venue

4 **Writing Check** Look again at the map on page 92. Write directions from Washington Library to City Bank.

_____

_____

_____

5 Work with a partner. Check your directions in Exercise 4.

6 Draw a map. Show your home and your school.

7 Write directions from your home to your school. Ask a partner to follow your directions using your map in Exercise 6.

_____

_____

_____

_____

_____

1 Complete the conversation. Use the correct simple present form of the verbs in parentheses and short answers.

SAL: **(1. feel)** ____Do____ you ___feel___ sick today?

TARA: Yes, **(2.)** ___I do___. I **(3. feel)** _____ terrible, Sal.

I **(4. have)** _____ a headache, and my throat

(5. hurt) _____.

SAL: I **(6. be)** _____ sorry. Julio **(7. feel)** _____ sick today, too.

TARA: **(8. have)** _____ he _____ a headache and a sore throat?

SAL: No, **(9.)** _____. He **(10. have)** _____ a stomachache.

TARA: And how about you, Sal? **(11. feel)** _____ you _____ sick today, too?

SAL: No, **(12.)** _____. I **(13. feel)** _____ great!

2 Read about the people's problems. What can they do? What can't they do? Write sentences. Use the words in parentheses.

a. Pam has a sore arm. **(play basketball/go to school)**
   She can't play basketball. She can go to school.

b. Carlo has a stomachache. **(eat pizza/drink juice)**
   _____

c. Barbara has a sore throat. **(sing/read)**
   _____

d. Mr. Li has a sore foot, and Mrs. Li has a backache. **(watch TV/ride their bikes)**
   _____

3 Complete the conversations with *a/an*, or *some*.

1. A: Would you like ____a____ hot dog?
   B: No, thanks. I want _____ vegetable soup and _____ small salad.

2. A: Do you want _____ milk?
   B: Yes, please. I'd like _____ carton of milk and _____ chicken sandwich.

3. A: Do you want _____ pizza for lunch?
   B: No, thanks. I'd like _____ cheeseburger and _____ order of fries.

4 Look at the map on page 87. Complete the sentences with *across from, between, next to, on,* or *past.*

a. The drugstore is ___on___ the corner of Park Avenue and Center Street.

b. The post office is _____ Center Street, _____ Lake Avenue and Park Avenue.

c. The bank is _____ the post office.

d. The fire station is _____ the drugstore and _____ the police station.

5 Write the negative sentences.

a. Write your name on the board.
   Don't write your name on the board.

b. Use the teacher's computer.
   _____

c. Speak Spanish in English class.
   _____

d. Turn right at the corner.
   _____

e. Eat in the cafeteria.
   _____

f. Go to school on Saturday.
   _____

6 Answer the questions. Write short answers.

a. Can you cook?   *Yes, I can.*

b. Can you drive a car? _____

c. Do you like fast food? *No, I don't.*

d. Do your friends like pizza? _____

e. Do you feel happy today? _____

f. Can you speak Spanish? _____

g. Do you like chicken soup? _____

h. Does your teacher walk to school? _____

i. Can you play the guitar? _____

j. Can you swim? _____

k. Can your parents speak English? _____

GETTING STARTED

Warm Up

 1 Listen.

 2 Listen and repeat.

3 Work with a partner. Ask and answer the questions.

    a. What does Samira's father do?

    b. What does her mother do?

    c. What does Samira want to be?

Building Vocabulary

Occupations

 1 Listen and repeat.

a. She's a principal. She helps students and teachers.

b. She's a doctor. She helps sick people.

c. He's a teacher. He teaches English.

d. She's a student. She studies English, math, and other subjects.

e. He's a cashier. He takes money and makes change.

f. He's a librarian. He helps people find and take out books.

2 Work with a partner. Ask and answer questions.

Example:

A: What does she do?

B: She's a principal. She helps students and teachers.

More Occupations

 Listen and repeat.

a. He's a salesperson.
He sells computers at a
computer store.

b. She's a nurse.
She helps sick people.

c. She's a firefighter.
She puts out fires.

d. She's a mail carrier.
She delivers and picks up mail.

e. He's a police officer.
He protects people.

f. She's a dentist.
She fixes people's teeth.

g. He's a bus driver.
He drives a bus.

4 Work with a partner. Ask and answer questions.

Example:

A: What does he do?

B: He's a salesperson. He sells computers at a computer store.

5 **Vocabulary Check** Write the sentences under the pictures. Then write the occupations.

> She delivers the mail.
> He sells things at a store.
> He helps people take out books.
> She protects people.
>
> She drives a bus.
> She fixes people's teeth.
> She puts out fires.
> He helps students and teachers.

a. *She fixes people's teeth.*
She's a dentist.

b. _____

c. _____

d. _____

e. _____

f. _____

g. _____

h. _____

6 Where do the people work? Complete the sentences.

fire station	police station	hospital
post office	library	school

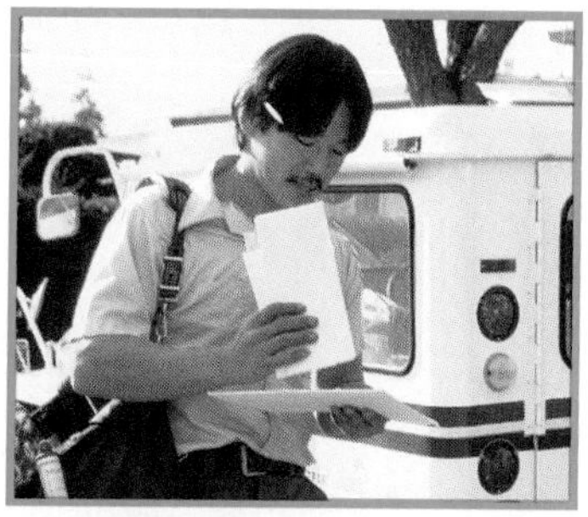

a. He _works at a post office._

b. She ______________

c. He ______________

d. She ______________

e. She ______________

f. He ______________

STRATEGY **Write irregular plurals.**
Most English nouns form their plural by adding *–s* or *–es*. Some nouns have special plural forms. Make a note.

Singular
salesperson
Plural
salespeople

GRAMMAR

Verb + Infinitive

  1 Listen.

What **do** you **want to be**?	I **want to be** a dentist.
What **does** Alma **want to be**?	She **wants to be** a teacher.
What **do** you **like to do**?	I **like to play** soccer.
	I **don't like to play** baseball.
What **does** Yuri **want to do**?	He **wants to have** lunch.
	He **doesn't want to study**.

2 Read the sentences. Answer the questions.

a. David wants to help sick people. What does he want to be?
  He wants to be a doctor.

b. Francine likes to help her classmates learn math. What does she want to be?

_____

c. Carlos is a salesperson at a computer store. What does he like to do?

_____

d. John and Rita are hungry. What do they want to do?

_____

e. Alex is tired. What does he want to do?

_____

f. What do you want to be?

_____

3 What do you like to do? Write a check (✓) on the line. Write another activity you like. Then work with a partner. What does your partner like to do? Write a check (✓) on the line.

Example:

A: Do you like to draw?

B: Yes, I do./No, I don't.

		I like to ...	My partner likes to ...
a.	draw	_____	_____
b.	write	_____	_____
c.	help people	_____	_____
d.	go to the movies	_____	_____
e.	go shopping	_____	_____
f.	play soccer	_____	_____
g.	go swimming	_____	_____
h.	_____	_____	_____

4 Tell the class about your partner.

Example:

_____ doesn't like to draw.

He/She likes to write.

Why?/Because

 5 Listen.

Questions	Answers
Why do you **want to be** a doctor?	**Because** I **like to help** people.
Why does Ana **want to go** to the mall?	**Because** she **wants to buy** new shoes.

6 Write questions with *Why*.

a. she/want to be a police officer?

Why does she want to be a police officer?

b. they/want to go to the cafeteria?

_____

c. you/want to learn English?

_____

d. he/want to go to the supermarket?

_____

e. she/want to be a nurse?

_____

7 Work with a partner. Ask the questions in Exercise 6. Make up
answers with *Because*.

Example:

A: Why does she want to be a police officer?

B: Because she wants to protect people.

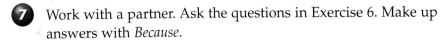

LISTENING and SPEAKING

1 Listen. Look at the picture. Is the sentence true or false? Circle **T** for
True or **F** for False.

a. T   F

b. T   F

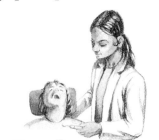

c. T   F

d. T   F

e. T   F

f. T   F

g. T   F

Listen and repeat.

a. What does your father do, Tony? — He's a dentist.

b. Really? Where does he work? — He works at an office downtown.

c. And what does your mother do? — She doesn't have a job. She takes care of my little sister. — Well, that's a job! — Yes, you're right. She's a homemaker.

d. And what do you want to be, Tony? — I want to be a police officer because I want to protect people.

STRATEGY **Show interest.**

A: What does your father do?

B: He's a dentist.

A: Really? Where does he work?

B: He works in an office downtown.

3 Work with a partner. Practice the conversation in Exercise 2. Then talk about yourself. Take turns.

READING and WRITING

 Read about Linda.

My name is Linda Mills. My mother is a nurse. She likes her job because she likes to help people. My father is a mail carrier. He likes his job because he meets many different people. I want to be a librarian.

2 Complete the chart. Why do you think Linda wants to be a librarian?

Name	Occupation	Reason for Occupation (Why?)
Mrs. Mills	_____	_____
Mr. Mills	_____	_____
Linda	_____	_____

STRATEGY ▶ **Join sentences. Use *and, but,* and *because*.**

- I can read in English. I can write in English, too.
  I can read in English, **and** I can write in English, too.
- I like to go to the movies. I don't like to watch TV.
  I like to go to the movies, **but** I don't like to watch TV.
- I want to go to the library. I need a book.
  I want to go to the library **because** I need a book.

☑ **3** **Writing Check** Join these sentences. Use *and, but,* or *because*.

a. He wants to be a teacher. He likes to help children.

_____

_____

b. She likes to swim. She doesn't like to run.

_____

_____

c. We want to eat in a restaurant. We want to see a movie, too.

_____

_____

4 Work with a partner. Check your sentences in Exercise 3.

5 Fill in the chart about yourself and your family or about other people you know.

Name	Occupation	Reason for Occupation (Why?)
_____	_____	_____
_____	_____	_____
_____	_____	_____

6 Write about the people in your chart in Exercise 5.

_____

_____

_____

_____

_____

GETTING STARTED

Warm Up

 1 Listen.

 2 Listen and repeat.

3 Work with a partner. Ask and answer the questions.

  a. Where are Ann and Rosa?
  b. Where's Amanda?
  c. Where do Ann and Rosa want to go?

Building Vocabulary

Free-Time Activities

 1 Listen and repeat.

a. Eva and Ron are playing frisbee. **b.** Mr. Soto is riding a bike.

c. Ms. Jones is jogging. **d.** Mr. and Mrs. Carter are skating.

e. Paulo is playing a computer game. **f.** Ken and Lin are swimming.

g. Kimiko is working out.

2 Work with a partner. Ask and answer questions.

Examples:

A: What are Eva and Ron doing? **A:** What's Mr. Soto doing?

B: They're playing frisbee. **B:** He's _____.

Ballgames

  3 Listen and repeat.

The girls are playing softball.

a. Ana is throwing the ball.

b. Barb is hitting the ball.

c. Now Barb is running, and Carla is catching the ball.

The boys are playing football.

d. Dan is kicking the ball.

e. Ed is catching the ball.

f. Now Ed is running with the ball.

4 Work with a partner. Ask and answer questions.

Examples:

A: What are the girls doing?

B: They're playing softball.

A: What's Ana doing?

B: She's throwing the ball.

Vocabulary Check Write the words under the pictures.

catching a ball	riding a bike
hitting a ball	skating
jogging	swimming
kicking a ball	throwing a frisbee
playing a computer game	working out

a. _swimming_

b. _____ **c.** _____ **d.** _____

e. _____ **f.** _____ **g.** _____

h. _____ **i.** _____ **j.** _____

STRATEGY **Learn new words.**

Add *–ing* to most verbs. Some verbs have spelling changes. Make a note.

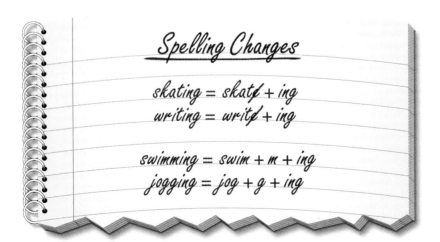

Spelling Changes

skating = skat~~e~~ + ing
writing = writ~~e~~ + ing

swimming = swim + m + ing
jogging = jog + g + ing

GRAMMAR

Present Progressive Tense: Information Questions

 1 Listen.

Questions	Statements
What **are** you **doing**?	I'**m listening** to music.
What'**s** Dan **doing**?	He'**s watching** TV.
What'**s** Cam **doing**?	She'**s doing** her homework.
What **are** you and Bob **doing**?	We'**re playing** basketball.
What **are** June and Tara **doing**?	They'**re swimming**.

2 Work with a partner. Look at the pictures and words.
Ask and answer questions.

Olga

Examples:

A: What's Olga doing?

B: She's swimming.

A: Do you like to swim?

B: Yes, I do./No, I don't.

a. Maya   Marian   **b.** Juan   **c.** Rosa   Luz

d. Bao   **e.** Robert   **f.** Bill   Jerry

g. you   **h.** you and I

Present Progressive Tense: Yes/No Questions

  Listen.

Questions	Answers/Statements
Are you **eating** now?	Yes, I **am**. (Yes, I**'m eating** now.)
	No, I**'m not**. (No, I**'m not eating** now.)
Is Fatima **studying**?	Yes, she **is**. (Yes, she**'s studying**.)
	No, she **isn't**. (No, she **isn't studying**.)
Are you and Bob **having** fun?	Yes, we **are**. (Yes, we**'re having** fun.)
	No, we **aren't**. (We **aren't having** fun.)
Are the students **reading**?	Yes, they **are**. (Yes, they**'re reading**.)
	No, they **aren't**. (No, they **aren't reading**.)
	The boys **are reading**, but the girls **are writing**.

Contractions

you aren't = **you're not**	we aren't = **we're not**
he isn't = **he's not**	they aren't = **they're not**
she isn't = **she's not**	

4 Complete the conversations.

1. **A:** _____*Are*_____ the students
   _____*playing*_____ soccer? **(play)**

   B: Yes, they _____.
   They _____ soccer
   in the park. **(play)**

2. **A:** _____ Peter _____? **(skate)**
   B: No, he _____. He _____ his
   bike. **(ride)** He _____ to school. **(go)**

3. A: _____ Tom _____? **(read)**

B: Yes, he _____. He _____ his homework. **(do)**

4. A: _____ Gino and Ken _____? **(work out)**

B: No, they _____. They _____ basketball. **(play)** They _____ fun. **(have)**

5 Work with a partner. Ask a question using the words. Your partner looks at page 108 for the answer. Take turns.

Example:

Ms. Jones/skate

A: Is Ms. Jones skating?

B: No, she isn't. She's jogging.

a. Mr. Soto/swim

b. Mr. and Mrs. Carter/jog

c. Ken and Lin/skate

d. Eva and Ron/play frisbee

e. Paulo/play a computer game

f. Kimiko/work out

LISTENING and SPEAKING

  1 Listen. What is each person doing? Write the number.

a. Rob _____4_____

b. David _____

c. Bobby _____

d. Rita _____

e. Teresa _____

f. Carmen's father _____

g. Carmen's mother _____

1.    **2.**

3.    **4.**

5.    **6.**

2 Listen and repeat.

STRATEGY **Check information.**

A: What's Connie doing?

B: Who?

A: Connie.

B: Oh. She's jogging.

3 Work with a partner. Practice the conversation in Exercise 2.

4 Work with a partner. Look at Picture A below and Picture B on page 115. Ask your partner questions about Tran, José, Carol, and Tom. Then answer your partner's questions about Carl, Connie, Joanne, and Julia.

Example:

A: What's Tran doing?

B: He's playing basketball.

Picture A

Unit 11

114

Picture B

READING and WRITING

 1 Read Jason's letter.

> *July 12, _____*
>
> *Dear Alex,*
>   *Hi! How are you? It's a beautiful day, but I'm home because I have a sore throat. My brother Tom is playing soccer at the park, and my brother Kent is skating. My sister Laura is buying clothing at the mall with my parents.*
>   *How are you and your family? Is your mother teaching English this year? Is your sister studying at the university? Write soon.*
>
>   *Your friend,*
>   *Jason*

2 Complete the chart.

Activity	Who is doing this?	Activity	Who is doing this?
a. playing soccer		**d.** teaching English	
b. skating		**e.** studying	
c. buying clothing		**f.** writing a letter	

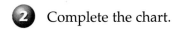

Start a letter with a greeting:	**End a letter with a closing:**
• *Dear Alex,*	• *Your friend,* *Jason*

3 **Writing Check** What's your family doing now? Write a letter to a friend. Tell about yourself and your family. Use a greeting and a closing. Write the date!

_____

_____

_____

_____

_____

_____

_____

_____

_____

_____

_____

_____

_____

_____

_____

_____

_____

_____

_____

4 Work with a partner. Check your letters in Exercise 3.

GETTING STARTED

Warm Up

 1 Listen.

 2 Listen and repeat.

3 Work with a partner. Ask and answer the questions.
  a. What's the girl looking for?
  b. What's wrong with the brown jacket?
  c. How much is the green jacket?

Building Vocabulary

Clothes

 1 Listen and repeat.

2 Work with a partner. You and your partner are a salesperson and a customer in a clothing store. Ask and answer questions. Take turns.

Example:

A: May I help you?

B: Yes. I'd like to buy this jacket. How much is it?

A: Seventy-nine ninety-five.

A: May I help you?

B: Yes. I'd like to buy these jeans. How much are they?

A: Twenty-two ninety-five.

Colors

 3 Listen and repeat.

a. red   **b.** orange   **c.** yellow   **d.** brown   **e.** tan   **f.** white

g. black   **h.** gray   **i.** blue   **j.** green   **k.** pink   **l.** purple

4 Work with a partner. You buy the clothes in the picture on page 118. Tell your partner about your new clothes. Take turns.

Examples:

A: I have a new T-shirt.

B: Really? What color is it?

A: It's orange.

A: I have some new shoes.

B: Really? What color are they?

A: They're brown.

5 Work with a partner. Walk around the classroom. Find the colors in Exercise 3.

Example:

A: Our desks are brown.

B: The teacher's skirt is pink.

Problems with Clothes

6 Listen and repeat.

a. This shirt is too big!   **b.** This jacket is too small!   **c.** This skirt is too long!   **d.** These jeans are too short!

7 Work with a partner. Ask and answer questions.

Example:

A: What's wrong with her shirt?

B: It's too big.

Opinions about Clothes

 8 Listen and repeat.

a. This dress is beautiful. **b.** This hat is pretty. **c.** These pants are great.

d. These boots are nice. **e.** This coat is ugly. **f.** These sneakers are awful.

9 Work with a partner. Ask questions about clothes. Give your opinions.

Example:

A: Do you like this dress?

B: Yes, I do. It's beautiful. / No, I don't. It's ugly.

 10 **Vocabulary Check** Work with a partner. Give your opinions about the clothes in Exercise 2.

Examples:

A: I think these brown shoes are nice.

B: I think this gray jacket is great.

11 Look at the pictures. What are the people saying? Complete the sentences.

a. I can't buy this ___jacket___.
It's too ___big___!

b. I don't want to buy these _____.
They're too _____!

c. I don't like this _____.
It's too _____!

d. I like these _____,
but they're too _____!

e. We can't buy these _____.
They're too _____!

STRATEGY **Learn new words.**
Write words with their opposites.

Adjectives

big — small
great — awful
long — short
pretty — ugly

GRAMMAR

Demonstrative Adjectives

1 Listen.

Singular

I like **this** shirt.   I don't like **that** shirt.

Plural

I like **these** shoes.   I don't like **those** shoes.

2 Write questions with *Do you like ... ?* Use *this, that, these,* or *those.*

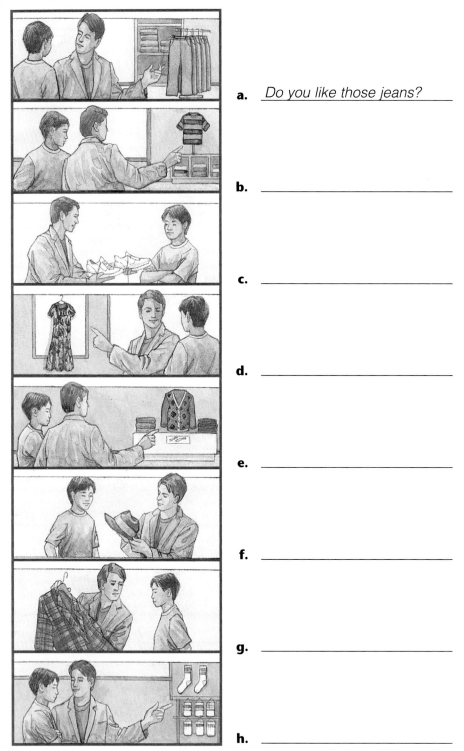

a. *Do you like those jeans?*

b. _____

c. _____

d. _____

e. _____

f. _____

g. _____

h. _____

3 Work with a partner. Ask and answer the questions in Exercise 2.

Example:

A: Do you like those jeans?

B: Yes, I do. They're nice./No, I don't. They're awful.

Adjectives

  4 Listen.

> I want **a green** jacket.   I'm wearing **black-and-white** shoes.
> She has **a small** book bag.   He's wearing **blue** jeans.
> She's wearing **a white** shirt, **an orange-and-white** skirt, and **white** shoes.

5 Work with a partner. What are these people wearing?
Ask and answer questions.

Example:

A: What's she wearing?

B: She's wearing a red T-shirt, blue jeans, and red sneakers.

a.   b.   c.   d.   e.

6 Work with a partner. What are you wearing?

LISTENING and SPEAKING

1 Listen and write each person's name.

Alex   Andy   Randy   Lee   Chris

a. _____*Randy*_____   b. _____   c. _____

d. _____   e. _____

Unit 12

123

Listen and repeat.

a. **May I help you?** / **Yes. I'm looking for a T-shirt.**

b. **OK. What color do you want?** / **Gray.**

c. **Do you like this T-shirt?** / **Yes, I do. It's very nice.**

d. **How much is it?** / **It's fifteen ninety-five.** / **OK. Here's twenty.**

 STRATEGY **Don't say just "yes" or "no." Give more information.**

> **A:** Do you like this T-shirt?
>
> **B:** Yes, I do. It's very nice.

3 Work with a partner. Practice the conversation in Exercise 2.

4 Work with a partner. You and your partner are a salesperson and a customer at a clothing store. Talk about things you want to buy. Take turns.

READING and WRITING

1 Read about Hiroshi.

Hiroshi Tanaka is ordering some clothes from the catalogue on page 125. He is circling the things he wants to buy. Hiroshi lives at 232 James Street, Andover, Massachusetts 01810. His phone number is (781) 555-4901.

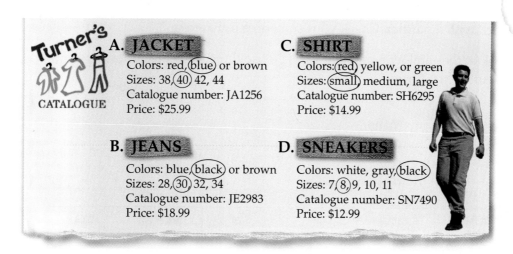

Turner's CATALOGUE

A. JACKET
Colors: red, (blue) or brown
Sizes: 38, (40) 42, 44
Catalogue number: JA1256
Price: $25.99

C. SHIRT
Colors: (red) yellow, or green
Sizes: (small) medium, large
Catalogue number: SH6295
Price: $14.99

B. JEANS
Colors: blue, (black) or brown
Sizes: 28, (30) 32, 34
Catalogue number: JE2983
Price: $18.99

D. SNEAKERS
Colors: white, gray, (black)
Sizes: 7, (8) 9, 10, 11
Catalogue number: SN7490
Price: $12.99

2 Complete the catalogue form for Hiroshi.

Turner's CATALOGUE

Name _____
Address _____
City _____ State _____ ZIP Code _____
Phone Number _____
(Area Code)

Clothing Item	Catalogue Number	Color	Size	How Many	Price
jacket	JA1256	blue	40	1	25.99
				Total Price	

STRATEGY **Always check your writing.**
Read your writing. Ask these questions.

- Is the punctuation correct?
- Is the spelling correct?
- Are the capital letters correct?

- Is the grammar correct?
- Is the information correct?

 3 **Writing Check** Correct these sentences.

a. I̶ want buy a new sweater.
   (with corrections: capital I, "to" inserted)

b. do you like this sneakers

c. I like go to the mall on saturdays

d. you do want to play soccer after scool?

e. youre wearing a great jaket

f. we dont like these shoe becuse theire too small

Unit 12

125

4 Work with a partner. Check your sentences in Exercise 3.

5 Look at the catalogue on page 125. Choose three things to order.
Complete the form.

Turner's
CATALOGUE

Name _____
Address _____
City _____ State _____ ZIP Code _____
Phone Number _____
　　　　　　　　　　　(Area Code)

Clothing Item	Catalogue Number	Color	Size	How Many	Price
				Total Price	

6 Work with a partner. You are ordering the clothes on your catalogue
form by telephone. Your partner works for Turner's, and he or she
fills out the form. Take turns.

A: Turner's. May I help you?

B: Yes. I'd like to order some clothes.

A: (Ask for the person's name, address, and phone number.)

B: _____ .

A: (Ask for the clothing item, catalogue number, color, and size. Ask
how many and the price.)

B: _____ .

Turner's
CATALOGUE

Name _____
Address _____
City _____ State _____ ZIP Code _____
Phone Number _____
　　　　　　　　　　　(Area Code)

Clothing Item	Catalogue Number	Color	Size	How Many	Price

1 What are the people doing? Write sentences with the present progressive form of the verbs in the box.

buy new sneakers	shop
have lunch	swim
jog	take out a book
play basketball	watch TV

a. My sister and I are at home. _We're watching TV._

b. Carmen and Tony are in the cafeteria. _____

c. Sandra is at the supermarket. _____

d. Mark is at the library. _____

e. Suzy and I are at the pool. _____

f. Greg and Kris are in the gym. _____

g. I'm at the shoe store. _____

h. My friends and I are in the park. _____

2 Match the answers with the questions. Write the letters.

1. _b_ What's he wearing?
2. ____ What does he do?
3. ____ What's he doing?
4. ____ What does he want to do?
5. ____ Why does he want to be a teacher?
6. ____ Where does he work?

a. He's a salesperson.
b. He's wearing jeans.
c. Because he likes children.
d. He's looking for a new jacket.
e. He wants to be a teacher.
f. He works at the mall.

3 Complete the story with the correct simple present form of the verbs in the box. Use one verb four times.

deliver	put out
fix	teach
help	want
like	

I think I **(1.)** _want_ to be a firefighter.

A firefighter **(2.)** _____ people and

(3.) _____ fires. Or maybe I can be a dentist.

A dentist **(4.)** _____ people's teeth. My sister **(5.)** _____

to be a mail carrier. Mail carriers **(6.)** _____ the mail. My brother

(7.) _____ to be a doctor because he **(8.)** _____ to help

sick people. My friend Sally **(9.)** _____ to be an English teacher.

An English teacher **(10.)** _____ children to speak, read, and

write in English.

4 Put the words in order. Write questions. Then look at the picture and answer the questions. Use capital letters and punctuation correctly.

a. Sue is driving car her? _Is Sue driving her car?_
No, she isn't. She's riding her bike.

b. and Dan Ron baseball playing are? _____

_____

c. Lou walking is? _____

_____

d. swimming is Ben? _____

_____

5 Rewrite the sentences. Use pronouns and words with opposite meanings.

a. The clothing store isn't on the left.
It's on the right.

b. Your jeans aren't too short.

_____

c. Her new dress isn't pretty.

_____

d. Those shoes aren't too big.

_____

6 Answer the questions. Write complete sentences.

a. What do you like to do on weekends?

_____

b. What are you wearing today?

_____

c. Where and when do you like to do your homework?

_____

d. Who's sitting next to you today?

_____

THE INTERNATIONAL PHONETIC ALPHABET

IPA SYMBOLS

Consonants

/b/	**b**a**b**y, clu**b**		/s/	**s**alt, medi**c**ine, bu**s**
/d/	**d**own, to**d**ay, sa**d**		/š/	**s**ugar, spe**c**ial, fi**sh**
/f/	**f**un, pre**f**er, lau**gh**		/t/	**t**ea, ma**t**erial, da**t**e
/g/	**g**ood, be**g**in, do**g**		/θ/	**th**ing, heal**th**y, ba**th**
/h/	**h**ome, be**h**ind		/ð/	**th**is, mo**th**er, ba**th**e
/k/	**k**ey, cho**c**olate, bla**ck**		/v/	**v**ery, tra**v**el, o**f**
/l/	**l**ate, po**l**ice, mai**l**		/w/	**w**ay, any**o**ne
/m/	**m**ay, wo**m**an, swi**m**		/y/	**y**es, on**i**on
/n/	**n**o, opi**n**ion		/z/	**z**oo, cou**s**in, alway**s**
/ŋ/	a**n**gry, lo**ng**		/ž/	mea**s**ure, gara**g**e
/p/	**p**aper, ma**p**		/č/	**ch**eck, pi**c**ture, wat**ch**
/r/	**r**ain, pa**r**ent, doo**r**		/ǰ/	**j**ob, refri**g**erator, oran**g**e

Vowels

/ɑ/	**o**n, h**o**t, f**a**ther		/o/	**o**pen, cl**o**se, sh**ow**
/æ/	**a**nd, c**a**sh		/u/	b**oo**t, d**o**, thr**ough**
/ɛ/	**e**gg, s**ay**s, l**ea**ther		/ʌ/	**o**f, y**ou**ng, s**u**n
/ɪ/	**i**n, b**i**g		/ʊ/	p**u**t, c**oo**k, w**ou**ld
/ɔ/	**o**ff, d**augh**ter, dr**aw**		/ə/	**a**bout, penc**i**l, lem**o**n
/e/	**A**pril, tr**ai**n, s**ay**		/ɚ/	mo**ther**, Sat**ur**day, doct**or**
/i/	**e**ven, sp**ea**k, tr**ee**		/ɜ/	**ear**th, b**ur**n, h**er**

Diphthongs

/ɑɪ/	**i**ce, st**y**le, l**ie**		/ɔɪ/	**oi**l, n**oi**se, b**oy**
/ɑʊ/	**ou**t, d**ow**n, h**ow**			

THE ENGLISH ALPHABET

Here is the pronunciation of the letters of the English alphabet, written in International Phonetic Alphabet symbols.

a	/e/		n	/ɛn/
b	/bi/		o	/o/
c	/si/		p	/pi/
d	/di/		q	/kyu/
e	/i/		r	/ɑr/
f	/ɛf/		s	/ɛs/
g	/ǰi/		t	/ti/
h	/eč/		u	/yu/
i	/ɑɪ/		v	/vi/
j	/ǰe/		w	/ˈdʌbəlˌyu/
k	/ke/		x	/ɛks/
l	/ɛl/		y	/wɑɪ/
m	/ɛm/		z	/zi/

UNIT VOCABULARY

STARTING OUT

Nouns
board
book
desk
door
page
pen
pencil
picture
window

Classroom Instructions
Close your book.
Look at the picture.
Open your book.
Raise your hand.
Repeat.
Sit down.
Stand up.
Work with a partner.
Write on the board.

Expressions
Good morning.
Goodbye.
Hello.
Hi.
What's your name?
I'm _____.
What's this?
It's a _____.
I don't know.
I'm sorry. I don't understand.

UNIT 1

Nouns
alphabet
book bag
chalk
country
desk
door
eraser
letter
map
notebook
number
paper
question
sentence
student
word

Articles
a
an

Numbers
zero
one
two
three
four
five
six
seven
eight
nine
ten

Expressions
How do you spell that?
It's nice to meet you.
Nice to meet you, too.
What's this?
It's a/an _____.
What's your first name?
My name is _____.
Where are you from?
I'm from _____.

UNIT 2

Nouns
address
boy
chair
girl
homework
ID card
locker
man/men
(first/last) name
table
wastebasket
woman/women

Numbers
eleven
twelve
thirteen
fourteen
fifteen
sixteen
seventeen
eighteen
nineteen
twenty

Possessive Adjectives
my
your
his
her

Prepositions
in
on
under

Expressions
I'm sorry. Is it _____?
No, it's _____.
This is _____.
What are these?
They're _____.
Where's _____?
It's _____.
Where are _____?
They're _____.

UNIT 3

Nouns
cafeteria
cashier
(English) class
gym
librarian
library
office
phone number
principal
principal's office
restroom
school
(English/PE) teacher

Numbers
thirty
forty
fifty
sixty
seventy
eighty
ninety
one hundred

Adjective
PE (class)

Subject Pronouns
I
you
he
she
it
they

UNIT 3 continued

Article
the

Preposition
at

Verb
be

Expressions
Who's this?
It's/He's/She's _____.

Who are they?
They're _____.
What's _____'s address?
It's _____.

And what's _____ phone number?
It's (area code) _____.
Oh, OK. Thanks.

UNIT 4

Nouns
bathroom
bedroom
brother
cat
children
daughter
dining room

family
father
garage
grandfather
grandmother
husband
kitchen
living room

mother
parents
sister
son
wife
yard

Possessive Adjectives
its
our
their

Expressions
How old _____?
_____ year(s) old.

UNIT 5

Nouns
bed
breakfast
computer
dinner
home
homework
lunch
math

PE
routine
schedule
science
social studies
time

Verbs
do
have

get up
go

Adverbs
here
(over) there
too
after

Expressions
What time is it?
When _____?
At _____.
How/What about you?

UNIT 6

Nouns
afternoon
art
band
baseball
basketball
classmate
day
evening
letter
(shopping) mall
morning
movies
music
newspaper
night
park

practice
soccer
street
television
TV
week
weekday
weekend

Days of the Week
Sunday
Monday
Tuesday
Wednesday
Thursday
Friday
Saturday

Adjectives
busy
every
free
new
weekly

Verbs
come
eat
listen to
play
read
study
watch
work
write

Adverbs
always
before
never

Expressions
When _____?
_____ in the morning/
in the afternoon/
in the evening/
at night.
_____ on Monday/on the weekend.
Let's _____.
OK. How about _____?
Sorry.

UNIT 7

Nouns
arm
back
backache
bike
doctor
drugstore
finger
flu
foot
guitar
hand
head
headache
leg

medicine
stomach
stomachache
temperature
toe
throat

Adjectives
great
happy
hungry
left
right
sad
sick

sore
terrible
thirsty
tired

Verbs
can/can't
cook
drive
feel
get
hurt
look at
ride
run

say
sing
speak
swim
use
walk

Expressions
How do you feel today?
What's the matter?
That's right.
Oh, sorry. I mean _____.
Thank you.
You're welcome.

UNIT 8

Nouns
apple
bottle
bowl
carton
cent
cheese
cheeseburger
chicken
dollar
drink
(french) fries

hamburger
hot dog
(apple/orange) juice
milk
money
order
piece
pizza
price
(green) salad
sandwich
sausage

slice
(tomato) soup
vegetable

Adjectives
fried
large
small
some

Verbs
drink
want

would like

Prepositions
of
with

Expressions
What would you like?
I'd like _____, please.
Here you go.
How much _____?

UNIT 9

Nouns
avenue
bank
block
building
clothing store
corner
directions
drugstore
fire station
hospital

nurse
police station
post office
sign
supermarket
telephone
thing
turn

Verbs
come in
enter

stop
turn

Adverbs
across from
next to
up

Prepositions
between
from
past

Conjunctions
and
or

Expressions
Excuse me.
What does _____ mean?
It means _____.

UNIT 10

Nouns
bus
bus driver
change
dentist
downtown
fire
firefighter
homemaker
mail
mail carrier
occupation

police officer
reason
restaurant
salesperson
security guard
shoe(s)
subject

Verbs
buy
deliver
draw

find
fix
go shopping
go swimming
help
learn
make
pick up
protect
put out
sell
take

take care of
take out
teach

Conjunctions
because
but

Expressions
Why _____?
Because _____.
Really?

UNIT 11

Nouns
ball
football
frisbee
fun

(computer) game
softball

Verbs
catch

hit
jog
kick
skate

throw
work out

Expression
Who?

UNIT 12

Nouns
blouse
boot(s)
catalogue
clothes
clothing store
coat
colors
customer
dress
hat
item
jacket
jeans
large
medium
opinion

pants
problem
shirt
size
skirt
sneaker(s)
sock(s)
sweater
T-shirt

Adjectives
awful
beautiful
big
black
blue
brown
gray

great
green
long
nice
orange
pink
pretty
purple
red
short
small
tan
that
those
ugly
white
yellow

Verbs
circle
look for
order
try
wear

Adverbs
too
very

Expressions
May I help you?
What color _____?
How about _____?
Let me _____.
What's wrong with _____?
I think _____.

INDEX

SCOTT FORESMAN ENGLISH

ON YOUR MARK 2

INTRODUCTORY

Second Edition

Karen Davy

Longman

On Your Mark 2, Second Edition

Pearson Education, 10 Bank Street, White Plains, NY 10606

Vice president, director of publishing: Allen Ascher
Editorial director: Louise Jennewine
Acquisitions editor: Bill Preston
Vice president, director of design and production: Rhea Banker
Senior development editors: Sherri Arbogast, Marilyn Hochman
Production manager: Alana Zdinak
Production supervisor: Liza Pleva
Executive managing editor: Linda Moser
Senior production editor: Virginia Bernard
Associate production editor: Sylvia Dare
Director of manufacturing: Patrice Fraccio
Senior manufacturing buyer: Edith Pullman
Photo research: Quarasan
Cover design: Charles Yuen
Text design and composition: Quarasan
Photo and illustration credits: See page vi.

Library of Congress Cataloging-in-Publication Data
Davy, Karen
    On your mark 2: introductory / Karen Davy.—2nd ed.
        p. cm.—(Scott Foresman English)
    Includes index.
    ISBN: 0-201-66394-5
    1. English-language textbooks for foreign speakers. I. Title. II. Series

PE 1128.D3562 2000
428.2′4—dc2l

99-33871
CIP

2 3 4 5 6 7 8 9 10—WC—04 03 02 01 00

CONTENTS

SUMMARY OF SKILLS

Theme	Vocabulary and Grammar	Listening and Speaking	Reading and Writing
Unit 1 **When Is Your Birthday?** Page 1	➡ Learn new words. Simple Present Tense + Frequency Adverbs; *There is/There are*	**Listening:** Identifying Dates **Speaking:** Asking for and Giving Information about Birthdays ➡ Check information.	**Reading:** A Letter to a Pen Pal **Writing:** A Letter to a Friend ➡ Use capital letters.
Unit 2 **The Carrots Look Delicious!** Page 11	➡ Learn new words. *Some/Any;* Count and Non-count Nouns	**Listening:** Identifying Quantities of Food **Speaking:** Asking for and Giving Information about Food Quantities ➡ Check information.	**Reading:** The Food Guide Pyramid **Writing:** A Note about One's Eating Habits ➡ Use punctuation marks.
Unit 3 **What Do You Have to Do Today?** Page 21	➡ Learn new words. *Go/Go to/Go to the;* *Have to*	**Listening:** Understanding Daily Routines and Sequence **Speaking:** Asking for and Giving Information about Daily Routines and Obligations ➡ Ask for an explanation. Give an explanation.	**Reading:** A Narrative about a Weekday Routine **Writing:** A Narrative about One's Weekday Routine ➡ Join sentences with *and, but, so,* and *because.*

Review (Units 1–3)

Theme	Vocabulary and Grammar	Listening and Speaking	Reading and Writing
Unit 4 **What Do You Want to Buy?** Page 33	➡ Learn new words. *One/Some;* Questions with Verb + Infinitive; Demonstrative Adjectives: Review	**Listening:** Identifying Wants and Needs **Speaking:** Asking for and Giving Information about Shopping ➡ Stop to think before you give information.	**Reading:** A Map **Writing:** A Paragraph about One's Neighborhood; A Map ➡ Know when to use capital letters and when *not* to use them.
Unit 5 **It's an Emergency!** Page 43	➡ Learn new words. Simple Past Tense: Regular Verbs and Irregular Verbs; Simple Past Tense: Information Questions	**Listening:** Understanding Emergency Phone Calls **Speaking:** Describing Accidents ➡ Express interest.	**Reading:** An Accident Report **Writing:** Filling out an Accident Report ➡ Don't repeat the same nouns. Use pronouns when possible.
Unit 6 **Did You Study for the Test?** Page 53	➡ Learn new words. Object Pronouns; Simple Past Tense: Statements; Simple Past Tense: Yes/No Questions	**Listening:** Identifying Students' Activities **Speaking:** Asking for and Giving Information about School Activities ➡ Say the same thing is true about yourself.	**Reading:** A School Newspaper Article **Writing:** A Newspaper Article about a School Event ➡ Make sure each sentence has a subject. The subject tells *who* or *what* the sentence is about.

Review (Units 4–6)

CREDITS

Introductions

1 Listen.

2 Listen and repeat.

3 Work with a partner. Take turns introducing yourselves.

A: Hi. I'm _____. What's your name?
B: _____.
A: What's your last name?
B: _____.
A: It's nice to meet you, _____.
B: Nice to meet you, too.

4 Work in groups of three. Take turns introducing your partner to another student.

A: Hi, _____.
B: Hi, _____.
A: _____, this is _____.
B: Hi, _____. It's nice to meet you.
C: Nice to meet you, too.

Countries of the World

5 Listen and repeat.

6 Work with a partner. Point to the pictures. Take turns asking and answering questions.

A: Where's he/she from?

B: He's/She's from _____.

Things to Say

7 Listen and repeat.

8 Work with a partner. Take turns asking and answering the questions.

    a. Where are you from?   **d.** What's your phone number?

    b. Where do you live?   **e.** How old are you?

    c. What's your address?   **f.** What class are you in? Who's your teacher?

ix

Forms

9 Read the form.

NEW STUDENT INFORMATION FORM

Name: _Yamamoto_ _Kenji_
      Last   First

Address: _3557 West 66th Street_

New York, NY 10023

Phone Number: _(212) 555-0420_

Age: _16_   Native Country: _Japan_

Class: _English 200_   Teacher: _Mr. Morgan_

10 Work with a partner. Ask and answer the questions about the form in Exercise 9.

a. What's the boy's first name?
b. What's his last name?
c. What's his address?
d. Does he have a phone? What's his number?

e. How old is he?
f. Where is he from?
g. What class is he in?
h. What's his teacher's name?

11 Fill out the form with information about yourself.

NEW STUDENT INFORMATION FORM

Name: _____
      Last   First

Address: _____

_____

Phone Number: _____

Age: ___   Native Country: _____

Class: _____   Teacher: _____

WHEN IS YOUR BIRTHDAY?

GETTING STARTED

Warm Up

 1 Listen.

2 Listen and repeat.

3 Work with a partner. Ask and answer the questions.
   a. When is Alma's birthday?
   b. When is Tomiko's birthday?
   c. Is Alma's party today?
   d. Does Tomiko want to go to the party?

Building Vocabulary

Ordinal Numbers

 1 Listen and repeat.

1st	first	11th	eleventh	21st	twenty-first
2nd	second	12th	twelfth	22nd	twenty-second
3rd	third	13th	thirteenth	23rd	twenty-third
4th	fourth	14th	fourteenth	24th	twenty-fourth
5th	fifth	15th	fifteenth	25th	twenty-fifth
6th	sixth	16th	sixteenth	26th	twenty-sixth
7th	seventh	17th	seventeenth	27th	twenty-seventh
8th	eighth	18th	eighteenth	28th	twenty-eighth
9th	ninth	19th	nineteenth	29th	twenty-ninth
10th	tenth	20th	twentieth	30th	thirtieth

40th	fortieth	70th	seventieth	100th	one hundredth
50th	fiftieth	80th	eightieth		
60th	sixtieth	90th	ninetieth		

2 Work with a partner. Say ten cardinal numbers. Your partner says the ordinal numbers. Take turns.

Example:

A: Three.
B: Third. One.
A: First.

Months of the Year

 3 Listen and repeat.

4 Work with a partner. Ask and answer questions.

Example:

A: What's the first month of the year?
B: January. What's the sixth month of the year?

Holidays in the United States

  Listen and repeat.

a. Martin Luther King Day
3rd Monday in January

b. Valentine's Day
February 14

c. St. Patrick's Day
March 17

d. Earth Day
April 22

e. Mother's Day
2nd Sunday in May

f. Father's Day
3rd Sunday in June

g. Independence Day
July 4

h. Labor Day
1st Monday in September

i. Halloween
October 31

j. Thanksgiving
*4th Thursday
in November*

k. Christmas
December 25

6 Work with a partner. Ask and answer questions.

Examples:

A: When is Martin Luther King Day?
B: It's the third Monday in January.

A: When is Valentine's Day?
B: It's on February fourteenth.

Vocabulary Check Look at the calendars. Complete the sentences.

MAY

Sunday	Monday	Tuesday	Wednesday	Thursday	Friday	Saturday
	1	2	3	4	5	6
7	8	9	10	11	12	13
14 Mother's Day	15	16	17	18	19	20
21	22	23	24	25	26	27
28	29	30	31			

a. In the U.S., Mother's Day is always in ____May____ .

b. Mother's Day is always on ____Sunday____ .

c. On this calendar, Mother's Day is on ____May 14____ .

June

Sunday	Monday	Tuesday	Wednesday	Thursday	Friday	Saturday
				1	2	3
4	5	6	7	8	9	10
11 Father's Day	12	13	14	15	16	17
18	19	20	21	22	23	24
25	26	27	28	29	30	

d. We celebrate Father's Day in _____ .

e. Father's Day is always on _____ .

f. On this calendar, Father's Day is on _____ .

October

Sunday	Monday	Tuesday	Wednesday	Thursday	Friday	Saturday
1	2	3	4	5	6	7
8	9	10	11	12	13	14
15	16	17	18	19	20	21
22	23	24	25	26	27	28
29	30	31 Halloween UNICEF Day				

g. Halloween and UNICEF Day are in _____ .

h. On this calendar, Halloween and UNICEF Day are on _____ .

i. Halloween and UNICEF Day are always on _____ .

November

Sunday	Monday	Tuesday	Wednesday	Thursday	Friday	Saturday
			1	2	3	4
5	6	7	8	9	10	11
12	13	14	15	16	17	18
19	20	21	22	23 Thanksgiving Day	24	25
26	27	28	29	30		

j. Thanksgiving is always in _____ .

k. Thanksgiving is always on the fourth _____ in November.

l. On this calendar, Thanksgiving is on _____ .

8 Work with a partner. Tell him or her about a holiday in your country. Tell the dates. Take turns.

STRATEGY **Learn new words.** Write new words in categories.

Months of the Year	U.S. Holidays	Ordinal Numbers
January	New Year's	first
February	Valentine's Day	second

GRAMMAR

Simple Present Tense + Frequency Adverbs

1 Listen.

> Do you ever eat pizza on Thanksgiving?
>
> No, I don't. I **never** eat pizza on Thanksgiving.
>
> Does he ever eat hamburgers on Independence Day?
>
> Yes, he does. He **sometimes** eats hamburgers on Independence Day.
>
> Does she ever have a party on her birthday?
>
> Yes, she does. She **often** has a party on her birthday.
>
> Do we ever go to school on our birthdays?
>
> Yes, we do. We **usually** go to school on our birthdays.
>
> Do they ever stay home from school on Thanksgiving?
>
> Yes, they do. They **always** stay home from school on Thanksgiving.

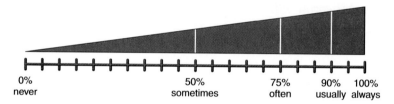

0%			50%		75%	90%	100%
never			sometimes		often	usually	always

2 Write the correct words. (The % tells you the frequency adverb to use.)

a. 0% We (**have/has**) _never have_ school on January 1.

b. 75% Our teacher (**give/gives**) _____ his students candy on Valentine's Day.

c. 90% I (**go/goes**) _____ to bed late on December 31.

d. 50% We (**go/goes**) _____ to a fireworks show on July 4.

e. 100% My father (**cook/cooks**) _____ a turkey on Thanksgiving.

f. 0% My friend and I (**go/goes**) _____ to school on Martin Luther King Day.

3 Work with a partner. Tell him or her what you do on holidays. Take turns.

Example:

On Mother's Day, we always go to my grandmother's house. I usually give my mother and my grandmother presents. My father sometimes gives my mother a present, too.

Unit 1

5

There is/There are

4 Listen.

> **There's** a holiday in May.
>
> **Is there** a holiday in September?   Yes, **there is**.
>
> **Is there** a holiday this Monday?   No, **there isn't**.
>
> **There are** thirty days in June.
>
> **Are there** thirty days in September?   Yes, **there are**.
>
> **Are there** thirty days in February?   No, **there aren't**.
>
> **Contraction**
>
> there is = there's

5 Look at the calendar below. Complete the questions with *Is there* or *Are there*.

    a. ___Are there___ thirty days in May?

    b. _____ two holidays on May 5?

    c. _____ a Japanese holiday on the calendar?

    d. _____ an African holiday in May?

    e. _____ a holiday for fathers in May?

    f. _____ an Independence Day on the calendar?

MAY

SUNDAY	MONDAY	TUESDAY	WEDNESDAY	THURSDAY	FRIDAY	SATURDAY
	1	2	3	4	5 Children's Day (Japan), Cinco de Mayo (Mexico)	6
7	8	9	10	11	12	13
14 Mother's Day	15	16	17	18	19	20
21	22	23	24	25 African Freedom Day, Independence Day (Argentina)	26	27
28	29 Memorial Day	30	31			

6 Work with a partner. Ask and answer the questions in Exercise 5.

Example:

    A: Are there thirty days in May?

    B: No, there aren't. There are thirty-one days in May.

LISTENING and SPEAKING

  1 Listen. Circle the correct date.

a.	March 3	March 13	(March 23)
b.	June 7	June 17	June 27
c.	April 3	August 3	October 3
d.	January 4	June 14	July 4
e.	February 7	February 17	February 27
f.	February 4	February 14	February 24
g.	September 2	September 7	September 17
h.	November 12	November 22	November 27

2 Listen and repeat.

a. When is your birthday, Sue? — It's April 26th.

b. April 25th? — No. April 26th.

c. Oh. And what do you usually do on your birthday? — My parents always have a big party for me.

d. What do you do at the party? — We usually sing, dance, and eat.

STRATEGY **Check information.**

A: When is your birthday?
B: It's April twenty-sixth.
A: April twenty-fifth?
B: No. April twenty-sixth.

3 Work with a partner. Practice the conversation in Exercise 2. Use your own information.

1 Read Laura's letter to her pen pal.

Laura Hansen
3506 Harlem Ave.
Chicago, IL 60634
USA

 AIRMAIL

Ms. Sofía Elena Castro
Av. 5 de mayo, No. 554
Aguascalientes, Mexico

January 18, _____

Dear Sofía Elena,

Hi! How are you?

I don't have school tomorrow because tomorrow is Martin Luther King Day here in the U.S. Do you celebrate that holiday? I don't think you do. When I have a day off, I usually get up at around nine o'clock. Then I go to my friend Polly's house or Polly comes to visit me. We always play video games. Then we usually go to the park and play basketball. We sometimes go to the shopping mall or to the movies.

What do you usually do when you have a day off from school? Do you go shopping with your friends? Do you go to the movies?

I hope you can visit me someday here in Chicago. Or maybe I can visit you in Aguascalientes. I'd love to meet you and your family.

Please write soon.

Your friend,
Laura

2 Fill in the chart about Laura.

What does Laura usually do on school holidays?
a. *She usually gets up at around nine o'clock.*
b.
c.
d.
e.

3 Fill in the chart about yourself.

What do you usually do on school holidays?
a.
b.
c.
d.
e.

STRATEGY **Use capital letters.**

- the first word of a sentence:
  He's in school today.
- the pronoun *I*:
  At the park, **I** usually play basketball.
- names of days and months:
  Saturday
  May
- names of holidays:
  Halloween
  Mother's Day
- names of people:
  Julio
  Margaret

 4 **Writing Check** Rewrite these sentences. Use capital letters correctly.

a. tomorrow is jessica's birthday.
Tomorrow is Jessica's birthday.

b. today is tuesday, march 3.

_____

c. i love valentine's day because i always get candy from my friends.

_____

d. my friend sally always has a party on earth day.

_____

e. what do you do on your favorite holiday?

_____

5 Work with a partner. Check your sentences in Exercise 4.

6 Write a letter to a friend. Tell what you usually do on school holidays. Use your information from Exercise 3. Be sure to use capital letters correctly.

_____

Dear _____,

_____

_____

_____

_____

_____

_____

_____

_____

_____

_____

_____

_____

_____

_____

_____

_____

_____

_____

_____

         _____,

         _____

THE CARROTS LOOK DELICIOUS!

TODAY'S MENU
Fish $2.09
Chicken $2.09
Carrots $.49
Rice $.49

Potatoes $.49
Orange $.45
Apple $.45
Banana $.45

Orange Juice $.49
Milk $.49
Bread $.29

1. Can I help you, Anita?

2. Yes. I'd like some chicken and some rice.

3. Would you like some carrots? — Yes, please. They look delicious!

4. Would you like a banana, an apple, or an orange? — I'll have a banana.

5. Would you like something to drink? — A glass of orange juice, please.

6. Chicken, rice, carrots, a banana, and a glass of orange juice. That will be $4.01. — Here's $5.00.

7. OK. Ninety-nine cents is your change. — Thank you.

GETTING STARTED

Warm Up

 1 Listen.

 2 Listen and repeat.

 3 Work with a partner. Ask and answer the questions.

    a. What is Anita eating for lunch today?

    b. What is she drinking?

    c. How much does her lunch cost?

Building Vocabulary

Fruits and Vegetables

  1 Listen and repeat.

2 Work with a partner. Ask and answer questions.

Examples:

A: Do you like apples?
B: Yes, I do. I love them./No, I don't. I hate them.
A: Do you like cabbage?
B: Yes, I do. I love it./No, I don't. I hate it.

Other Foods

  3 Listen and repeat.

4 Work with a partner. Ask and answer questions.

Example:

A: Do you ever eat chicken for breakfast?
B: No, I don't. I never eat chicken for breakfast. I sometimes eat it for lunch or dinner.

Amounts of Food

 Listen and repeat.

a. a loaf of bread

b. a carton of milk/eggs

c. a bottle of juice

d. a jar of pasta sauce

e. a bag of chips

f. a can of beans

g. a box of cereal

h. a package of cheese/cookies

i. a piece of chicken

j. a pound of meat/fish

6 Work with a partner. You're at the supermarket. What are you buying? Tell your partner. Take turns.

Example:

I'm buying a loaf of bread, a package of cookies, a box of rice, a pound of fish, a carton of milk, three tomatoes, and two cans of beans.

STRATEGY **Learn new words.**

Write new words. Draw pictures to go with them.

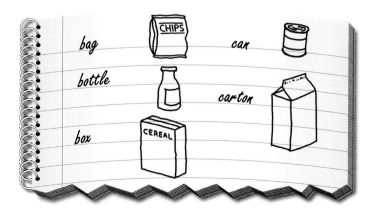

Unit 2

7 **Vocabulary Check** Write the words. Add *a* or *an* when necessary.

apple	bread	egg	orange	tomato
bananas	carrots	grapes	potato	

a. ____carrots____   **b.** ____an orange____   **c.** _____

d. _____   **e.** _____   **f.** _____

g. _____   **h.** _____   **i.** _____

8 Complete the sentences. Use the words in the box.

bag	box	carton	package
bottle	can	jar	pound

a. I need a ____carton____ of milk.
b. Let's buy a _____ of cereal and a _____ of chips.
c. We need a _____ of meat, a _____ of pasta, and a _____ of pasta sauce.
d. I want to buy a _____ of tomato juice and a _____ of corn.

GRAMMAR

Some/Any

 1 Listen.

Question	Statements
Do we have **any** fruit?	Yes, we do. We have **some** fruit.
	Yes. We have **some** grapes, **an** orange, and **a** banana.
	No, we don't. We don't have **any** fruit.
	No. We need **some** fruit.

2 Work with a partner. Look at the picture. Make conversations.

Examples:

vegetables

A: Do we have any vegetables?

B: Yes, we do. We have some lettuce, some carrots, and a tomato.

milk

A: Do we have any milk?

B: No, we don't have any milk.

a. bread	**e.** juice
b. eggs	**f.** cheese
c. fruit	**g.** meat
d. cookies	**h.** pizza

Unit 2

15

Count and Non-count Nouns

> **Count Nouns**
>
> | **Singular** | **Plural** |
> |---|---|
> | an egg | (some) eggs |
> | a sandwich | (some) sandwiches |
> | **How many** eggs do we have? | We have six eggs. |
> | **How many** sandwiches do you want? | I want one sandwich. |
>
> **Non-count Nouns**
>
> | | |
> |---|---|
> | (some) bread | |
> | (some) meat | |
> | **How much** bread do we have? | We have one loaf. |
> | **How much** meat do you want? | I want two pounds. |

4 Complete the chart. Write the words in the correct lists.

> | bananas | cake | chicken | juice | peaches | sauce |
> |---|---|---|---|---|---|
> | beans | carrots | cookies | milk | potatoes | soup |
> | bread | cheese | fish | oranges | rice | tomatoes |

Count Nouns	**Non-count Nouns**

5 Add two more nouns to each list in Exercise 4. Then work with a partner and compare your lists.

6 Complete the conversation. Write *how much* or *how many*.

MARIO: Let's make some sandwiches for lunch.

LUCY: Good idea. **(1.)** <u>How many</u> sandwiches do you want to make?

MARIO: I don't know. Let's see. **(2.)** _____ chicken do we have?

LUCY: There are six pieces here. **(3.)** _____ pieces do we need?

MARIO: Six is fine. And **(4.)** _____ tomatoes do we have?

LUCY: We have five tomatoes.

MARIO: Good. And **(5.)** _____ bread is there?

LUCY: There's a new loaf of bread. It isn't even open.

MARIO: OK. Oh, I'd like to make a fruit salad. **(6.)** _____ fruit is there?

LUCY: We have a bag of apples. There are some oranges and some peaches, too.

MARIO: Good. **(7.)** _____ oranges and peaches do we have?

LUCY: We have three large oranges and five peaches.

MARIO: Great! Let's get to work!

7 Work with a partner. Practice the conversation in Exercise 6.

LISTENING and SPEAKING

1 Listen. Complete the shopping list. Write the amounts.

THINGS I NEED AT THE STORE

Amounts	Items
1 carton	milk
	bananas
	mangoes
	beans
	rice
	bread

🎧 ② Listen and repeat.

STRATEGY **Check information.**

A: How many potatoes do we need?
B: Buy four potatoes.
A: I'm sorry. How many?
B: Four.

③ Work with a partner. Make a shopping list of three things. Practice the conversation in Exercise 2. Take turns.

THINGS I NEED AT THE STORE

Amounts	Items

READING and WRITING

1 The Food Guide Pyramid shows the foods we need to eat every day. Read about how many servings from each food group we need to eat.

FOOD GUIDE PYRAMID

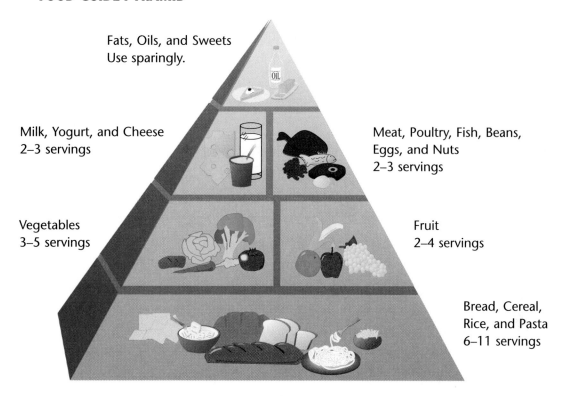

Fats, Oils, and Sweets
Use sparingly.

Milk, Yogurt, and Cheese
2–3 servings

Meat, Poultry, Fish, Beans,
Eggs, and Nuts
2–3 servings

Vegetables
3–5 servings

Fruit
2–4 servings

Bread, Cereal,
Rice, and Pasta
6–11 servings

2 Work with a partner. Look at the pictures in the pyramid. Which of these foods do you eat? Which of these foods do you *not* eat?

3 Read Michael's note to his friend Min Ho.

> October 4, _____
>
> Dear Min Ho,
>   It's lunchtime, and I'm having lunch in the school cafeteria. My friend Jason isn't in school today, so I'm eating alone. I'm very hungry today. I'm eating two pieces of chicken, a piece of bread and some butter, some rice, some green beans, a tomato salad, and an orange. I'm drinking a glass of milk.
>   Where do you usually have lunch? What do you usually eat and drink?
>   Write soon.
>
>   Your friend,
>   Michael

4 Match the foods in Michael's lunch with their food groups.
Write the correct numbers. You may use a number more than one time.

a. chicken ___3___   **1.** fats, oils, sweets
b. bread _____   **2.** milk, yogurt, cheese
c. butter _____   **3.** meat, poultry, fish, beans, eggs, nuts
d. rice _____   **4.** vegetables
e. green beans _____ **5.** fruit
f. tomatoes _____   **6.** bread, cereal, rice, pasta
g. an orange _____
h. milk _____

 Use punctuation marks.

Use a period (.):
• statements: I love green beans.
• titles: Mr. Jensen Mrs. Turner Ms. Blanco

Use a question mark (?):
• questions: How are you?

Use a comma (,):
• lists with *and*: I'm having a sandwich, an apple, and some orange juice.
• lists with *or*: I don't like eggs, butter, or cheese.
• two sentences joined with *and, so,* or *but*:
    I'm eating a piece of pizza, and I'm drinking a glass of milk.
    I'm hungry, so I'm eating a big lunch.
    We're hungry, but we're not thirsty.

5 Writing Check Add punctuation marks to these sentences.

a. What are you having for lunch today?
b. Do you want rice pasta or potatoes for dinner
c. Sue likes rice but she doesn't like pasta
d. Dario's mother is cooking fish rice and green beans for lunch
e. Mr Soto can't cook so he always eats in restaurants

6 Work with a partner. Check your sentences in Exercise 5.

7 At lunchtime, write a note to a friend. Tell him or her what you're
eating and drinking.

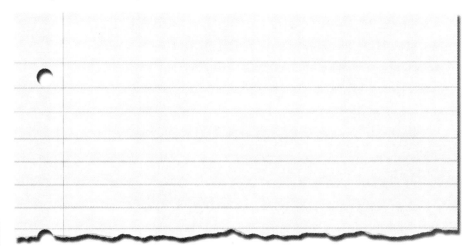

WHAT DO YOU HAVE TO DO TODAY?

Unit 3

The comic panels:

1. Do you ever watch *The Late Show* on TV, Marc?

No, I never do. I can't stay up late on weeknights because I have to get up early in the morning.

2. What time do you get up?

At 6:00.

3. Why so early?

Well, I have to take a shower, get dressed, have breakfast, and brush my teeth. I have to leave for school by 7:20. My first class starts at 8:00.

4. That's early! My first class is at 8:30. I live only three blocks from school, so I don't have to leave until 8:15.

You're lucky, Carlos!

GETTING STARTED

Warm Up

1. Listen.

2. Listen and repeat.

3. Work with a partner. Ask and answer the questions.

Example:

A: Why can't Marc stay up late on weeknights?

B: He has to get up early in the morning.

a. What time does Marc get up in the morning?

b. What does Marc do before he leaves for school?

c. What time does Marc's first class start?

d. Who lives close to school, Marc or Carlos?

Unit 3

21

Building Vocabulary

Breakfast, Lunch, and Dinner

  1 Listen and repeat.

    a. It's 7:30 in the morning. Lucy is having breakfast. Today she's having two eggs, two pieces of bread, and a glass of milk.

    b. It's noon. Lucy is having lunch in the school cafeteria. Today she's having a chicken sandwich, a salad, an apple, and a carton of milk.

    c. It's 4:00 in the afternoon. Lucy is doing her homework and having a snack. Today she's having a banana and a carton of orange juice.

    d. It's 6:30 in the evening. Lucy is having dinner at home with her family. They're having fish, rice, carrots, and salad.

2 Work with a partner. Cover the sentences next to the pictures. Tell about Lucy's meals. Take turns.

3 Work with a partner. Take turns asking and answering questions about your meals.

    a. What time do you usually have breakfast? lunch? dinner?

    b. What do you usually have for breakfast? for lunch? for dinner?

Daily Routines

4 Listen and repeat.

a. Andrew gets up at 5:00 in the morning.

b. First, he takes a shower.

c. After he takes a shower, he gets dressed.

d. Then he combs his hair.

e. After he has breakfast, he brushes his teeth.

f. Then he leaves for school.

g. He gets home from school in the afternoon. Then he does his homework.

h. He has dinner at 6:30 in the evening.

i. Before he goes to bed, he watches TV.

j. He goes to bed at 10:00 at night.

5 Work with a partner. Ask and answer questions about Andrew's routine.

Examples:

A: What time does Andrew get up?

B: He gets up at five o'clock in the morning. What does he do first?

A: First, he takes a shower. What does he do after that?

B: He _____.

6 **Vocabulary Check** The sentences are about Paula's daily routine.
Match the sentences to the pictures. Write the letters on the lines.

a.	She gets dressed.	e.	She has dinner.
b.	She goes to bed.	f.	She eats breakfast.
c.	She brushes her teeth.	g.	She gets up.
d.	She takes a shower.	h.	She combs her hair.

 6 _____ c _____

 ☐ _____

 ☐ _____

 ☐ _____

 ☐ _____

 ☐ _____

 ☐ _____

☐ _____

7 Work with a partner. Look at the pictures in Exercise 6. Put the
pictures in order. Write the numbers in the boxes. Talk about Paula's
routine. What does she do first? Then what does she do?

Example:

A: First, she gets up.

B: Then she _____ .

8 Work with a partner. Talk about Jenny's morning routine. Make sentences with *before* and *after*.

Example:

Jenny takes a shower at 7:00. She gets dressed at 7:15.

A: Before she gets dressed, she takes a shower.

B: After she takes a shower, she gets dressed.

a. Jenny gets dressed at 7:15. She combs her hair at 7:20.

b. She eats breakfast at 7:30. She brushes her teeth at 8:00.

c. She brushes her teeth at 8:00. She goes to school at 8:15.

d. She goes to her locker at 8:30. She goes to her first class at 8:40.

9 Work with a partner. Talk about Mike's afternoon routine. Make sentences with *before* and *after*.

a. Mike goes to math class at 12:45. He has PE at 1:30.

b. He goes to his locker at 2:15. He goes home at 2:30.

c. He eats a snack at 3:00. He plays basketball at 3:15.

d. He plays basketball at 3:15. He watches TV at 5:00.

10 Work with a partner. Take turns asking and answering questions about your routines. Use the words below or your own ideas.

Example:

before/have breakfast

A: What do you do before you have breakfast?

B: Before I have breakfast, I get dressed.

a. after/have breakfast
d. before/eat dinner

b. before/go to school
e. after/eat dinner

c. after/get home from school
f. before/go to bed

STRATEGY **Learn new words.** Write whole expressions.

Routines
brush your hair/teeth
comb your hair
get dressed
get up
have breakfast/lunch/dinner/a snack

GRAMMAR

Go/Go to/Go to the

 1 Listen.

go	
I usually **go home** after school.	I sometimes **go downtown**.
go to	
He **goes to school** every day.	He **goes to bed** late every night.
He **goes to class** in the morning.	On Saturdays, he **goes to soccer practice**.
After school, he **goes to work**.	
go to the	
We like to **go to the library** after school.	On Saturday, we always **go to the supermarket**.
We often **go to the shopping mall**.	
We usually **go to the movies** on Friday night.	Sometimes we **go to the post office**, too.

2 Complete the story with the correct forms of *go, go to,* and *go to the.*

Weekdays are very busy at my house. In the morning, my sister and I **(1.)** ___*go to*___ school. My mother is studying English, so she **(2.)** _____ class an hour after we leave. My father **(3.)** _____ work in the afternoon, so he usually **(4.)** _____ supermarket before work to buy food for dinner.

On Mondays and Wednesdays, I **(5.)** _____ downtown after school. I **(6.)** _____ library because I have a part-time job there. I sometimes **(7.)** _____ post office to mail letters for the librarian.

On Tuesdays and Thursdays, I **(8.)** _____ band practice after school. Friday is my favorite weekday because it's the beginning of the weekend! I **(9.)** _____ home after school. After we have a snack, my friends and I usually **(10.)** _____ mall. We sometimes **(11.)** _____ movies on Friday night. We always **(12.)** _____ home late on Fridays. I never **(13.)** _____ bed before midnight.

3 Make a list of places you go every week. Then work with a partner. Tell your partner where you go.

Example:

On Monday and Wednesday, I go to English class. After class, I go to the library. On Tuesday, Thursday, and Friday, I go to work. On the weekend, I usually go to the mall or to the park.

Have to

4 Listen.

> **Do** I **have to wash** the dishes tonight?
>
> Yes, you **do**. You **have to wash** the dishes after dinner.
>
> No, you **don't**. You **don't have to wash** the dishes tonight.
>
> **Do** you **have to go** home now?
>
> Yes, I **do**. I **have to be** home by 8:00.
>
> No, I **don't**. I **don't have to be** home until 9:00.
>
> **Does** Jason **have to get up** early every day?
>
> Yes, he **does**. He **has to get up** at 6:00.
>
> No, he **doesn't**. He **doesn't have to get up** early on the weekend.
>
> **Do** you and Sue **have to work** today?
>
> Yes, we **do**. We **have to go** to work at noon.
>
> No, we **don't**. We **don't have to work** this week.
> _____
> What time **does** Diana **have to leave** for school?
>
> She **has to leave** at 7:45.
>
> What **do** your parents **have to do** today?
>
> They **have to go** to work.

5 Complete the conversations with forms of *have to*. Then practice the conversations with a partner.

1. **A:** Martin's father works at night.
   B: ___*Does*___ he ___*have to*___ get up early in the morning?
   A: No, he _____.
   B: What time _____ he _____ get up?
   A: He _____ get up at 3:00 in the afternoon.

2. **A:** I feel sick. _____ I _____ go to school today?
   B: No, you _____. You _____ go to the doctor.

3. **A:** This is fun. When _____ we _____ leave?
   B: I'm sorry, but we _____ leave right now.

4. **A:** Why can't Wendy come with us to the party tonight? What _____ she _____ do?
   B: She _____ study.

1 Listen to the conversation. Read the sentences.
Circle **T** for True or **F** for False.

a.	Elena can go to the basketball game.	**T**	(**F**)
b.	She has band practice in the morning.	**T**	**F**
c.	She has to get up at 6:00 tomorrow morning.	**T**	**F**
d.	Judy always gets up at 6:00 in the morning.	**T**	**F**
e.	Elena eats breakfast before she walks her dog.	**T**	**F**
f.	Judy puts her books in her book bag after she eats breakfast.	**T**	**F**

2 Listen and repeat.

STRATEGY ▶ **Ask for an explanation. Give an explanation.**

A: Do you want to go to the movies tomorrow?
B: I'd like to go, but I can't.
A: How come?
B: I have to clean my room.

3 Work with a partner. Practice the conversation in Exercise 2. Use your own information.

4 What do you have to do this week? Make a list. Then work with a partner. Tell your partner what you have to do. Take turns.

5 Work in groups of three. Tell what your partner has to do this week.

READING and WRITING

 Read about Connie's weekday routine.

My name is Connie. I have a lot to do in the morning before I go to school. I have to get up at 7:00 every day. After I take a shower, I fix my hair. Then I have to make breakfast for my little brother and sister. After breakfast, I have to wash the dishes and clean the kitchen. Then I brush my teeth. I have to leave the house before 8:30. The bus comes at 8:45, and I have to walk to the bus stop. I get to school at around 9:00.

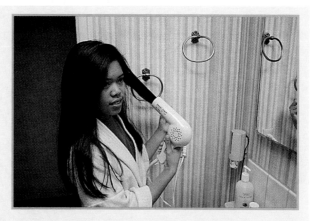

After I get out of school at 3:30, I go to the library. I have to use the computer at the library because I don't have a computer at home. I have to be home by 5:30, so I usually leave the library at 5:00. When I get home, I help my mother make dinner. We eat at 6:30. After dinner, I wash the dishes and clean the kitchen again. My brother and sister usually help me. Then, if I don't have to do homework, I watch TV or I call my friends on the phone. At 10:00, I put on my pajamas, brush my teeth, and go to bed.

 Work with a partner. List Connie's weekday activities. Include the time of day if possible.

Before School	After School
gets up at 7:00	gets out of school at 3:30

Join sentences with *and, but, so,* and *because*.

- I wash the dishes. I clean the kitchen.
  I wash the dishes **and** clean the kitchen.

- I have to go to bed early on weeknights.
  I can go to bed late on weekends.
  I have to go to bed early on weeknights, **but**
  I can go to bed late on weekends.

- I need a book. I'm going to the library.
  I need a book, **so** I'm going to the library.

- I'm leaving now. I have to be home by 9:00.
  I'm leaving now **because** I have to be home by 9:00.

3 Writing Check Join these sentences with *and, but, so,* or *because*.

a. Maggie has to be at the bus stop by 8:15. The bus comes at 8:15.

   _____

b. I'd like some cereal. We don't have any milk.

   _____

c. Raisa's parents work at night. She makes dinner for her brother.

   _____

d. I have to wash my face. I have to brush my teeth.

   _____

4 Work with a partner. Check your sentences in Exercise 3.

5 List your weekday activities in the chart. Include times if possible.
   Use the chart for Exercise 2 on page 29 for help.

Before School	After School

6 On your own paper, write two paragraphs about your weekday
   activities. Use your notes from the chart in Exercise 5.

1 Write the dates in long form.

  a. 6/3 _____June 3_____
  b. 12/25 _____
  c. 2/27 _____
  d. 5/1 _____
  e. 10/12 _____

2 Write the dates in short form.

  a. April 26 _____4/26_____
  b. November 20 _____
  c. August 4 _____
  d. January 10 _____
  e. March 13 _____

3 Complete each question with the correct simple present form of the verb. Then answer the question with the adverb of frequency in parentheses.

  1. A: (watch) ____Do____ you ever ____watch____ TV on weekdays?
   B: (always) __Yes, I always watch TV on weekdays.__
  2. A: (mail) _____ Tracy ever _____ her letters at the post office?
   B: (never) _____
  3. A: (shop) _____ you and your friends ever _____ on Saturdays?
   B: (often) _____
  4. A: (study) _____ Karl and Thomas ever _____ in the library?
   B: (sometimes) _____
  5. A: (have) _____ you ever _____ a party on your birthday?
   B: (usually) _____

4 Match the questions with the answers. Write the letters.

  1. Would you like some cherries? __c__
  2. Do you like cheese? ____
  3. Do you like carrots? ____
  4. Would you like some pizza? ____

  a. Yes, I do. I love them.
  b. No, thanks. I don't like it.
  c. Yes, please. They look delicious!
  d. No, I don't. I hate it.

5 Complete the conversations. Choose the correct words to complete each sentence.

  1. A: (Is there/Are there) _____Are there_____
   (some/any) _____any_____ eggs in the refrigerator?
   B: No, (there isn't/there aren't) _____ (some/any) _____ eggs.

2. A: Do we have (**some/any**) _____*any*_____ juice?

B: (**How much/How many**) _____ juice do you want?
(**There's/There are**) _____ (**a/some**) _____
bottle of apple juice in the cabinet.

3. A: (**How much/How many**) _____ sandwiches do we
have to make?

B: (**How many/How much**) _____ students are in our class?

A: (**There's/There are**) _____ seven students, so we have to
make seven sandwiches.

B: So (**how much/how many**) _____ bread do we need?

A: Let's buy (**a/some**) _____ loaf of French bread.

6 Look at Tony's Saturday routine. He always has to go to
the same places and do the same things. Write sentences.

a. _Tony has to go downtown in the morning._

b. _____

c. _____

d. _____

e. _____

f. _____

g. _____

h. _____

SATURDAY

downtown in the morning

karate class at 11:00

work at 1:00

basketball practice at 6:00

dinner at 7:30

Scott's house at 8:30

home at 12:00

bed at 12:30

7 Answer the questions. Write complete sentences.

a. Do you stay up late on weeknights?

_____

b. What time do you have to get up on weekdays?

_____

c. What do you have to do before you leave for school?

_____

d. Do you comb or brush your hair?

_____

e. What time do you leave for school?

_____

f. What time do you get home from school?

_____

g. What do you have to do after you get home?

_____

WHAT DO YOU WANT TO BUY?

Unit 4

GETTING STARTED

Warm Up

 1 Listen

 2 Listen and repeat.

3 Work with a partner. Ask and answer the questions.

a. What is Chen doing downtown?
b. Where does he need to go?
c. Where is Alex going?
d. What does Alex want to buy?

e. Does Chen like the group The Baby Dolls?
f. Does Chen have enough money for a new CD?

Unit 4

33

Building Vocabulary

Things to Buy

  1 Listen and repeat.

2 Work with a partner. Take turns buying things at the store.

Example:

A: Can I help you?

B: Yes. I'd like to buy these two CDs and this hairbrush.

A: OK. That will be $34.39.

Places in the Neighborhood

 3 Listen and repeat.

4 Work with a partner. Take turns reading about Sam and Carmen and saying where they need to go.

Example:

A: Sam doesn't have any bread, and he wants to make some sandwiches.

B: He needs to go to the grocery store.

a. Sam wants to rent a video.

b. Sam's car has only a little gas, and he wants to drive to school tomorrow.

c. Sam wants to buy a toothbrush and a comb.

d. Carmen would like to buy a CD for her friend.

e. Carmen's brother is using her car, so she has to take the bus to work.

f. Carmen wants to buy some new jeans.

5 **Vocabulary Check** Write the words.

bananas	comb	hairbrush	toothbrush
book	compact disc (CD)	magazine	toothpaste
cassette	gas	newspaper	video

a. _____   **b.** _____   **c.** _____

d. _____   **e.** _____   **f.** _____

g. _____   **h.** _____   **i.** _____

j. _____   **k.** _____   **l.** _____

6 Work with a partner. Where can you buy the things in Exercise 5?
Take turns asking and answering questions. Use information about
your neighborhood.

Example:

A: Where can I buy a comb?

B: You can buy a comb at Hedge's Drugstore or at Walgreen's.

STRATEGY **Learn new words.**

A compound noun is a noun made up
of two words.

Examples:

toothbrush = tooth + brush

toothpaste = tooth + paste

Write related compound nouns.

Compound Nouns
hairbrush
hairdo
hairdryer
hairstyle
hairstylist

GRAMMAR

One/Some

 1 Listen.

Singular Count Nouns	I need a new comb.
	You can buy **one** at the drugstore.
Plural Count Nouns	I need (some) stamps.
	You can get **some** at the post office.
Non-count Nouns	I need (some) bread.
	You can get **some** at the supermarket.

2 Work with a partner. Ask and answer questions. Use the cues and the map.

Examples:

video

A: Where can I get a video?
B: You can get one at Star Video.
A: Where's Star Video?
B: It's at the corner of Main Street and First Avenue.

milk

A: Where can I buy milk?
B: You can buy some at Quick Stop Grocery Store.
A: Where's Quick Stop Grocery Store?
B: It's on Main Street, between the gas station and the drugstore.

a. toothbrush
b. T-shirt
c. gas
d. fruit
e. magazines
f. CD
g. toothpaste
h. new clothes

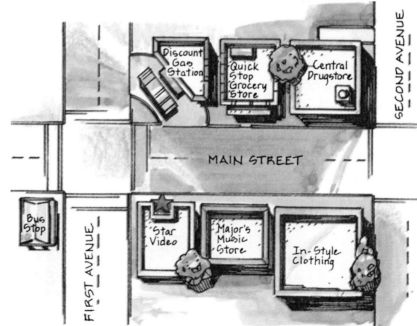

Questions with Verb + Infinitive

  **3** Listen.

Questions	Answers
Where **does** Ruben **want to go**? Why **does** he **want to go** there?	He **wants to go** to the music store. Because he **wants to buy** a CD.
Do you **want to rent** a video? **Does** Mei **need to go** to the bank?	Yes, I **do**. I **want to rent** *Star Wars*. No, she **doesn't**. She **doesn't have to go out** today.

4 Read the answers. Write the questions.

  a. Question: _____*Do you want to go to the movies?*_____
      Answer: No, I don't. I don't want to go to the movies.

  b. Question: _____
      Answer: He wants to go to his favorite restaurant.

  c. Question: _____
      Answer: Yes, she does. She needs to get a toothbrush.

  d. Question: _____
      Answer: I want to go to Jan's Clothing Store.

  e. Question: _____
      Answer: I want to go to Jan's because I need a new sweater.

  f. Question: _____
      Answer: No, he doesn't want to go to the video store.

  g. Question: _____
      Answer: Yes, I do. I need to go to the supermarket.

  h. Question: _____
      Answer: She wants to go to the library because she needs to study.

5 Work with a partner. Use the cues to make questions to ask your partner. Take turns asking and answering. Answer with your own information.

Example:

Where/want/go for lunch?

A: Where do you want to go for lunch?
B: I want to go to Hamburger House.

  a. Where/need/go after this class?
  b. What/want/do after school today?
  c. Do/have/do any homework for tomorrow?
  d. Do/want/go to the shopping mall on Saturday?
  e. What/want/have for dinner?
  f. What/need/buy at the drugstore?
  g. Do/need/buy new shoes?

Demonstrative Adjectives: Review

6 Listen.

> I want to buy **this** CD and **these** cassettes. I want to buy **that** newspaper and **those** magazines.

7 Complete the sentences with *this*, *these*, *that*, or *those*.
Then practice the sentences with a partner.

a. I want to buy _____*that*_____ newspaper.

b. Does _____ bus go to the park?

c. Please take _____ bags to my car.

d. I want to buy _____ brown shoes.

e. Can I rent a movie from _____ video store?

f. I want to take out _____ book.

1 Listen to each conversation. Circle the correct information.

Conversation 1

a. The woman needs to buy a _____.   magazine   newspaper

b. She needs to go to _____.   Better Grocery   Better Drugstore

c. It's on _____.   Fourth Avenue   Main Street

Conversation 2

a. The man wants to buy a _____.   cassette   CD

b. He needs to go to _____.   Central Department Store   Mac's Music

c. It's on _____.   Main Street   High Street

Conversation 3

a. The woman wants to buy a _____.   T-shirt   sweater

b. She needs to go to _____.   The Clothes Closet   The Music Man

c. The store is _____.   in the shopping mall   on High Street

  2 Listen and repeat.

STRATEGY **Stop to think before you give information.**

A: Where is Ladybug Fashions?

B: Uh … it's on Center Street, um … next to the movie theaters.

Unit 4

3 Work with a partner. Practice the conversation in Exercise 2.
Use your own information.

4 Where does your family buy food? Do you like to rent videos? If yes,
where do you rent them? Do you like to buy cassettes or CDs? Where
do you go to buy them? Work with a partner. Ask and answer these
questions. Take turns.

5 Work in groups of three. Tell about your partner's answers to the
questions in Exercise 4.

READING and WRITING

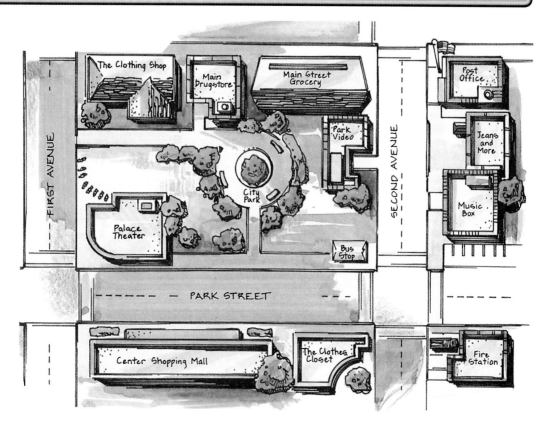

1 Look at the map. Work with a partner. Ask and answer the questions.
Take turns.

   a. What's the name of the music store?
   b. Where's the bus stop?
   c. Where can you go to buy toothpaste?
   d. Where's the movie theater?
   e. What's next to the music store?
   f. Where can you go to buy milk?
   g. What's across the street from The Clothing Shop?
   h. Where can you go to buy a sweater?

Know when to use capital letters and when *not* to use them.

- Capitalize names of specific people, places, and things:

  José Canseco

  Camelot Music Store

  Main Street

- Don't capitalize words that are not names—unless they come at the beginning of the sentence:

  He's a **m**an.

  It's a **m**usic **s**tore.

  There's a video store on this **s**treet.

- Capitalize names of days, months, and holidays:

  Monday

  January

  Thanksgiving Day

- Don't capitalize words such as *today*, *tomorrow*, *week*, or *day*—unless they come at the beginning of the sentence.

 2 **Writing Check** Rewrite the sentences. Use capital letters correctly.

  a. We saw the movie *Last Chance* at the palace theater.

  _____

  b. We go to the Movies every Weekend.

  _____

  c. Is there a good Clothing Store on Center street?

  _____

  d. Which Newspaper do you like to read on sundays?

  _____

  e. We always rent our videos at a store called video library.

  _____

  f. I mail my letters and packages at the Post Office across the Street.

  _____

3 Work with a partner. Check your sentences in Exercise 2.

4 Where do you do things in your neighborhood? First, read Angela's paragraph about her neighborhood. Then, on your own paper, write about your neighborhood. Draw a map that shows the places you describe.

My name is Angela. I can do a lot of things in my neighborhood. I can buy and rent videos at Park Video. I can mail letters and packages at the post office. My favorite store is Jeans and More. I buy almost all my clothes there. When I have some extra money, I like to go to Music Box. I love music, and I like to buy the new CDs when they come out. My favorite place in the neighborhood is the Palace Theater. My friends and I like to see new movies there.

IT'S AN EMERGENCY!

1. Oh, no! What's wrong, Sam? There's a fire in the garage. Call 911!

2. Emergency Operator. What's your address? Help! There's a fire in our garage! 54 North Elm Street.

3. What's your name? Jin Bong. B-O-N-G. And your phone number? 555-9931.

4. OK. Stay calm. A fire truck will be there in a few minutes.

GETTING STARTED

Warm Up

 1 Listen.

 2 Listen and repeat.

3 Work with a partner. Ask and answer the questions.

    a. What does Sam see?

    b. What does Jin do to help?

    c. What does the emergency operator ask Jin?

    d. What will happen next?

Building Vocabulary

Emergencies

  1 Listen and repeat.

a. My car is on fire!   **b.** Our garage is on fire!   **c.** Our neighbor's house is on fire!

d. Someone stole my wallet!   **e.** Someone stole my purse!   **f.** A burglar broke into our apartment!

2 Work with a partner. Take turns making and receiving telephone calls about the emergencies in Exercise 1.

Examples:

A: 911.
B: Help! My car is on fire!
A: Where are you?
B: On Cherry Street, next to the supermarket.
A: A fire truck will be there soon.

A: Police Department.
B: Someone stole my wallet!
A: Where are you now?
B: 436 North Broadway.
A: OK. A police officer will be there soon.

More Emergencies

  3 Listen and repeat.

a. There's an accident! A truck hit a car, and the driver of the car is bleeding.

b. She's unconscious! She's hardly breathing!

c. He can't breathe! He's choking on something!

d. She fell off her bike! I think she broke her leg!

4 Work with a partner. Take turns making and receiving telephone calls about the emergencies in Exercise 3.

Example:

A: 911, Emergency.

B: Yes. I just saw an accident. A truck hit a car, and the driver of the car is bleeding.

A: Where's the accident?

B: On Interstate 94, near the Lake Street exit.

A: OK. An ambulance will be there in a few minutes.

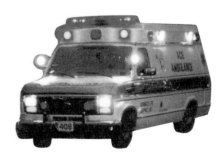

Action: Emergencies and Accidents

 5 Listen and repeat.

a. A burglar **broke into** a store and stole some money.

b. The burglar **ran into** me.

c. I **fell down** and hurt my knee.

d. When I **got up**, I didn't have my wallet. I think the burglar **picked up** my purse and **took out** my wallet.

6 Complete the conversations. Write the words. Then practice the conversations with a partner.

broke into	got up	ran into
fell down	picked up	took out

1. A: There's a terrible accident on Main Street.
   B: What happened?
   A: A car ___ran into___ a building.

2. A: Where's your television set?
   B: A burglar _____ my apartment and stole it.

3. A: How did you hurt your leg?
   B: I _____ in the gym. When I _____, the PE teacher took me to the nurse's office. She put a bandage on it.

4. A: Where's your wallet?
   B: I _____ my wallet at the store, and someone stole it. I had $25.00 in it.

5. A: I'm so angry!
   B: Why?
   A: Someone _____ my book bag and took out my new glasses!

STRATEGY

Learn new words.

Write two-word verbs.

Two-Word Verbs
break into/broke into
pick up/picked up
fall down/fell down
run into/ran into
get up/got up
take out/took out

  7 **Vocabulary Check**

Complete the sentences.
Write the words.

accident	burglar	emergency	purse	wallet
ambulance	car	fire truck	truck	

a. My _____
is on fire!

b. A _____
broke into our house.

c. Someone stole my
_____.

d. Help! This is an
_____! My
house is on fire.

e. We saw an
_____.

f. The _____
went off the road.

g. Someone stole
my mother's
_____.

h. The _____
is on its way now!

i. The _____
will be there in a
few minutes.

8 Work with a partner. Look again at the sentences in Exercise 7. Take
turns completing the sentences using different words. Use your own
ideas.

Example:

A: My computer is on fire!

B: My kitchen is on fire!

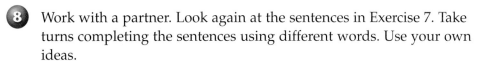

GRAMMAR

Simple Past Tense

  Listen.

Regular Verbs	
Simple Present Tense	**Simple Past Tense (verb + –*ed*)**
I always **call** 911 in an emergency.	I **called** 911 yesterday.
Accidents sometimes **happen** here.	An accident **happened** on our street this morning.

Irregular Verbs	
Simple Present Tense	**Simple Past Tense**
I sometimes **break** things.	I **broke** a glass yesterday.
Marta sometimes **falls down**.	She **fell down** last night.
We sometimes **see** accidents.	We **saw** a car accident yesterday.
Trucks sometimes **hit** cars.	A truck **hit** a car this morning.
Ben sometimes **takes** the bus.	Ben **took** the bus yesterday.
Burglars often **steal** things.	A burglar **stole** our TV set last night.
Jenny **runs** every morning.	This morning, she **ran** for an hour.
I usually **get** to school early.	Yesterday I **got** to school late.
We usually **go** to Rob's Grocery.	On Friday, we **went** to Best Grocery.
My friends sometimes **come** to visit.	Last night, my friends **came** to visit.

2 Complete the stories. Write the past tense forms of the verbs.

a. I **(1. see)** _____*saw*_____ an accident yesterday. It
(2. happen) _____ on the corner of
Lake Street and Fifth Avenue. A small truck
(3. hit) _____ a road sign. A police car
(4. get) _____ there five minutes after
the accident.

b. Hillel **(5. run)** _____ to the bus stop because
he was late. He **(6. fall down)** _____ as
he **(7. get on)** _____ the bus. He
(8. break) _____ his leg, so the bus driver
(9. call) _____ 911. An ambulance
(10. come) _____ really fast.

c. A burglar **(11. steal)** _____ our CD player
last week. We think he **(12. get)** _____ in
and **(13. go)** _____ out through the window.
He didn't know our CD player was broken!

Unit 5

48

Simple Past Tense: Information Questions

 **3** Listen.

Questions	Answers
What did you **see?**	I **saw** an accident. A blue car **hit** a green car.
Where did it **happen?**	It **happened** in front of my school.
When did it **happen?**	It **happened** at about 3:00 this afternoon.
How did it **happen?**	The green car **turned** left at a red light.

4 Complete the conversation. Write the correct form of the verbs.
(Remember to use *did* in past tense questions.) Then practice the
conversation with a partner.

A: What **(1. do)** ____did____ you ____do____ last night?

B: I **(2. go)** ____went____ to the movies.

A: Who **(3. go)** _____ you _____ to the
movies with?

B: I **(4. go)** _____ with my friend Lori.

A: What movie **(5. see)** _____ you _____?

B: We **(6. see)** _____ *Emergencies*.

A: How **(7. like)** _____ you _____ it?

B: We **(8. love)** _____ it. In one accident scene, a car
(9. run into) _____ a building.

A: What happened?

B: The driver **(10. break)** _____ his leg. An ambulance
(11. come) _____ and **(12. take)** _____ him
to the hospital.

A: What time **(13. get)** _____ you _____ home?

B: Well, after the movie, Lori and I **(14. go)** _____ to Rose's
Restaurant for a snack. I **(15. take)** _____
Lori home at around 11:00, and I
(16. get) _____ home at 11:15.

1 Listen to each 911 call. Circle the correct information.

Caller 1

a. Peter is reporting _____.

   an accident   a fire   a burglary

b. The person on the floor is _____.

   choking   unconscious   bleeding

c. The _____ will be there in a few minutes.

   police   fire truck   ambulance

Caller 2

a. Elsa called 911 to report _____.

   a fire   an accident   a burglary

b. The neighbor's _____ is on fire.

   house   truck   garage

c. The _____ will be there in 15 minutes.

   ambulance   police   fire truck

Caller 3

a. Darren wants _____ to come.

   a police car   a fire truck   an ambulance

b. The emergency is at _____.

   his house   his store   his neighbor's house

c. Darren has to wait _____.

   an hour   half an hour   15 minutes

  2 Listen and repeat.

a. I saw something terrible yesterday.

What did you see?

b. A girl fell off her bike and broke her leg.

Really? So what did you do?

c. I called 911.

Then what happened?

An ambulance came and took her to the hospital.

Express interest.

> **A:** A girl fell off her bike and broke her leg.
>
> **B:** Really? So what did you do?

3 Work with a partner. Practice the conversation in Exercise 2.

4 Did you ever have an accident? Did you ever see an accident? What happened? How did it happen? Where did it happen? When did it happen? Work with a partner. Take turns telling about an accident that you had or saw.

READING and WRITING

1 Read the accident report.

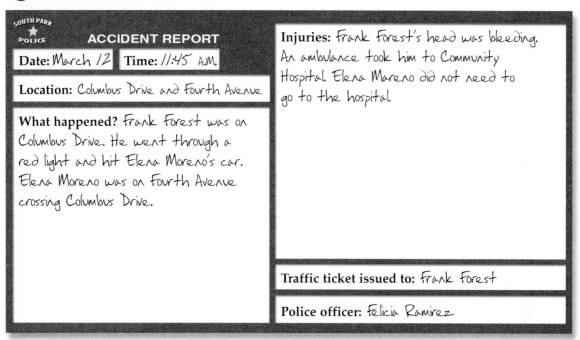

2 Work with a partner. Ask and answer the questions. Take turns.

a. When did the accident happen?

b. Where did it happen?

c. What happened?

d. What were the injuries?

e. Why did Frank Forest get a ticket?

STRATEGY **Don't repeat the same nouns. Use pronouns when possible.**

- Mr. Columbo saw an accident, so Mr. Columbo called the police.
  Mr. Columbo saw an accident, so **he** called the police.

- The three friends went to the mall, and the three friends saw a good movie.

- The three friends went to the mall, and **they** saw a good movie.

Writing Check Rewrite the sentences. Change nouns to pronouns when possible.

    a. The two burglars broke into a store, and the two burglars stole a computer.

    _____

    _____

    b. The woman is choking, and the woman can't breathe.

    _____

    _____

    c. John saw the fire, so John called 911.

    _____

    _____

    d. The man is getting a ticket because the man went through a red light.

    _____

    _____

    e. My brothers broke their legs when my brothers fell out of a tree.

    _____

    _____

4 Work with a partner. Check your sentences in Exercise 3.

5 You work in the emergency room at Community Hospital. Look at the pictures. Then fill out the accident report about Juana Cruz's accident.

Community Hospital

EMERGENCY ROOM REPORT

Patient's name: Juana Cruz

Date: April 11   Time:

Location:

Injuries:

What happened?

Emergency room clerk's signature:

DID YOU STUDY FOR THE TEST?

GETTING STARTED

Warm Up

 1 Listen.

 2 Listen and repeat.

3 Work with a partner. Ask and answer the questions.
   a. Where did Scott and Julio go on Friday night?
   b. Who did Scott go with?
   c. Who did Julio go with?
   d. What did Julio do all night?

Building Vocabulary

School Activities

  1 Listen and repeat.

a. On Monday morning, the students attended an assembly in the auditorium.

b. On Tuesday morning, they voted in an election.

c. On Tuesday evening, they went to a concert.

d. On Wednesday morning, they attended a student council meeting.

e. On Wednesday afternoon, they went to a volleyball game.

f. On Thursday afternoon, they went to a science fair.

g. On Friday night, they went to a dance.

2 Work with a partner. Take turns asking and answering questions.

Example:

A: What did the students do on Monday morning?

B: They attended an assembly in the auditorium.

More School Activities

 Listen and repeat.

a. They decorated the gym.

b. They danced to the band.

c. They marched on the field.

d. They cheered for their team.

e. They ran for student council.

f. They voted in the school election.

g. She ran in the race.

h. He entered the science fair.

 Work with a partner. Cover the sentences under the pictures. Ask, "What did he/she/they do?" Take turns asking and answering questions.

Example:

A: What did they do?

B: They decorated the gym.

5 **Vocabulary Check** Complete the sentences. Write the words.

assembly	dance	science fair
auditorium	election	student council
band	game	

a. There are no students in the _____ today.

b. The students voted in the school _____.

c. Many students entered the _____.

d. The students in the _____ marched on the football field.

e. Five students attended a _____ meeting.

f. On Friday night, all the students went to the school _____.

g. We went to the baseball _____ to see our team play.

h. The principal talked to the students at the school _____ on Monday morning.

6 Work with a partner. Look again at the pictures in Exercise 5. Take turns asking and answering questions about places and activities at your own school. Use your own ideas.

Example:

A: Is there an auditorium at our school?

B: Yes, there is. Does our school ever have elections?

STRATEGY **Learn new words.**

Think about nouns that go with certain verbs.

go to…

… a game   … a concert
… a science fair   … a dance

Write new verbs and different nouns that go with them.

attend …
 an assembly
 a meeting

enter …
 the science fair
 the race

GRAMMAR

Object Pronouns

 **1** Listen.

Subject Pronouns	Object Pronouns	
I	**me**	Lin went to the game with **me**.
you	**you**	Rosa and I looked for **you**.
he	**him**	I voted for **him**.
she	**her**	Some students voted for **her**.
it	**it**	Ed saw the race, but I didn't see **it**.
we	**us**	Please come to the dance with **us**.
they	**them**	Meg and Al went to the dance. I saw **them** there.

2 Complete the story. Write the correct object pronouns. (Use each pronoun only one time.)

My friend Marie wanted to go to the volleyball game on Friday, so I went to the game with **(1.)** _____*her*_____. We saw Marie's brother at the game, so we sat with **(2.)** _____. We looked for you, but we didn't see **(3.)** _____.

Our team hit the ball a lot, but the other team didn't hit **(4.)** _____ very much. We like the players on our team, so we cheered for **(5.)** _____.

Would you like to go to the next game with **(6.)** _____? Maybe Marie can go with **(7.)** _____, too.

3 Work with a partner. You're at a school dance, and you're looking for your friends. Use the picture to ask and answer questions. Take turns.

Example:

A: Do you see Jack?

B: No, I don't see him. Do you see Pedro?

A: Yes, I see him.

Simple Past Tense: Statements

4 Listen.

Affirmative	Negative
I **cheered** for the team last night.	I **didn't cheer** for the team yesterday.
You **went** to the Valentine's Day dance.	You **didn't go** to the Halloween dance.
She **planned** the trip yesterday.	She **didn't plan** the trip yesterday.
We **marched** in the band last year.	We **didn't march** in the band this year.
They **studied** for their English test.	They **didn't study** for their science test.

Past Tense Spellings

cheered = cheer + ed	studied = study + ed	planned = plan + n + ed

5 Work with a partner. Who did these activities? Who didn't do them? Look at the pictures. Take turns saying what Pablo and Amy did and didn't do.

Pablo

Amy

Examples:

vote

A: Pablo voted yesterday.

B: Amy voted yesterday, too.

play volleyball

A: Amy played volleyball yesterday.

B: Pablo didn't play volleyball yesterday.

a. call a friend on the phone

b. march in the band

c. decorate the school gym

d. go to the school dance

6 Work with a partner. What did you do yesterday? What didn't you do? Tell your partner.

Example:

A: Yesterday I studied English, and I played soccer. I didn't study math. How about you?

B: I played the piano, and I went to the mall. I didn't study at all.

Simple Past Tense: Yes/No Questions

 **7** Listen.

Questions	Answers
Did you **study** for your math test?	Yes, I **did**.
Did you **talk** to Ines?	No, I **didn't**.
Did Mayra **march** in the band?	Yes, she **did**.
Did she **cook** dinner?	No, she **didn't**.
Did all the students **vote**?	Yes, they **did**.
Did all of them **attend** the assembly?	No, they **didn't**.

8 Read each question and answer. Write *did* or *didn't* and the correct verbs from the box. Then practice the conversations with a partner.

attend	go	talk
cook	study	vote

1. **A:** _____*Did*_____ Dimitri _____*talk*_____ to you last night?

   B: Yes, he _____*did*_____. He called me at 7:00.

2. **A:** _____ Elena _____ the assembly in the auditorium?

   B: No, she _____. She had to go to the doctor's office.

3. **A:** _____ Jeff _____ dinner last night?

   B: Yes, he _____. He made a pizza.

4. **A:** _____ Lourdes _____ for you?

   B: No, she _____. She voted for her boyfriend.

5. **A:** _____ Steve and Suk _____ to the volleyball game?

   B: No, they _____. They had to do their homework.

6. **A:** _____ Akina _____ for the history test?

   B: Yes, she _____. She studied for three hours.

9 Work with a partner. Ask five questions about yesterday. Answer with *Yes, I did* or *No, I didn't*. Take turns.

Examples:

A: Did you come to school yesterday?

B: Yes, I did.

A: Did you cook dinner last night?

B: No, I didn't.

LISTENING and SPEAKING

  Listen to the conversation. What did Luz, Sam, Carol, and Kim do on Friday night? Check (✔) their activities.

	Luz	Sam	Carol	Kim
a. played in the band	✔			
b. went to the football game				
c. went to the science fair				
d. studied for a test				
e. went to the dance				

  Listen and repeat.

a.
I'm really tired today.

Why? Did you go to bed late last night?

b.
No, I didn't. I just had a really busy week.

Oh, I did, too. What did you do?

c.
After school, I went to band practice on Monday and Wednesday and to soccer practice on Tuesday and Thursday. I studied every night until 10:00.

You're right. You had a very busy week! Maybe I didn't have a busy week after all!

Say the same thing is true about yourself.

> **A:** I had a really busy week.
>
> **B:** Oh, I did, too.

3 Work with a partner. Practice the conversation in Exercise 2.

4 Work with a partner. Did you have a busy week?
Take turns telling about your weeks.

READING and WRITING

1 Read the article from a school newspaper.

AND THE WINNER IS . . .

DIAZ IS NEW STUDENT COUNCIL PRESIDENT

The student council election was on September 16.

Here is how we voted. Ana Díaz won the election for president. She got 104 votes, and Juan Gómez got 87 votes. For vice-president, Tuan Lee got 145 votes and won the election. Lucas Silva got 121 votes. Congratulations, Ana and Tuan!

Our secretary and treasurer are returning from last year. The secretary is Amina Chandar, and the treasurer is LaToya Miller. The first student council meeting is on October 2.

2 Who won the election? How many votes did each student get?
Fill in the chart.

	Name	Number of Votes
President		
Vice-president		

3 Answer the questions.

   a. When was the election?

   b. Who are the four officers?

   c. When is the first student council meeting?

**Make sure each sentence has a subject.
The subject tells *who* or *what* the sentence is about.**

- Didn't go to the dance.
  Jack didn't go to the dance.
- Went to the movies last night.
  We went to the movies last night.
- Where did go last night?
  Where did **you** go last night?

 4 **Writing Check** Correct these sentences. Add subjects. Use your own ideas.

a. Had to go to the principal's office this afternoon.

_____

b. Did study for the English test last night?

_____

c. When did decorate the gym for the dance?

_____

d. Worked all day and went to the movies in the evening.

_____

e. Didn't talk to my friends on the phone today.

_____

5 Work with a partner. Check your sentences in Exercise 4.

6 You write articles for your school newspaper.
Write notes about an activity at school.

a. What happened? _____

_____

_____

b. Where did it happen? _____

_____

_____

c. When did it happen? _____

_____

_____

d. Who attended the activity? _____

_____

_____

7 On your own paper, write your newspaper article.
Use your notes from Exercise 6.

1 Complete the conversations with *a/an*, *some*, *one*.

1. A: I want to buy _____*a*_____ new CD.
 B: You can get _____ at Flower Records.

2. A: Where can I buy _____ jeans?
 B: You can find _____ at Mike's Jeans.

3. A: I'd like to make _____ cookies, but I don't have _____ egg.
 B: I can get _____ from the neighbors.

4. A: Where can I get _____ gas for my car?
 B: You can get _____ at the Chess Station on the corner.

2 Put the words in order. Write questions. Then answer the questions. Write sentences about yourself.

a. you do like rent to videos ?
 Do you like to rent videos?
 Yes, I do. I love to watch movies.

b. do like you where eat to lunch ?

c. need do to you today do homework ?

d. where clothes like you to do buy ?

e. need to you do this week go to supermarket the ?

3 Write sentences with the opposite meanings.

a. I don't like those sneakers.
 I like these sneakers.

b. We never take this bus.

c. They don't want to rent that movie.

d. I don't want these apples.

4 Complete the conversation. Use the simple past tense of the verbs in parentheses and short answers.

A: What **(1. do)** ___*did*___ you ___*do*___ last night?

B: My brother and I **(2. go)** _____ to the movies.

A: What **(3. see)** _____ you _____?

B: We **(4. see)** _____ the new Brad Pitt movie.

A: **(5. like)** _____ you _____ it?

B: Yes, we **(6. do)** _____. We **(7. love)** _____ it! How about you? **(8. go)** _____ you _____ out last night?

A: No, I **(9. do)** _____. I **(10. stay)** _____ home and **(11. read)** _____ a good book. I also **(12. watch)** _____ TV and **(13. talk)** _____ to my parents.

5 Change these sentences from the present to the past. Use the time expressions.

a. I usually get home at 5:00.
(yesterday) _I got home at 5:00 yesterday._

b. We often take the bus to school.
(last week) _____

c. Our teacher always comes to school early.
(yesterday) _____

d. We sometimes run in the park.
(this morning) _____

e. My baby brother often falls down.
(last night) _____

6 Now write the simple past sentences in Exercise 5 again.
This time, write negative sentences.

a. _I didn't get home at 5:00 yesterday._

b. _____

c. _____

d. _____

e. _____

7 Complete the conversation. Write *me, you, him, her, it, us,* or *them.*

SUSAN: I want to go to the mall tomorrow, and Julio wants to go with **(1.)** ___*me*___. Would you like to go with **(2.)** _____?

PAUL: I can't. I have a lot of homework, and I have to do **(3.)** _____ tomorrow. I think Mike is free tomorrow. Call **(4.)** _____.

SUSAN: That's a good idea. And Sharon likes to shop. I can call **(5.)** _____, too.

PAUL: Maybe Kate and Leon would like to go with **(6.)** _____. Why don't you invite **(7.)** _____, too?

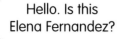

Hello. Is this Elena Fernandez?

Yes, it is.

Hi, Elena. My name is Jenny Cox. You don't know me, but I know your sister, Ana. She and I met at volleyball camp.

Oh, yes. She told me about you. Ana is away at college.

1.

Yes, I know. I'm in town for a volleyball game at Central High School. Would you like to meet me after the game?

2.

Sure. I can meet you by the door to the gym. What do you look like?

I'm tall and thin. I have short blond hair and blue eyes. What do you look like?

I'm short. I have curly brown hair and brown eyes. I wear glasses.

3.

OK. I'll look for you after the game.

OK. See you later, Jenny. Thanks for calling.

4.

GETTING STARTED

Warm Up

 1 Listen.

 2 Listen and repeat.

3 Work with a partner. Ask and answer the questions.

  a. Who does Jenny call?

  b. Why is Jenny in town?

  c. Where is Ana?

  d. What does Jenny look like?

  e. What does Elena look like?

Building Vocabulary

Personal Appearances

  Listen and repeat.

a. Eric is heavy. **b.** Gerard is thin. **c.** Mike is tall. **d.** Cathy is short.

e. Lee has long hair. It's wavy. **f.** Carla has short hair. **g.** Joe has straight hair. **h.** Dan has curly hair.

2 Work with a partner. Take turns asking and answering questions.

Example:

A: Is Eric heavy or thin?

B: He's heavy.

3 Work with a partner. Take turns asking and answering the questions.

a. Are you heavy or thin?

b. Are you tall or short?

c. Is your hair long or short?

d. Is your hair straight, curly, or wavy?

Unit 7

66

STRATEGY **Learn new words.**

Write new adjectives and
their opposites.

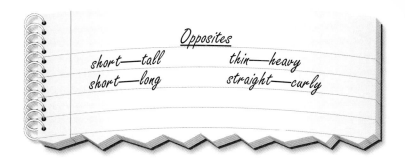

Opposites

short — tall   thin — heavy
short — long   straight — curly

Descriptions of People

 4 Listen and repeat.

a. What does Peter look like?

He's tall and heavy.
He has short brown hair.
He has blue eyes.
He's wearing blue jeans.

b. What does Nancy look like?

She's of average height.
She has long, straight blond hair.
She has blue eyes.
She's wearing a purple skirt.

c. What does Teresa look like?
She's of average height.
She has short, curly black hair.
She wears glasses.
She's wearing a purple, pink, and blue skirt.

5 Work with a partner. Look at the picture. Take turns asking and
answering questions about Kenji, Gary, and Fatima.

Example:

A: Is Kenji tall?

B: No, he isn't. He's short.

A: Does he wear glasses?

B: Yes, he does.

A: Is he wearing jeans?

B: No, he isn't. He's wearing brown pants.

Unit 7

6 **Vocabulary Check** Complete the sentences. Write the words.

black	brown	glasses	long	short	tall	wavy
blond	curly	heavy	red	straight	thin	

Sharon **Joe** **Carmen** **Kim**

Chen **Al** **Pat** **Crystal** **Robert**

a. Sharon wears _____ because she wants to see clearly.

b. Joe is tall and _____.

c. Carmen is _____ and thin.

d. Kim has _____ brown hair. Her hair is _____.

e. Chen has short _____ hair. His hair is _____.

f. Al has straight _____ hair.

g. Pat is tall and _____. She has short _____ hair.

h. Crystal has short _____ hair. It's _____.

i. Robert is _____ and a little heavy.

7 Work with a partner. Look again at the picture in Exercise 6. Take turns asking and answering questions about the people's clothes.

Example:

A: What's Sharon wearing?

B: She's wearing a pink blouse, a brown vest, a brown skirt, and brown shoes.

GRAMMAR

Be/Have/Wear

 1 Listen.

Be	Have	Wear
I'm **short**.	I **have long hair**.	I **wear glasses**.
Marcos **is sixteen years old**.	He **has brown eyes**.	He **doesn't wear glasses**.
She's **tall**.	She **has long legs**.	She **wears glasses**.
My sisters **are thin**.	They **have curly hair**.	They **don't wear glasses**.

2 Look at the picture and complete the story. Write the correct forms of *be*, *have*, and *wear*.

My name **(1.)** _____ Ross. I **(2.)** _____ fifteen years old. I **(3.)** _____ of average height, and I **(4.)** _____ thin. I **(5.)** _____ short brown hair and blue eyes. I **(6.)** _____ glasses.
My friend Bob **(7.)** _____ the same age as I am. He **(8.)** _____ fifteen. He **(9.)** _____ short and a little heavy. He **(10.)** _____ long brown hair, and he **(11.)** _____ glasses. His parents **(12.)** _____ glasses, too. Bob and his parents **(13.)** _____ brown eyes.

3 Work with a partner. Take turns describing yourself and two other people.

Example:

My friend Hal is eighteen. He's tall and thin. He has black hair and brown eyes. He doesn't wear glasses, but sometimes he wears sunglasses.

Simple Present Tense vs. Present Progressive Tense

 4 Listen.

> **Simple Present Tense**
>
> Use the simple present tense to tell about things that happen often.
>
> | | |
> |---|---|
> | **Do** you **wear** glasses? | Yes, I **do**. I **need** them to see clearly. |
> | | No, I **don't**. I **don't need** glasses. |
> | What do you usually **wear** to school? | I almost always **wear** jeans and a T-shirt. |
>
> **Present Progressive Tense**
>
> Use the present progressive tense to tell about things that are happening right now.
>
> | | |
> |---|---|
> | **Are** you **wearing** your glasses today? | Yes, I **am**. I can't see without them. |
> | | No, I**'m not**. I left them at home. |
> | What **are** you **wearing** today? | I**'m wearing** blue jeans and a red T-shirt. |
>
> (*Note:* We almost always use *be, have, like, need,* and *want* in the simple present tense. However, we often use expressions like *have lunch* and *have fun* in the present progressive tense. For example: *I'm having* lunch in the cafeteria today. *Are you having* fun in school today?)

5 Complete the letters. Write the correct forms of the verbs in parentheses. Use the simple present tense or the present progressive tense.

a.

Dear Chun,

   I **(1. write)** _____ you this letter at home. I **(2. be,** *neg.***)** _____ in school this morning because I **(3. have to)** _____ go to the eye doctor. I **(4. wear)** _____ glasses because I can't see very well without them. . . .

b.

Dear Eliza,

   How **(1. be)** _____ you? What **(2. do)** _____ you _____ today? Today is Saturday. I **(3. watch)** _____ my little sister. She **(4. want)** _____ to play outside all day. . . .

c.

Dear Oliver,

   Hi. How **(1. be)** _____ Chicago? **(2. like)** _____ you _____ your new school? **(3. have)** _____ you _____ fun with your new friends? Rick and I **(4. want)** _____ to see you again. . . .

Order of Adjectives

  **6** Listen.

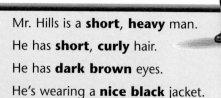

Sonia is a **tall**, **thin** girl.

She has **long**, **straight** hair.

She has **big blue** eyes.

She's wearing a **pretty red** sweater.

Mr. Hills is a **short**, **heavy** man.

He has **short**, **curly** hair.

He has **dark brown** eyes.

He's wearing a **nice black** jacket.

7 Add the words to the sentences.

a. He's a boy. (heavy/short)

   He's a short, heavy boy.

b. It's a jacket. (nice/green)

c. She's a woman. (thin/tall)

d. They're kittens. (white/cute)

e. She has short hair. (curly)

f. They have brown eyes. (beautiful)

8 Work with a partner. Complete the sentences about the two friends in the picture. Use adjectives in the correct order.

a. Alicia is a _____*tall*_____, _____*thin*_____ girl.

b. She has _____, _____ hair.

c. She's wearing a _____ _____ jacket.

d. Jack is a _____, _____ boy.

e. He has _____, _____ hair.

f. He's wearing a _____ _____ jacket.

LISTENING and SPEAKING

🎧 **1** Listen to the conversations. Write *1* under the person described in Conversation 1, *2* under the person described in Conversation 2, and *3* under the person described in Conversation 3.

a. _____ b. _____ c. _____ d. _____ e. _____

🎧 **2** Listen and repeat.

a. Let's play a guessing game. — OK. You go first.

b. OK. Who am I thinking of? — Well, is the person a girl or a boy? — It's a girl.

c. Is she tall or short? — She's short. — Does she wear glasses? — Yes, she does.

d. Is she wearing a pink blouse? — Yes, she is. — Is it Dina? — Yes, it is!

Unit 7

72

STRATEGY ➤ **Make a suggestion.**

> **A:** Let's play a guessing game.
>
> **B:** OK.

3 Work with a partner. Practice the conversation in Exercise 2. Then take turns thinking of classmates and guessing who they are.

READING and WRITING

1 Read these ads for pen pals.

PEDRO RAMÍREZ, 16, lives in Mexico. He has straight black hair and green eyes. He likes to play soccer and go to the movies.

DALIA SCHWARTZ, 16, lives in Israel. She has curly brown hair and brown eyes. She likes to listen to music. She also likes to dance and play sports.

DILLON YEATS, 17, lives in Ireland. He has straight red hair and blue eyes. He likes to read, write, and hike.

YOKO TANAKA, 16, lives in Japan. She has straight black hair and brown eyes. She likes to go to restaurants, museums, and movies.

2 Answer the questions about the ads.

a. Where does Yoko live?

b. How old is Dillon?

c. What does Pedro look like?

d. What does Dalia like to do?

3 Read this letter to a new pen pal.

> 745 Washington Street
> Boston, MA 02215
> September 5, ____
>
> Dear Pedro,
>
> Hi! I'd like to be your new pen pal.
>
> My name is Michael Baker. I live in Boston, Massachusetts. I am sixteen years old—the same age as you. I have straight brown hair and blue eyes. Like you, I like to play soccer. I also like to play baseball and listen to music.
>
> Please write to me soon.
>
> Sincerely yours,
> Michael

4 Answer the questions about the letter.

a. Where does Michael live?

b. How old is he?

c. What does he look like?

d. What does he like to do?

5 Fill in the chart with information about yourself. Then compare charts with a partner.

Name	
Age	
Country	
Height	
Weight	
Hair and eyes	
I like to …	

 Follow these rules when you write a friendly letter.

- Put your address and the date in the right-hand corner.

- Start with a greeting. Don't forget the comma.

  Dear Joachim,

- Write an introduction.

  Hi! I'm writing to you from my hotel in Jakarta.

- Write your information, with one paragraph for each idea.

- Write a conclusion.

  Please write to me soon.

- End with a closing and your name. Don't forget the comma.

  Your friend,/ Sincerely yours,/ Love,

  Michael

6 **Writing Check** On your own paper, follow the instructions above to write a letter to a new pen pal. Use the chart in Exercise 5 to help you. Choose one of the people from Exercise 1 or make up your own pen pal.

HOW WAS YOUR VACATION?

GETTING STARTED

Warm Up

 1 Listen.

 2 Listen and repeat.

3 Work with a partner. Ask and answer the questions.

    a. Where did Luis and his parents go on vacation?

    b. How long were they there?

    c. What did they do in Mexico City?

    d. What other city in Mexico did Luis and his parents visit?

    e. How did they get there?

Building Vocabulary

Vacation Activities

 1 Listen and repeat.

a. travel by plane

b. stay at a hotel

c. sit on the beach

d. swim in the ocean

e. hike in the mountains

f. visit a museum

g. see a ballet

2 Work with a partner. Take turns asking and answering questions.

Example:

A: Did they travel by plane?

B: Yes, they did.

Locations in North America

  Listen and repeat.

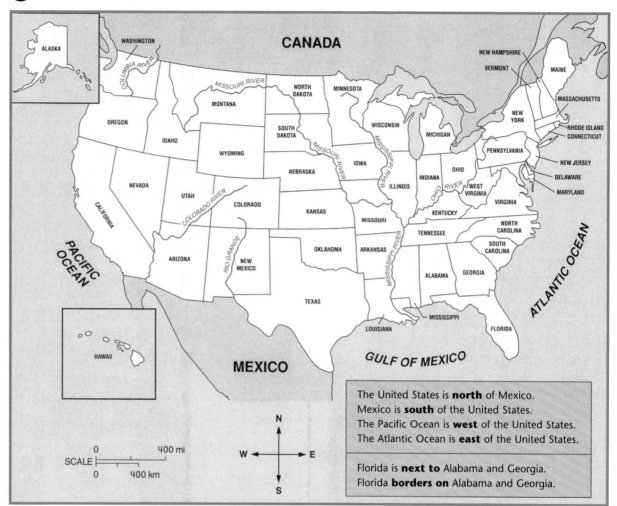

The United States is **north** of Mexico.
Mexico is **south** of the United States.
The Pacific Ocean is **west** of the United States.
The Atlantic Ocean is **east** of the United States.

Florida is **next to** Alabama and Georgia.
Florida **borders on** Alabama and Georgia.

 Work with a partner. Take turns asking and answering the questions.
(There is more than one correct answer to some questions.)

Example:

A: Where is Utah?

B: Utah is west of Colorado.

a. Where is California?
b. Which states border on Mexico?
c. Where is North Carolina?
d. Where is New Mexico?
e. Which states border on Kansas?
f. What are two states west of Idaho?
g. Which three states border on the Pacific Ocean?
h. What country is north of the United States?

Transportation

 5 Listen and repeat.

A: How did you get to Seattle?

B: I got there …

a. by bike **b.** by train **c.** by motorcycle **d.** by plane **e.** by car

6 Work with a partner. Take turns asking and answering the questions.

Example:

A: How did Roberto get to the beach?

B: He got there by car.

a. How did Roberto get to school?

b. How did David and his family get to New York City?

c. How did Mei get to California?

d. How did Michael get to Chicago?

e. How did Casey get to Washington, D.C.?

STRATEGY **Learn new words.**

Use new words and expressions to write true sentences about yourself.

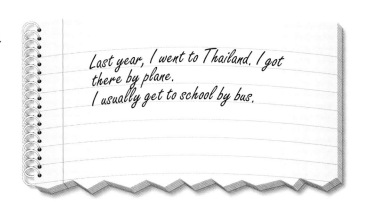

Last year, I went to Thailand. I got there by plane.
I usually get to school by bus.

7 **Vocabulary Check** Complete the sentences. Write the words.

ballet	hotel	museum	plane
beach	mountains	ocean	

a. The Tanaka family went to California on vacation. They got there by _____.

b. They stayed at a _____.

c. They went to the _____ almost every day.

d. They swam in the _____.

e. One day, they drove to the _____.

f. They visited a _____.

g. On Friday night, they saw a _____.

8 Work with a partner. Look again at the pictures in Exercise 7. Take turns asking and answering questions about the Tanakas' vacation.

Example:

A: How did the Tanakas get to California?

B: They got there by plane. Where did they stay?

A: They _____.

GRAMMAR

Simple Past Tense of *Be*: Information Questions and Statements

 1 Listen.

Questions	Statements
Where **were** you last week?	I **was** on vacation last week.
Where **was** Susan last week?	She **was** on vacation, too.
How long **was** Greg on vacation?	He **was** on vacation for ten days.
How **was** your vacation?	It **was** fun!
Where **were** you and Nan yesterday?	We **were** at the park.
Where **were** Fred and Max yesterday?	They **were** at the soccer game.

2 Complete the story with *was* or *were*.

Last week I **(1.)** _____ on vacation with my family. We **(2.)** _____ in Hawaii. My mother and I **(3.)** _____ there for one week. My father **(4.)** _____ there for two weeks. He went there early because he had to do some work there.

We loved Hawaii. The ocean **(5.)** _____ beautiful. The water **(6.)** _____ warm, and the waves **(7.)** _____ huge. The mountains **(8.)** _____ beautiful, too. Our hotel **(9.)** _____ on the beach. We **(10.)** _____ near a lot of nice stores and restaurants, too.

3 Complete the questions and answers with *was* or *were*. Then practice the conversation with a partner.

A: Where **(1.)** _____ you last month?

B: I **(2.)** _____ in Italy. I went there with my grandmother.

A: How long **(3.)** _____ you there?

B: We **(4.)** _____ there for three weeks. I celebrated my birthday there.

A: Really? When **(5.)** _____ your birthday?

B: It **(6.)** _____ on June 8.

A: Where in Italy **(7.)** _____ you?

B: We **(8.)** _____ in Venice, Florence, and Rome.

A: How **(9.)** _____ the people in Italy?

B: They **(10.)** _____ very friendly.

A: And how **(11.)** _____ the food?

B: It **(12.)** _____ delicious!

Simple Past Tense of *Be*: Yes/No Questions and Short Answers

🎧 **4** Listen.

Questions	Answers	
Were you sick yesterday?	Yes, I **was**.	No, I **wasn't**.
Was Sam at the game last night?	Yes, he **was**.	No, he **wasn't**.
Were you and Rita at the theater?	Yes, we **were**.	No, we **weren't**.
Were Ted and Luis in class today?	Yes, they **were**.	No, they **weren't**.
Contractions		
was + not = wasn't	were + not = weren't	

5 Work with a partner. Take turns asking questions with *was* or *were*. Use the map to answer the questions.

KEY
- •—•—• Kim and Tracy's trip
- +—+—+ Antonio's trip

Example:

Kim and Tracy in San Diego

A: Were Kim and Tracy in San Diego?

B: Yes, they were.

a. Antonio in Los Angeles
b. Antonio in Palm Springs
c. Kim and Tracy in Fresno
d. Antonio in San Jose
e. Kim and Tracy in San Francisco
f. Kim and Tracy in Palm Springs

San Francisco • San Jose • Fresno • Santa Barbara • Los Angeles • Palm Springs • San Diego

How Long Does/Did It Take?

🎧 **6** Listen.

Questions	Answers
How long does it take to get from Los Angeles to Chicago?	**It takes** about four hours by plane.
How long did it take you to get from Los Angeles to San Francisco?	**It took** me eight hours by bus.

7 Read the conversations. Complete the questions with *How long does it take* or *How long did it take*. Then practice the conversations with a partner.

1. **A:** _____ you to get to school yesterday?
   B: It took me ten minutes.
2. **A:** _____ to get from here to the park?
   B: It takes about five minutes by car.
3. **A:** _____ to get to New York by train?
   B: It takes forty-five minutes.
4. **A:** _____ you to get to the airport last night?
   B: It took us about an hour.

Unit 8

1 Listen to the conversation. Fill in the chart about Samira's travel plans.

Date	From	To	Departure Time	Arrival Time	Travel By
June 1	New York City	London		6:25 a.m.	
June 3		Canterbury			
June 10	London	New York City			

2 Listen and repeat.

STRATEGY **Express surprise. Ask a question.**

A: I was in Puerto Rico.

B: Puerto Rico? Why were you there?

3 Work with a partner. Practice the conversation in Exercise 2. Then take turns telling about one of your vacations.

READING and WRITING

 Read about Samira's vacation.

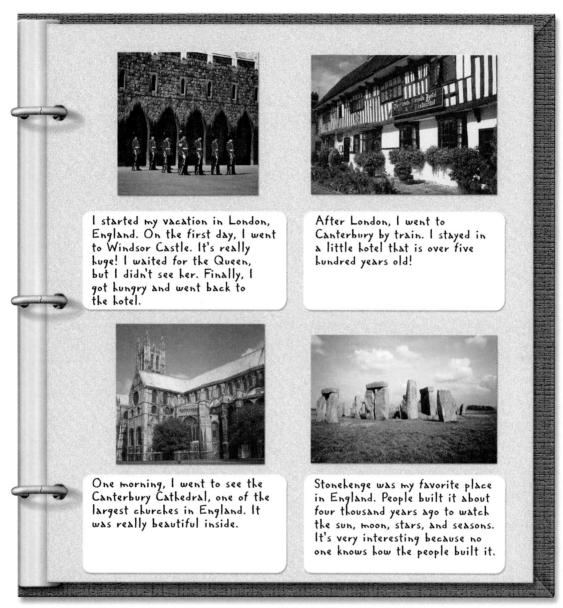

I started my vacation in London, England. On the first day, I went to Windsor Castle. It's really huge! I waited for the Queen, but I didn't see her. Finally, I got hungry and went back to the hotel.

After London, I went to Canterbury by train. I stayed in a little hotel that is over five hundred years old!

One morning, I went to see the Canterbury Cathedral, one of the largest churches in England. It was really beautiful inside.

Stonehenge was my favorite place in England. People built it about four thousand years ago to watch the sun, moon, stars, and seasons. It's very interesting because no one knows how the people built it.

2 Answer the questions.

- **a.** What country did Samira visit on her vacation?
- **b.** What did she do at Windsor Castle?
- **c.** How did Samira get to Canterbury?
- **d.** How old was the hotel in Canterbury?
- **e.** What was Samira's favorite place in England?
- **f.** When and why did people build Stonehenge?

Make sure the verb form is correct for the subject of your sentence.

Incorrect	Correct
We ~~was~~ sick yesterday.	We **were** sick yesterday.
He ~~don't~~ like the beach.	He **doesn't** like the beach.

✓ ③ **Writing Check** Correct these sentences. Make sure the verb form is correct for the subject.

a. Where was you yesterday?

_____

b. Joanne love to travel.

_____

c. My mother are in Brazil.

_____

d. They goes on vacation every year.

_____

e. Why weren't Ricardo in school yesterday?

_____

④ Work with a partner. Check your sentences in Exercise 3.

⑤ Read Samira's postcard.

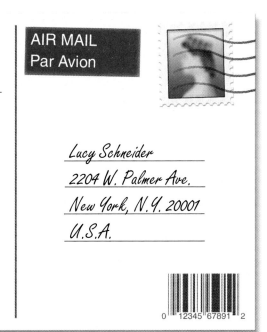

British Museum:
London, England
A famous landmark
in London.

December 8, _____

Dear Lucy,

How are you? I miss you, but I'm having a good time in England. This morning I went to the British Museum and saw many ancient objects. There was so much to see! I got tired and went to eat lunch and write letters. The food here is good, but I miss my mom's cooking at home. I'll buy a present for you while I'm here.

Love,
Samira

AIR MAIL
Par Avion

Lucy Schneider
2204 W. Palmer Ave.
New York, N.Y. 20001
U.S.A.

0 12345 67891 2

⑥ Pretend that you're on vacation. On your own paper, write a postcard to a friend.

GETTING STARTED

Warm Up

 1 Listen.

 2 Listen and repeat.

3 Work with a partner. Ask and answer the questions.

    a. What was the weather like in the morning?

    b. What was the weather like when Tracy and Sylvia stopped to rest?

    c. Why did Tracy and Sylvia run to the car?

    d. Why does Tracy want the storm to end soon?

    e. Why does Sylvia say "Don't worry" to Tracy?

Building Vocabulary

The Weather and Temperature

 1 Listen and repeat.

30°F / –1°C

a. It's cold and snowy.

65°F / 18°C

b. It's rainy and windy.
It's very stormy.

90°F /32°C

c. It's clear. It's hot and sunny, too.

50°F /10°C

d. It's cool and windy.

40°F /4°C

e. It's cloudy and cold.

2 Work with a partner. Point to the pictures. Take turns asking and answering questions.

Example:

A: What's the weather like?

B: It's cold and snowy.

A: What's the temperature?

B: The temperature is 30 degrees Fahrenheit/minus 1 degree Celsius.

The Seasons of the Year

  Listen and repeat.

a. winter

b. spring

c. summer

d. fall

4 Work with a partner. Take turns asking and answering the questions.

a. What season is it now?

b. What months are winter in your country? What months are spring? summer? fall?

c. What's the weather like in the winter in your country? What's the weather like in the spring? in the summer? in the fall?

d. What's your favorite season of the year? Why?

e. What do you like to do in the winter? What do you like to do in the spring? in the summer? in the fall?

f. Do you go to school in the summer? If not, what do you do?

 STRATEGY **Learn new words.**

Write words in groups.

winter	spring	summer	fall
December	March	June	September
January	April	July	October
February	May	August	November
March	June	September	December

5 **Vocabulary Check** Complete the sentences. Write the words.

clear	hot	stormy
cloudy	rainy	sunny
cold	snowy	windy

a. It's a _____ day.

b. The weather is _____, _____, and _____.

c. It's _____ today.

d. There's no school today because it's _____ and _____.

e. Today it's _____.

f. It's not raining, but it's very _____.

6 Work with a partner. Look again at the pictures in Exercise 5. Take turns making and responding to suggestions.

Example:

A: Let's go to the park today.

B: We can't go to the park today. It's stormy.

GRAMMAR

Future with *Going to*: Information Questions and Statements

  1 Listen.

Questions	Statements
What **are** you **going to do** tomorrow?	**I'm going to swim** in the ocean.
	I'm not going to do homework.
What**'s** Ted **going to do**?	He**'s going to hike** in the mountains.
	He **isn't going to go** to the library.
What**'s** the weather **going to be** like?	It**'s going to rain**.
	It **isn't going to be** a nice day.
Where **are** you and Rita **going to go** tonight?	We**'re going to go** to the dance.
	We **aren't going to go** to the movies.
Where **are** Ed and Barb **going to be**?	They**'re going to stay** home.
	They **aren't going to go** to the dance.

2 Work with a partner. What is everyone going to wear? Take turns asking and answering the questions. Use the clothing words or your own ideas.

dress	jacket	jeans	raincoat

shorts	sweater	shirt	T-shirt

Example:

A: It's rainy today. What are the friends going to wear?

B: They're going to wear their raincoats.

1. A: It's cold outside. What are you going to wear?

B: _____

2. A: Jack wants to go outside, but it's hot. What's he going to wear?

B: _____

3. A: What's Maria going to wear to the dance tomorrow?

B: _____

4. A: What are you and your friends going to wear to the mall?

B: _____

3 Work with a partner. Take turns asking and answering the questions.

   a. What are you going to wear tomorrow?
   b. What are you going to do tomorrow?
   c. What are you going to do this weekend?
   d. What are you going to do next week?

Future with *Going to*: Yes/No Questions and Short Answers

4 Listen.

Questions	Answers
Are you **going to study** English tomorrow?	Yes, I **am**.
Are you **going to go** to school tomorrow?	No, I**'m not**.
Is Lin **going to play** volleyball on Saturday?	Yes, she **is**.
Is she **going to play** with Jack?	No, she **isn't**.
Is the weather **going to be** nice tomorrow?	Yes, it **is**.
Is it **going to be** rainy?	No, it **isn't**.
Are your friends **going to be** at the park?	Yes, they **are**.
Are they **going to be** at the movies?	No, they **aren't**.

5 Complete the conversations. Use the future with *going to*. Then practice the conversations with a partner.

   1. A: (go) _____*Are*_____ you __*going to go*__ to the bank at 2:00?

      B: Yes, _____ .

   2. A: (be) _____ Raúl and Teng _____ at the movies tonight?

      B: Yes, _____ .

   3. A: (study) _____ Maria _____ tonight?

      B: No, _____ .

   4. A: (play) _____ Ted _____ soccer this afternoon?

      B: Yes, _____ .

   5. A: (be) _____ it _____ sunny tomorrow?

      B: No, it _____ .

   6. A: (play) _____ you _____ in the game?

      B: No, _____ .

6 Work with a partner. Take turns asking and answering questions about the cities on the weather map. Use the cues to ask the questions and the map to answer the questions. Then make up your own questions about Los Angeles and Washington, D.C.

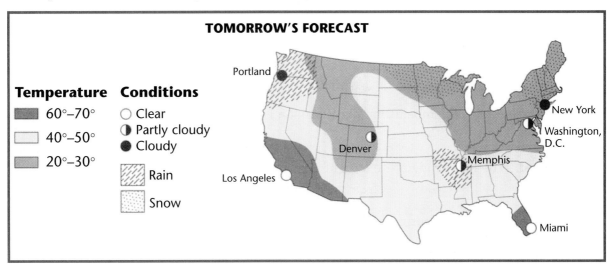

TOMORROW'S FORECAST

Temperature
- 60°–70°
- 40°–50°
- 20°–30°

Conditions
- ○ Clear
- ◑ Partly cloudy
- ● Cloudy
- Rain
- Snow

Portland
New York
Washington, D.C.
Denver
Memphis
Los Angeles
Miami

Example:

New York City: rainy and warm

A: Is the weather in New York City going to be rainy and warm tomorrow?

B: No, it isn't.

A: Well, what's the weather going to be like?

B: It's going to be cloudy, snowy, and cold.

a. Miami: rainy and warm

b. Memphis: snowy and cold

c. Denver: snowy and cold

d. Portland: clear and warm

1 Listen to the weather report. Circle the correct words.

    a. The weather in the morning is going to be _____.

        sunny   rainy   cloudy

    b. The weather in the afternoon is going to be _____.

        rainy   sunny   warm

    c. The high temperature this afternoon is going to be _____.

        85°   65°   60°

    d. The low temperature tonight is going to be _____.

        40°   50°   55°

    e. Tomorrow morning, it's going to be _____.

        sunny   rainy   cloudy

    f. Tomorrow afternoon, the skies are going to be _____.

        cloudy   rainy   clear

 2 Listen and repeat.

Extend an invitation. Accept an invitation.

> **A:** Do you want to go to the beach with my friends and me?
>
> **B:** Sure. Thanks for asking!

3 Work with a partner. Practice the conversation in Exercise 2. Then take turns telling about your weekend and inviting your partner to do something with you.

READING and WRITING

1 Read the weather forecast.

Today it's going to be warm and sunny in the morning and cool and rainy in the afternoon. The high temperature is going to be 82°. This evening, it will be cool and cloudy, with the low temperature around 60°. Tomorrow it's going to be windy and stormy in the morning, with the high temperature around 68°.

Tomorrow afternoon and evening, it will be clear and cool. On Wednesday, it's going to be sunny all day. The high temperature is going to reach 85°. The temperature on Wednesday evening will fall to around 70°. On Thursday, it's going to be hot all day—90°. On Friday, it's going to be hot, too, but it will start to cool off in the evening.

2 Complete the chart.

	Morning	**Afternoon**	**Evening**
Today	*warm and sunny*		
Tomorrow			
Wednesday			
Thursday			
Friday			

3 Use the weather forecast and the chart to decide if each statement below is true or false. Circle **T** for True or **F** for False.

a.	The high temperature is going to be 84° today.	**T** (**F**)
b.	The low temperature tonight is going to be around 60°.	**T** **F**
c.	Tomorrow morning is going to be a good time to go swimming.	**T** **F**
d.	Tomorrow evening is going to be a good time to be outside.	**T** **F**
e.	Wednesday is going to be a good day to go hiking.	**T** **F**
f.	Thursday and Friday are going to be good days to go to the mountains.	**T** **F**

Check your spelling. Use your dictionary.

- Say each word out loud.

- Try to find the word in the dictionary by the way it sounds. Don't forget about double letters (*rr*) and silent letters (*e*).

   - tomorow ⟶ **tomorrow**

   - tempratur ⟶ **temperature**

- Correct the spelling.

4 **Writing Check** Find the five misspelled words in the sentences below. Circle them. Find them in your dictionary. Then correct them.

forecast
Today's ⟨forcast⟩ says a huricane is going to pass near our city. We need to be prepard for vilent winds and hevy rains.

5 Work with a partner. Check the spelling of the words in Exercise 4.

6 What's the weather going to be like this week in your city or town? Read the newspaper or listen to a weather report on television. Then write your own weather report.

WEATHER WATCH

_____   _____
_____   _____
_____   _____
_____   _____
_____   _____
_____   _____
_____   _____
_____   _____
_____   _____
_____   _____
_____   _____
_____   _____

1 Complete the story with the correct forms of the verbs *be*, *have*, or *wear*. Use contractions when possible.

I **(1.)** ____'m____ Sally Mitchell. I **(2.)** _____ short blond hair and blue eyes. I **(3.)** _____ very tall and thin. I **(4.)** _____ seventeen years old, and I usually **(5.)** _____ dresses to school. On the weekends, I **(6.)** _____ jeans and T-shirts.

My friend's name **(7.)** _____ Natalia. She **(8.)** _____ sixteen. She **(9.)** _____ long brown hair. Her eyes **(10.)** _____ brown. Natalia **(11.)** _____ short and a little heavy. She **(12.)** _____ jeans and pretty blouses to school, but she **(13.)** _____ dresses on the weekends because she **(14.)** _____ a job at the mall.

2 Write the correct forms of the verbs. Use the simple present or the present progressive. Use contractions when possible.

a. We usually **(study)** ____study____ in the library, but today we ____'re studying____ at Joe's house.

b. It almost never **(snow)** _____ here, but it _____ today.

c. My family usually doesn't **(watch)** _____ TV on weekdays, but we _____ it tonight because there's a great show on Channel 6.

d. Sue **(call)** _____ her grandmother now, but she usually _____ her in the evening.

e. Mr. and Mrs. Gonzales usually **(shop)** _____ at the supermarket, but today they _____ at a small store.

3 Put the words in order. Write sentences.

a. my has sister curly hair blond .
   My sister has curly blond hair.

b. have you beautiful eyes blue .
   _____

c. is thin a tall boy Pablo .
   _____

d. green dress wearing she's a beautiful .
   _____

4 Complete the story with the correct simple past forms of *be*.

Yesterday **(1.)** ____was____ a holiday, so there **(2.)** _____ any school. I **(3.)** _____ at home. All my friends **(4.)** _____ at my house, too. It **(5.)** _____ my birthday, and my parents gave me a party. The party **(6.)** _____ fantastic, but we **(7.)** _____ all tired at the end of the day.

5 Complete the conversations. Use the correct simple past forms of *be* and short answers. Use contractions when possible.

1. A: Where **(1.)** ___were___ you yesterday?
   B: I **(2.)** _____ at home.

2. A: **(1.)** _____ you and your sister at this school last year?
   B: Yes, we **(2.)** _____. **(3.)** _____ you and Carlos here?
   A: No, we **(4.)** _____. I **(5.)** _____ at Central High School, and Carlos **(6.)** _____ at Western High School.

3. A: Who **(1.)** _____ your English teacher last year?
   B: I had two teachers last year: Ms. Fallon and Mr. Morgan.
   A: **(2.)** _____ they nice?
   B: Yes, they **(3.)** _____. They **(4.)** _____ great!

6 Complete the questions with *does* or *did*. Then answer the questions.

a. How long ___did___ it take you to get to school today?

_____

b. How long _____ it take you to get to your favorite store?

_____

c. How long _____ it take you to do Exercise 5?

_____

7 Complete the story with the correct future with *going to* forms of the verbs. Use contractions when possible.

   My friends and I **(1. have)** _are going to have_ a very busy weekend. My friend Monica **(2. be)** _____ in a play on Friday night, and we **(3. see)** _____ her. On Saturday, Ken and Larry **(4. play)** _____ in a big volleyball game at the park. I **(5. watch)** _____ them play. On Sunday, Larry's parents **(6. have)** _____ a party at the beach. We **(7. swim)** _____ all day. It **(8. be)** _____ a great weekend!

8 Complete the questions with the correct future with *going to* forms of the verbs. Then answer the questions with short answers. Use contractions when possible.

a. **(be)** _____ you _____ in class tomorrow?

_____

b. **(go)** _____ you and your family _____ on vacation next year?

_____

c. **(give)** _____ your teacher _____ the class a test this week?

_____

1.

The weather is terrible today. What are we going to do?

What *can* we do?

We can watch TV. Here's the TV guide.

OK, Ed. What's on?

2.

The Andy McCabe Show is on at 3:00.

What kind of show is that?

It's a great talk show. Andy McCabe is the host. Famous actors and actresses are the guests. They talk about their interesting lives.

3.

I don't like talk shows. I usually watch sports.

Well, there aren't any sports shows on right now. There's a game show on Channel 4, a sitcom on Channel 7, a movie on Channel 9, and a soap opera on Channel 12.

4.

Let's watch the game show. That's my favorite kind of show.

OK, and maybe we can watch a sports show after that!

GETTING STARTED

Warm Up

 1 Listen.

 2 Listen and repeat.

3 Work with a partner. Ask and answer the questions.

   a. What's the weather like?
   b. What can the friends do?
   c. What kinds of shows are on?
   d. What kind of show are they going to watch?
   e. What kind of show do you think Ed likes? Why?

Building Vocabulary

Kinds of TV Shows

🎧 **1** Listen and repeat.

a. a cartoon

b. a sitcom

c. a drama

d. the news

e. a game show

f. a soap opera

g. a talk show

h. a sports show

2 Work with a partner. Point to the pictures. Take turns asking and answering questions.

Example:

A: What kind of show are they watching?

B: They're watching a cartoon.

People on TV

3 Listen and repeat.

a. The actor and actress in the commercial are drinking coffee.

b. The game-show host is asking the contestant a question.

c. The talk-show host is talking to a guest.

d. The news reporter is talking about the weather.

e. The athlete is playing baseball.

4 Work with a partner. Point to the pictures. Take turns asking and answering questions.

Example:

A: What does she do?

B: She's an actress.

A: What's she doing?

B: She's drinking coffee.

A TV Guide

5 Listen and repeat.

EVENING TV SHOWS			
TIME	CHANNEL 4	CHANNEL 5	CHANNEL 7
6:00	**NEWS**	**NEWS**	**NEWS**
6:30		**Life with Dad** Dad and his three children go on vacation together.	**The Samsons** Cartoon with Paula, Ed, and Herman Samson.
7:00	**NFL Football**	**The Liz Ames Show** Laugh with Liz as she takes her first piano lesson.	**Gold Rush** A lucky contestant will win a trip to California.
7:30		**In Court** Lawyers find out the truth about a girl's murder.	**Win the Bank!** Contestants compete for $100,000.
8:00		**Police Stories** Exciting crime drama. Police look for stolen jewelry.	**True Lives** Listen to true stories about Hollywood's greatest stars.
8:30			
9:00		**Manhattan Bridge** Sara meets her boyfriend's family in this hilarious episode.	
9:30		**Talk Live** Guest: Frank Marshall.	
10:00	**NEWS**	**NEWS**	**NEWS**

6 Work with a partner. Take turns asking and answering questions. Use the information in the TV guide.

Example:

Channel 5/6:30

A: What's on Channel 5 at 6:30?

B: *Life with Dad.*

A: What's the show about?

B: It's about a father and his three children.

a. Channel 7/6:30   **d.**   Channel 5/8:00

b. Channel 5/7:30   **e.**   Channel 7/8:00

c. Channel 4/7:00

STRATEGY **Learn new words.**

Write examples of TV shows from your own life.

drama: *Law and Order*
game show: *Wheel of Fortune*
sitcom: *Spin City*

Complete the sentences.
Write the words.

actor	contestant	host	soap operas
actress	drama	news	sports show
athlete	game show	news reporter	talk show
cartoon	guests	sitcom	

a. *Happy Times* is a very funny
_____ about a large
family. I like the _____
and _____ who play the
parents on the show.

b. My favorite _____ is on
TV tonight, and Mitchell Jenkins
is my favorite _____.

c. I watch the _____ every
night at 6:00. Jessica Howard is the
best _____.

d. *Talk Live* is a great _____
and has a funny _____.
The _____ are always
interesting.

e. I'm going to be a _____
on a _____. I'm going to
win lots of money!

f. I never watch _____.
I like dramas better.

g. The children love to watch this
_____ in the morning.

h. The _____ *In Court*
is on Wednesday at 7:30 p.m.

Prepositions *At*, *In*, *On*: Review

 **1** Listen.

When is *Life with Dad* on TV?

Look **in** the TV guide. It's **on** the table **in** the kitchen.

Life with Dad is **on** Wednesday **at** 6:30 p.m. It's **on** Channel 5.

I really like the actors **on** that show.

2 Complete the conversation with *at*, *in*, or *on*.
Then practice the conversation with a partner.

A: What's **(1.)** _____ *on* _____ TV?

B: I don't know. Let's look **(2.)** _____ the TV guide.

A: Where is the TV guide?

B: It's **(3.)** _____ the table
(4.) _____ the kitchen.

A: Here it is. OK. **(5.)** _____ 4:30, we
can watch the news or a talk show.

B: Who's the guest **(6.)** _____ the talk show?

A: Lee Taylor. He's really interesting. Let's watch the talk show.

B: OK. And then there's news again **(7.)** _____ 5:00 and 6:00.

A: And **(8.)** _____ 7:00, *The Liz Ames Show* starts.

B: Oh, I love the actors **(9.)** _____ that show!

3 Work with a partner. Take turns asking and answering questions
about TV shows. Use your own information.

Example:

A: What do you watch
on Mondays?

B: On Mondays, I watch
Monday Night Sports.

A: What time is it on?

B: It's on at 9:00 p.m.

A: What channel is it on?

B: It's on Channel 6.

Direct and Indirect Objects

 4 Listen.

Indirect Object + Direct Object	Direct Object + Indirect Object
Could you please give **me the TV guide**?	Could you please give **the TV guide to me**?
I gave **you the TV guide**.	I gave **it to you**.
Did Ken give **her the book**?	Did Ken give **the book to her**?
No, she gave **him the book**.	No, she gave **it to him**.
Did Pam and Lucy show **you the pictures**?	Did Pam and Lucy show **the pictures to you**?
Yes, they showed **us the pictures**.	Yes, they showed **them to us**.
We showed **them some pictures**, too.	We showed **some pictures to them**, too.

5 Work with a partner. Take turns making and responding to requests. Use the cues and *Could you please* _____?

Example:

give/me/the TV guide

A: Could you please give me the TV guide?

B: Sure. Here it is.

a. show/your pictures/to him
b. tell/me/a story
c. give/her/this book
d. show/us/your pictures
e. give/the TV guide/to them
f. ask/him/about the pictures

6 Write the correct word or words.

a. The talk-show host asked **(her/to her)** _____ a question.
b. She didn't give **(him/to him)** _____ an answer.
c. The game-show host gave **(you/to you)** _____ a giant TV.
d. The Santiagos don't have a TV, so we're going to give our old TV **(them/to them)** _____.
e. The news reporter told **(us/to us)** _____ a great story.
f. He showed the newspaper **(me/to me)** _____.
g. I gave the TV guide **(you/to you)** _____.
h. Did you give it back **(me/to me)** _____?

1 Listen to each commercial. Circle the correct information.

Commercial 1

a. This commercial is for a new _____.

radio show   restaurant   television show

b. *Sunny Skies* is a _____.

talk show   sitcom   sports show

Commercial 2

a. This commercial wants to sell _____.

food   clothing   music

b. The Sugar Shack is a _____.

music store   drugstore   restaurant

Commercial 3

a. This commercial is for _____.

blue jeans   basketball shoes   basketballs

b. The brand name is _____.

Sky High   Mile High   High School

  2 Listen and repeat.

Ask for information about a story.

> **A:** My favorite show is *Life with Dad*.
>
> **B:** What's it about?
>
> **A:** It's about a single dad and his kids.

3 Work with a partner. Practice the conversation in Exercise 2. Use your own information.

4 What shows do you like to watch on television? Make a list, including the names, days, times, and channels of the shows. Work with a partner. Tell your partner about your favorite TV shows. Take turns.

5 Work in groups of three. Tell about the shows your partner likes.

READING and WRITING

1 Read the summary of *The Good Life*, a popular TV show.

Summary of *The Good Life*

Week 1: Last week on this exciting new drama, we attended the wedding of Monica and Paul Mosley. Wasn't it wonderful? Didn't you think that they were the happiest couple? But the very next day, Monica packed her bags and left! She wrote Paul a note saying that she was going home to her parents in Boston. She got into a taxi and left. Paul came home from work later that evening and saw the note. What a surprise!

Week 2: Well, Paul decided to drive to Boston to see Monica. But on the way, he

got into a car accident. He wasn't badly hurt, but he needed to stay in the hospital overnight. Paul called Monica from the hospital. She went to see him. They talked for a long time.

Tune in tonight for Week 3 of *The Good Life*.

2 Answer the questions.
   a. What kind of show is *The Good Life*?
   b. Who are the people on the show?
   c. What happened during Week 1?
   d. What happened during Week 2?

3 Work with a partner. Answer the questions.

   a. What do you think Monica and Paul talked about?
   b. What do you think is going to happen next?

4 Make up an ending to the story. Take turns telling your stories to the class.

STRATEGY **Use either the present tense or the past tense to write a summary of a story. Don't mix tenses.**

Incorrect	Correct
Monica **packs** her bags and ~~left~~.	Monica **packs** her bags and **leaves**.
Monica **packed** her bags and ~~leaves~~.	Monica **packed** her bags and **left**.

  5 **Writing Check** Watch a TV show. Write a summary of the show. Use either the present tense or the past tense. Don't mix tenses.

*Name of show:*_____

*Kind of show:*_____

*This is a summary of the show:*_____

_____

_____

_____

_____

_____

_____

_____

_____

_____

_____

_____

_____

_____

_____

_____

WHO WON THE GAME?

GETTING STARTED

Warm Up

 1 Listen.

 2 Listen and repeat.

3 Work with a partner. Ask and answer the questions.

   a. What sport are Ayo and his friends watching?
   b. Why does Tony think that the sport is dangerous?
   c. What sport do people love in Ayo's country?
   d. Where is Ayo from?
   e. What's Ayo's favorite sport?
   f. What sports do his friends like?

Building Vocabulary

Sports Scores

 1 Listen and repeat.

a. The Bears are winning three to two.

b. The Sharks are losing twenty to ten.

c. The Tigers and the Patriots are tied three all.

2 Work with a partner. Take turns asking and answering questions.

Examples:

A: What's the score of the Bears game?

B: The Bears are winning three to two.

A: What's the score of the Tornadoes game?

B: The Tornadoes are losing three to two.

3 Work with a partner. Take turns asking and answering questions about the basketball games.

Examples:

A: Did the Bulls win?

B: Yes, they did. They won one hundred ten to ninety-eight.

A: Did the Knicks win?

B: No, they didn't. They lost one hundred ten to ninety-eight.

Opinions

a. He likes to ride his bike. It's fun.

b. They like to play chess. It's interesting.

c. They love to ice-skate. It's exciting.

d. He likes to play tennis. It's great exercise.

e. They don't like to play hockey. It's dangerous.

f. She hates to play golf. It's boring.

g. She loves to swim. It's easy.

h. She likes to play baseball, but she thinks it's hard.

5 Work with a partner. Point to the pictures. Take turns asking and answering questions.

Example:

A: Does he like to ride his bike?

B: Yes, he does. He thinks it's fun.

6 **Vocabulary Check** What do the people in the pictures think about their activities? Complete each sentence with the best word.

boring	exciting
dangerous	fun
easy	interesting

a. He likes to ski, but he thinks it's _____.

b. They love to dance. They think it's _____.

c. They like to play chess because they think it's _____.

d. They like to watch soccer. They think it's _____.

e. She loves to ice-skate. She thinks it's _____.

f. She doesn't like golf. She thinks it's _____.

7 Work with a partner. Look again at the pictures in Exercise 6. Take turns asking for and giving opinions about the activities.

Example:

A: Do you like to ski?

B: Yes, I do. I think it's exciting. OR I don't know how to ski.

 STRATEGY **Learn new words.**

Write new words in categories.

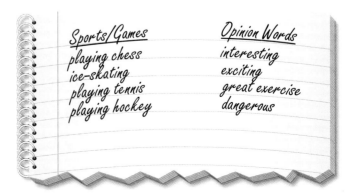

Sports/Games
playing chess
ice-skating
playing tennis
playing hockey

Opinion Words
interesting
exciting
great exercise
dangerous

GRAMMAR

Go + Verb + –ing

 **1** Listen.

> I **go shopping** every Saturday.　　We **go skiing** every winter.
>
> He likes to **go swimming** after school.　They **go dancing** on Friday nights.
>
> She **goes hiking** in the mountains.
>
> **Spellings**
> _____
>
> skiing = ski + ing
>
> shopping = shop + p + ing
>
> hiking = hike̸ + ing

2 Complete the sentences with *go* + verb + *–ing*.

a. In the winter, I like to ___go skiing___ in the mountains.

b. On Saturday nights, my friends and I _____.

c. Zola and Allen like to _____ after work.

d. In the afternoons, our neighbors like to _____ in their pool.

e. I like to _____ on weekends.

f. We _____ every Saturday afternoon.

It's + Adjective + Infinitive

  Listen.

> **It's fun to ice-skate**.
>
> **It's exciting to play** hockey.
>
> I think **it's hard to learn** a new sport.

Verb + *–ing* as Noun

 4 Listen.

> **Ice-skating** is fun.   I think **learning** a new sport is hard.
>
> **Playing** hockey is exciting.   I love **watching** TV.

5 Work with a partner. Take turns giving opinions and agreeing or disagreeing. Use *It's* + adjective + infinitive in your opinions and verb + *–ing* in your responses.

Example:

hard/play tennis

A: It's hard to play tennis.

B: I agree. Playing tennis is hard. OR
I disagree. I think playing tennis is easy.

a. easy/play soccer   **d.** interesting/ski

b. fun/play hockey   **e.** boring/play chess

c. exciting/play basketball **f.** hard/swim

6 Work with a partner. Take turns asking questions about the pictures below. Use the words in the box. Answer with your own opinions.

boring	fun
dangerous	hard
easy	interesting
exciting	

Example:

A: Do you think reading books about real people is interesting?

B: Yes, I do. OR No, I don't. I think it's boring to read books about real people.

1 Listen to the conversation. Circle the correct words.

a. First, Dan wants to go _____.

skating   shopping   swimming

b. Lisa thinks Dan's idea is _____.

exciting   dangerous   boring

c. Then Dan wants to go _____.

skiing   biking   swimming

d. Lisa likes _____.

sailing   biking   skating

e. Dan thinks sailing and windsurfing are _____.

fun   boring   hard

f. Dan and Lisa are going to go to the _____.

beach   park   mall

water-skiing   **windsurfing**   **sailing**

 2 Listen again to the conversation. Who wants to do what? Check (✔) the boxes. Then check the activities that you would like to do. Compare answers with a partner.

	Dan	Lisa	You
skating			
biking			
water-skiing			
windsurfing			
sailing			
swimming			

🎧 ③ Listen and repeat.

Hey, Jess? What do you like to do in your free time?

Do you like playing any sports?

No, not really. But I like watching tennis and golf on television.

a. Oh, lots of things. I love reading, writing, watching TV, and going to the movies.

b. You bet! I love playing soccer and basketball. How about you? Do you like playing any sports?

c.

STRATEGY **Show enthusiasm.**

A: Do you like playing any sports?

B: You bet! I love playing soccer and basketball.

④ Work with a partner. Practice the conversation in Exercise 3. Use your own information.

⑤ Work with a partner. Take turns asking and answering questions. Circle your partner's answers in the chart below. Then circle your own answers.

Example:

A: Do you like listening to rock music?

B: You bet! Do you?

A: No, not really.

Activities	Does my partner like __?		Do I like __?	
a. listen to rock music	Yes	No	Yes	No
b. ride a bike	Yes	No	Yes	No
c. swim in the ocean	Yes	No	Yes	No
d. play baseball	Yes	No	Yes	No
e. play soccer	Yes	No	Yes	No
f. go shopping	Yes	No	Yes	No
g. play chess	Yes	No	Yes	No
h. go running	Yes	No	Yes	No

victory

undefeated

championship

1 Read the article

Tigers Win Soccer Game

In an exciting win over the Westville Wildcats on Saturday, the Central High School Tigers showed that victory is sweet.

The final score was 12 to 10. Star player María Hernández scored two of the goals. We asked her what makes her a great soccer player. She said, "I love soccer. It's my favorite sport. I love going to soccer practice. It's so much fun!"

María Hernández

The Tigers are going to play the undefeated Park Forest Patriots next Tuesday. If they win that game, they will play in the state championship.

2 Answer the questions.

a. Who won the soccer game on Saturday?

b. Who played against the Tigers?

c. Who is the star player for the Tigers?

d. Why is she a good soccer player?

e. What do the Tigers have to do to get to the state championship?

> **When you write someone's exact words, use correct punctuation and capitalization.**

- Use quotation marks (" ").
- Start with a capital letter.
- Separate the exact words from the rest of the sentence by a comma, a question mark, or an exclamation mark.
- Use a punctuation mark at the end of the sentence.

Examples:

"We love soccer," she said.

"Do you like skiing?" Tom asked.

"Go Tigers!" Mary cheered.

③ Writing Check Correct these sentences. Add capital letters, punctuation marks, and quotation marks.

    "D   ?"

a. do you like swimming in the ocean the teacher asked.

b. my friends and I love going to the mall Carol said

c. do you think skating is fun Javier asked

d. Peter said ice-skating isn't very popular in my country

e. Dora's friend asked do you think tennis is hard or easy

④ Work with a partner. Check your sentences in Exercise 3.

⑤ Write an article about a game you played or watched. Who won? What was the score? Who was the star player? Was it exciting? Was it boring? Include someone's exact words.

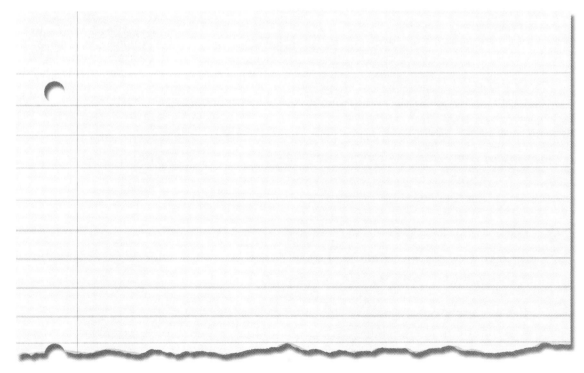

Welcome to the first meeting for the new school newspaper. Let's talk about the different jobs. Let's start with sports.

1.

I'd like to write about sports.

Great! Frank is going to be our sports writer. Who wants to write about other school events, like concerts or special class projects?

2.

I go to all the concerts. I'm also the president of the Art Club, so I can be the school events writer.

Thanks, Reiko. Now we need a photographer, an editor, and someone to draw and write the comics.

OK, Juan. Now all we need is an editor.

I think Lisa can be the editor. She always helps me with my English papers.

3.

I like to draw and write comics. And my friend Chen takes really good pictures. He can be our photographer.

4.

I'd love to be the editor!

Great! Thanks, Lisa.

GETTING STARTED

Warm Up

 1 Listen.

 2 Listen and repeat.

3 Work with a partner. Ask and answer the questions.

a. What are the students going to work on?
b. Who's going to write about sports?
c. What kinds of events do you think Reiko can write about?
d. Who's going to draw and write the comics?
e. Why can Chen be the photographer?
f. What does Lisa want to do?

Building Vocabulary

Parts of a Newspaper

  1 Listen and repeat.

a. front page
b. headline
c. photograph
d. article
e. column
f. comic strip
g. ad/advertisement

the LION'S ROAR

Friday, March 23, ___

LIONS WIN BIG GAME

In a spectacular win, the Central High Lions cruised to a victory over the Jefferson High School Rams. The Lions roared through the game, winning 72 to 52 in front of a cheering crowd.

Star player Peter Courtney said, "It was an unforgettable game. I scored 36 points. This was my best game ever. The whole team was awesome."

The Lions have to win next Tuesday's game against the Bulldogs to go to the state championship. If the Lions win, they will be the first state champions in Central High's history.

Coach Ken Burger is a happy man. "This team can't be beat. This is a dream come true for me," he said. Let's all show our school spirit and cheer for the Lions this Tuesday night.

---

the LION'S ROAR   Friday, March 23, ___   **Page 7**

March of the Snow People

BAKE SALE!

Please come to the PEP CLUB *bake sale.* We'll have lots of delicious pastries and coffee. This week in the main lobby.

Nancy's Advice

Dear Nancy,

My friends always come to my house after school. My mother doesn't want them to come here anymore because she doesn't like the music we listen to. What can I do?

Worried

Dear Worried,

Ask your friends if you can go to their houses. Try not to play the music too loud.

Nancy

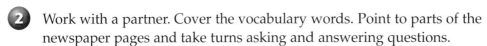

2 Work with a partner. Cover the vocabulary words. Point to parts of the newspaper pages and take turns asking and answering questions.

Example:

A: What's this?

B: It's the front page.

People Who Work on a Newspaper

  3 Listen and repeat.

a. She's a reporter.
She finds out the news.

b. She's a writer.
She writes articles.

c. She's an editor.
She corrects mistakes.

d. He's a photographer.
He takes pictures.

e. He's a cartoonist.
He draws and writes
comic strips.

4 Work with a partner. Take turns asking and answering questions.

Example:

A: What's her job?

B: She's a reporter.

A: What does a reporter do?

B: A reporter finds out the news.

5 Work with a partner. Look again at the pictures in Exercise 3. Take
turns saying something about each picture.

Example:

A: The reporter is talking to the principal.

B: The principal is smiling.

Special Newspaper Columns: Movie Review and Advice Column

6 Read the movie review and the advice column.

Movie Review

by Mike Plotsky

Big Bang–a Bust!

Big Bang is at the Bijou Movie Theater. The movie stars Miranda Marvel and Harvey Smart. It's about police in a big city.

Both the acting and the story are terrible. Don't go see this movie.

Lucy's Advice

Dear Lucy,

My little sister wears my clothes, and she listens to my telephone calls. She's a real pest. What can I do?

Angry Annie

Dear Angry Annie,

Give her your old clothes and a music CD she likes. She might stop bugging you.

Lucy

7 Work with a partner. Take turns asking and answering the questions.

   a. What's the movie review about?
   b. Who wrote the review?
   c. What's the advice column about?
   d. Who wrote the first letter? Who wrote the second letter?

 Learn new words.

Write related words.

Related Words

report	reporter
edit	editor
write	writer
cartoon	cartoonist
photograph	photographer
column	columnist

8 **Vocabulary Check** Complete the sentences. Write the words.

ad	comic strip	photographer	review
article	editor	pictures	writer
column	headline	reporter	

Janna's Advice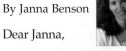

By Janna Benson

Dear Janna,

People are always angry at me because I never arrive anywhere on time. What can I do?

FOR SALE: Skates. Like new. $25.00. Call 555-2374.

Clara Barton is a book about the woman who started the American Red Cross.

It's a great story about an interesting woman. I recommend it highly.

a. Janna writes an advice _____.

b. This is an _____ for skates.

c. This book _____ is about *Clara Barton*.

Mom, this is my new friend Elliot.

Jets Win Championship!

Last night, the Hampton High School Jets won their first championship in ten years. The coach congratulated the players and showed them their trophy. Tomorrow at noon, there is going to be a victory parade on Main Street.

d. A cartoonist drew and wrote this _____.

e. This _____ is about the Jets. The _____ says, "Jets Win Championship!"

f. He's a _____. He loves to take _____.

g. This _____ works on a computer.

h. This _____ is talking to a football player.

i. The _____ is correcting mistakes in the article.

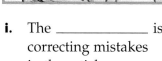

Verb Tense Review 1

 **1** Listen.

Present Progressive	**Are** you **writing** your newspaper article now?
Simple Past	No, but I **wrote** the first paragraph last night.
Simple Present	But you **work** at the newspaper every Monday, Tuesday, and Wednesday.
Verb + Infinitive	I know. But today I **want to work** on my science project.
Future	I'**m going to write** my article on Thursday.

2 Read the article Yolanda Cruz wrote for the school newspaper. Write the correct verb forms.

My name is Yolanda Cruz. I **(1. take/took)** _____ an interesting vacation last month. I **(2. went/go)** _____ to New York City. When I **(3. was/am)** _____ there, I **(4. visited/am visiting)** _____ the Metropolitan Museum of Art, the Museum of Modern Art, and the Statue of Liberty. I also **(5. to eat/ate)** _____ in nice restaurants and **(6. see/saw)** _____ two good plays.

My favorite place **(7. is going to be/was)** _____ the Museum of Modern Art because I want **(8. am/to be)** _____ an artist. I **(9. draw/to draw)** _____ pictures every day. I **(10. am going to show/showed)** _____ my drawings at the art fair in my town next Saturday.

Verb Tense Review 2

 **3** Listen.

Yes/No Questions	Short Answers
Is Carla **writing** the sports column now?	Yes, she **is**.
Did the computer **work**?	No, it **didn't**.
Were you at the meeting yesterday?	No, I **wasn't**.
Does Chen usually **go** to football games?	Yes, he **does**.
Is he tall and thin?	No, he **isn't**.
Are Kenji and Alma **going to be** here tomorrow?	Yes, they **are**.

4 Complete the short answers. Pay close attention to the verb tenses in the questions.

1. A: Did you go to the concert last night?
B: No, ___I didn't___ .

2. A: Was Maria at the concert?
B: Yes, _____ .

3. A: Do Peter and Teng often play frisbee?
B: Yes, _____ .

4. A: Is it going to rain tonight?
B: No, _____ .

5. A: Are you and Jake doing your homework?
B: No, _____ .

6. A: Are Pedro and his brother here today?
B: Yes, _____ .

Verb Tense Review 3

5 Listen.

Information Questions	Statements
How **was** your vacation in Florida?	It **was** great!
When **did** you and your family **go** there?	We **went** there last week.
What **did** you **do** on your vacation?	We **went** to the beach a lot.
Where **does** Lin usually **go** after school?	She usually **goes** home.
Why **isn't** Frank **going to be** at the meeting?	He**'s going to go** to the dentist.

6 Complete the conversation with the correct forms of the verbs. Then practice the conversation with a partner.

MEI: Hi, Rosa. How **(1. be)** _____ you?

ROSA: I **(2. be)** _____ fine, thanks. What
(3. do) _____ you _____ last night?

MEI: I **(4. play)** _____ volleyball. Why
(5. be, *neg.***)** _____ you at the game?

ROSA: I **(6. be)** _____ sick yesterday.

MEI: That's too bad. What **(7. do)** _____ you _____ next weekend?

ROSA: I **(8. work)** _____ next Saturday. My father always
(9. need) _____ me to work in his store on weekends.

MEI: Well, my sister and I **(10. go shopping)** _____ next Saturday. Maybe we can visit you at your store!

Listen to the news reports. Circle the correct words.

a. Tonight the weather is going to be _____.
rainy and cool   windy and cold   warm and sunny

b. The Lions played the Tigers _____.
last week   last night   last year

c. The score was _____.
Lions 62, Tigers 55   Lions 72, Tigers 65   Tigers 82, Lions 65

d. *Lost in Alaska* is at the _____.
Orion Cinema   Cinemax Theater   Regal Theater

e. The two men in the movie _____.
get lost in the mountains   drive a car across   play basketball
                            the country

 Listen and repeat.

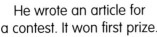

STRATEGY **Express surprise. Follow up with a question.**

A: There was an article about my brother on the front page.

B: You're kidding! What did he do?

3 Work with a partner. Practice the conversation in Exercise 2. Then take turns telling each other about something interesting, funny, sad, or exciting that you read about in the newspaper.

Read the newspaper article.

Mr. Smith's Class Welcomes New Student

by Jim Adams

Teresa Salazar is a new student at Central High School. Teresa is from the Philippines. She and her family moved to the United States last month. Mr. Smith's class had a party to welcome Teresa. Her hobbies are swimming, bike riding, dancing, and reading. Teresa said she misses her friends in the Philippines, but she is happy to be in the United States.

2 A news reporter asks these questions: *Who? What? When? Where?* and *How?* Fill in Jim's notes for his article.

Notes About the New Student	
Who is she?	
What is special about her?	
Where is she from?	
When did she move?	
What did Mr. Smith's class do?	
What are her hobbies?	
How does she feel about moving?	

3 First, read Melba's article. Then fill in her notes for her article.

Players Off to a Good Start

by Melba Sanders

The school drama club, The Players, held their first meeting of the year on September 9. Twenty-one members met in the auditorium.

At this meeting, club officers were elected. Sophia Levi is going to be the new president. Mark Griffin is going to be secretary/treasurer. The club sponsor is Ms. Foster.

Ms. Foster announced that the club is going to perform *The Quest* this year. The play is a drama about the Gold Rush. The Players invite all students in the school to help.

Notes About the School Drama Club	
When was the first meeting?	
Where was it held?	
How many members attended?	
Who is the president going to be?	
Who is the secretary/treasurer going to be?	
Who is the sponsor?	
What play is the club going to perform?	
What is the play about?	
Who can help?	

STRATEGY ▶ **Always check your writing.**

Check your writing. Ask these questions:

- Is the information correct?
- Did you use complete sentences?
- Is the grammar correct?

- Is the spelling correct?
- Did you use capital letters correctly?
- Is the punctuation correct?

  Writing Check Read Kim's notes for her sports article. Then, on your own paper, use the notes to write a sports article about the Tigers. Be sure to check your writing when you're finished.

> Notes About School Soccer Game
> Who? Tigers and Wildcats
> When? Last Saturday
> Where? Central High School
> What Score? Tigers 4, Wildcats 3
>
> How does coach feel? Coach Rooney said, "It was an exciting game. I think we can win the state championship next week."

5 Work with a partner. Check your articles in Exercise 4.

6 On your own paper, write something for a newspaper. It can be a news or sports article, an advice column, a weather report, or a review of a book, movie, CD, or TV show. Remember to check your writing when you're finished.

1 Complete the questions with *at*, *in*, or *on*. Then answer the questions. Write complete sentences about yourself.

a. What time do you get up __on__ weekdays?

_____

b. What time do you usually go to bed _____ the weekend?

_____

c. What's your favorite TV show? When is it _____? What channel is it _____?

_____

_____

2 Write new sentences with the same meanings.

a. Did Sheila show her pictures to Tom?
   Did Sheila show Tom her pictures?

b. Can you give some money to Jenny?

_____

c. Could you please give your English book to me?

_____

d. Did the teacher tell the story to the students?

_____

e. Let's give the menu to the waitress.

_____

f. Do you want to give the money to them?

_____

3 Write sentences with *go* + verb + *–ing*. Write about yourself, your friends, and your family. Use the verbs in parentheses.

Examples:

(dance) My friend Eva goes dancing every Saturday night.
         I love to go dancing at the Pine Club.

a. (dance) _____

b. (hike) _____

c. (jog) _____

d. (run) _____

e. (shop) _____

f. (skate) _____

g. (ski) _____

h. (swim) _____

4 Write sentences about the activities in the box. Use *It's* + adjective + infinitive.

dance	use a computer
play golf	watch TV
swim in a pool	write in English

Example:

It's fun to dance.

a. _____

b. _____

c. _____

d. _____

e. _____

f. _____

5 Rewrite your sentences from Exercise 4. Begin each sentence with verb + *–ing* as a noun.

Example:

Dancing is fun.

a. _____

b. _____

c. _____

d. _____

e. _____

f. _____

6 Complete the telephone conversation with the correct form of the verbs: present progressive, simple present, simple past, or future with *going to*.

A: Where **(1. be)** _____*are*_____ you _*going to be*_ tomorrow? **(2. be)** _____ you _____ home?

B: No, I **(3. go)** _____ to a hockey game with Sal.

A: Why **(4. go)** _____ you _____ to a hockey game? You **(5. hate)** _____ hockey!

B: Sal **(6. invite)** _____ me, so I **(7. say)** _____ yes. I **(8. think)** _____ the game **(9. be)** _____ very exciting!

A: Hockey **(10. be)** _____ very dangerous.

B: Yes, but I **(11. watch)** _____ the game; I **(12. play,** *neg.***)** _____ in it!

A: Well, I **(13. say)** _____ goodbye now. The doorbell **(14. ring)** _____ .

B: OK. Bye!

Consonants

/b/	**b**a**b**y, clu**b**	/n/	**n**o, opi**n**ion	/ð/	**th**is, mo**th**er, ba**th**e
/d/	**d**own, to**d**ay, sa**d**	/ŋ/	a**ng**ry, lo**ng**	/v/	**v**ery, tra**v**el, o**f**
/f/	**f**un, pre**f**er, lau**gh**	/p/	**p**a**p**er, ma**p**	/w/	**w**ay, any**o**ne
/g/	**g**ood, be**g**in, do**g**	/r/	**r**ain, pa**r**ent, doo**r**	/y/	**y**es, on**i**on
/h/	**h**ome, be**h**ind	/s/	**s**alt, medi**c**ine, bu**s**	/z/	**z**oo, cou**s**in, alway**s**
/k/	**k**ey, cho**c**olate, bla**ck**	/š/	**s**ugar, spe**c**ial, fi**sh**	/ž/	mea**s**ure, gara**g**e
/l/	**l**ate, po**l**ice, mai**l**	/t/	**t**ea, ma**t**erial, da**t**e	/č/	**ch**eck, pi**c**ture, wat**ch**
/m/	**m**ay, wo**m**an, swi**m**	/θ/	**th**ing, heal**th**y, ba**th**	/ǰ/	**j**ob, re**f**ri**g**erator, oran**g**e

Vowels

/ɑ/	**o**n, h**o**t, f**a**ther	/e/	**A**pril, tr**ai**n, s**ay**	/u/	p**u**t, c**oo**k, w**ou**ld
/æ/	**a**nd, c**a**sh	/i/	**e**ven, sp**ea**k, tr**ee**	/ə/	**a**bout, penc**i**l, lem**o**n
/ɛ/	**e**gg, s**ay**s, l**ea**ther	/o/	**o**pen, cl**o**se, sh**ow**	/ɚ/	mo**ther**, Satu**r**day, doct**or**
/ɪ/	**i**n, b**i**g	/u/	b**oo**t, d**o**, thr**ough**	/ɝ/	**ear**th, b**ur**n, h**er**
/ɔ/	**o**ff, d**au**ghter, dr**aw**	/ʌ/	**o**f, y**ou**ng, s**u**n		

Diphthongs

/aɪ/	**i**ce, st**y**le, l**ie**	/au/	**ou**t, d**ow**n, h**ow**	/ɔɪ/	**oi**l, n**oi**se, b**oy**

THE ENGLISH ALPHABET

Here is the pronunciation of the letters of the English alphabet, written in International Phonetic Alphabet symbols.

a	/e/	h	/eč/	o	/o/	v	/vi/
b	/bi/	i	/aɪ/	p	/pi/	w	/ˈdʌbəlˌyu/
c	/si/	j	/je/	q	/kyu/	x	/ɛks/
d	/di/	k	/ke/	r	/ɑr/	y	/waɪ/
e	/i/	l	/ɛl/	s	/ɛs/	z	/zi/
f	/ɛf/	m	/ɛm/	t	/ti/		
g	/ǰi/	n	/ɛn/	u	/yu/		

UNIT VOCABULARY

STARTING OUT

Nouns
address
(first/last) name
telephone number

Expressions
Hi./Hello.
I'm _____.

What's your name?
My name is _____.
I'm _____.
It's nice to meet you./
Nice to meet you, too.
Where are you from?
Where's he/she from?

I'm/He's/She's from _____.
Where do you live?
I live in _____.
What's your address?
My address is _____.
What's your phone number?

My number is _____.
Wow, that's interesting.
How old are you?
What class are you in?
Who's your teacher?

UNIT 1

Nouns
bed
birthday
cake
calendar
candy
date
friend
fun
game
grandmother
hamburger

holiday
house
ice cream
month
mother
music
party
people
present
school
(fireworks) show
turkey

week
year

Ordinal Numbers
(See page 2.)

Months of the Year
(See page 2.)

Adjectives
big
favorite
next
this

Verbs
celebrate
come
cook
dance
do
eat
get
give
go
have
invite

UNIT VOCABULARY

UNIT 1 continued

listen (to)
(would) love
play
sing
sound (like)
stay
want

Adverbs
always
ever
home
late
never
often
sometimes

today
tomorrow
too
usually

Prepositions
in (May/Brazil)
on (your birthday/
    Sunday)

Expressions
What's the date today?
Happy Birthday!
Thanks.
I'd love to _____.

UNIT 2

Nouns
afternoon
apple
bag
banana
(green) bean
bottle
box
bread
breakfast
butter
cabbage
can
carrot
carton
cent
cereal
change
cheese
cherry
chicken
chip
cookie
corn
dinner
egg
fish

food
fruit
glass
grape
jar
juice
lemon
lettuce
loaf
lunch
mango
meat
milk
onion
orange
order
package
pasta
peach
pepper
piece
potato
pound
rice
salad
sandwich
sauce

snack
soup
spinach
strawberry
supermarket
tomato
vegetable

Adjectives
any
delicious
fine
large
new
open
some

Verbs
buy
cost
drink
get
hate
(would) like
look
make
need
work

Adverbs
even
here
there

Conjunctions
and
but
or

Articles
a/an

Expressions
Can I help you?
I'd like _____.
Would you like _____?
Yes, please.
Thank you.
I'll have _____.
That will be _____.
Here's _____.
OK.
How many _____?
How much _____?
Let's _____.
Good idea.
I don't know.
Great!
I'm sorry. _____?

UNIT 3

Nouns
band
basketball
beginning
block
book bag
brother
bus
bus stop
cafeteria
computer
dish
doctor
dog
evening
face

family
father
hair
home
homework
hour
job
kitchen
letter
librarian
library
locker
(shopping) mall
math
midnight
morning

movies
night
noon
pajamas
parents
park
practice
post office
restaurant
room
sister
soccer
teeth
test
TV
weekday

weekend
weeknight
work

Adjectives
busy
lucky
part-time
sick

Verbs
brush
clean
comb
feel
get dressed
get out (of)
get up

UNIT 3 continued

go shopping
have to
leave (for)
mail
put
start
stay up
study
take (a shower)
walk

wash
watch

Adverbs
close to
downtown
early
often
only
right now

then
tonight

Prepositions
at (six o'clock/home/noon)
by (7:20)
for
in (the morning)
on (weeknights)
until
with

Conjunctions
after
because
before
so

Expressions
Why so _____?
How come?
That's too bad.
How about _____?

UNIT 4

Nouns
bank
brush
car
cassette
CD/compact disc
clothes
comb
department store
drugstore
fire station
gas
gas station
grocery store
group
hairbrush
jeans
magazine

mom
money
music store
neighborhood
newspaper
shoe
stamp
sweater
T-shirt
theater
thing
toothbrush
toothpaste
video

Adjectives
all
brown
extra

new
that
these
those

Verbs
ask
be on one's way (to)
drive
know
rent
shop
take (a bus)
take out
use

Adverbs
almost
downtown

Prepositions
across from
at (the corner of)
between
next to

Conjunction
if
when

Expressions
How are you doing?
I'm great.
How about you?
Everything's fine.
Sure.
See you.
Thanks a lot.
No problem.
Welcome (to the _____)!

UNIT 5

Nouns
accident
ambulance
apartment
bandage
bike
building
burglar
burglary
department
driver
emergency
fire
garage
girl
glasses
gym
hospital
knee
leg
man
minute
neighbor

nurse
office
operator
(CD) player
police officer
purse
radio
report
road
television set
(fire) truck
wallet
window

Adjectives
angry
blue
broken
calm
green
last
late
small

terrible
unconscious

Verbs
bleed
break
break into
breathe
call
choke
fall
fall down
fall off
get up
happen
help
hit
hurt
pick up
run
run into
see
steal
take out

think
turn
visit

Adverbs
around
early
fast
hardly
just
left
near
now
really
soon
yesterday

Prepositions
for (an hour)
in front of

Expressions
Oh, no!
What's wrong?
Help!

UNIT VOCABULARY

UNIT 6

Nouns
assembly
auditorium
ball
band
boyfriend
concert
dance
election
(science) fair
field
history

meeting
player
principal
student council
race
team
volleyball

Adjectives
many
right
tired

Verbs
attend
cheer
decorate
enter
look for
march
run for
talk
vote
win

Adverbs
a lot
maybe
together
very much

Expressions
I did, too.
Now I understand why
_____.
You're right.
_____ after all.

UNIT 7

Nouns
age
blouse
boy
camp
college
door
eye
guessing game
hair
height
jacket
kitten
pants
person
shirt

skirt
sunglasses
sweater
town
vest
weight
woman

Adjectives
(of) average (height)
beautiful
black
blond
curly
cute
heavy
long

nice
pink
pretty
purple
red
same
short
straight
tall
thin
wavy
white

Verbs
hike
hope
meet

read
wear
write

Adverbs
again
clearly
outside
(very) well

Preposition
without

Expressions
What do/does _____ look
  like?
See you later.
Thanks for calling.

UNIT 8

Nouns
airport
aunt
ballet
beach
bike
city
departure
hotel
motorcycle
mountain
museum
ocean
palace

place
plane
relative
state
time
train
trip
vacation
water
wave

Adjectives
east
fantastic

friendly
fun
huge
interesting
north
south
warm
west

Verbs
border (on)
build
fly
hike

sit
spend (time)
swim
travel

Prepositions
by (bike/motorcycle/
  plane/train/car)

Expressions
Welcome back!
How long does/did it
take?
How long _____?
How was _____?

UNIT 9

Nouns
cloud
country
degree
dress
fall
forecast

plan
raincoat
season
shorts
spring
storm
summer

sun
temperature
weather
winter

Adjectives
Celsius
clear

close
cloudy
cold
cool
Fahrenheit
glad

UNIT 9 continued

	Verbs	run	**Expressions**
hot	clear up	say	Wow!
low	end	speak	That was close!
rainy	go (hiking/swimming)	wait	Don't worry.
snowy	pass	**Preposition**	Not really.
stormy	rain	for (a while)	I'm not sure.
sunny			Thanks for asking!
windy			

UNIT 10

Nouns	host	**Adjectives**	show
actor	kind	the best	talk about
actress	life	better (than)	**Adverb**
answer	news	exciting	especially
athlete	picture	famous	**Preposition**
cartoon	question	funny	on (TV, Channel 6)
channel	reporter	giant	**Expressions**
coffee	(talk, game, sports) show	single	Could you please _____?
commercial	sitcom	terrible	What's it about?
contestant	soap opera	**Verbs**	What's on?
drama	sport	leave	Let's _____.
guest	story	pack	
(TV) guide	table		

UNIT 11

Nouns	run	rock (music)	skate
championship	score	tied	ski
chess	tennis	undefeated	think of
exercise	victory	**Verbs**	water-ski
goal	**Adjectives**	agree	windsurf
golf	boring	disagree	**Adverb**
hockey	dangerous	ice-skate	just
opinion	easy	know how (to)	**Expressions**
player	hard	lose	Hey, _____?
point	popular	sail	You bet!
pool	real		

UNIT 12

Nouns	event	**Adjectives**	learn
ad/advertisement	frisbee	front (page)	miss
article	headline	other	move
artist	hobby	sad	take pictures
cartoonist	mistake	special	work on
(art) club	paragraph	**Verbs**	**Adverbs**
(advice) column	photograph	arrive	highly
comic strip	photographer	cheer	very
comics	(first) prize	correct	**Expressions**
contest	project	decide	That's too bad.
dentist	(book/movie) review	draw	You're kidding!
drawing	writer	find out	
editor		get lost	

INDEX

Hemispheres 2

Diana Renn
Scott Cameron

Susan Iannuzzi
Consultant

Joe Loree
Contributor, Expansion Units

Hemispheres 2 Student Book

Published by McGraw-Hill ESL/ELT, a business unit of The McGraw-Hill Companies, Inc., 1221 Avenue of the Americas, New York, NY 10020. Copyright © 2008 by The McGraw-Hill Companies, Inc. All rights reserved. No part of this publication may be reproduced or distributed in any form or by any means, or stored in a database or retrieval system, without the prior written consent of The McGraw-Hill Companies, Inc., including, but not limited to, in any network or other electronic storage or transmission, or broadcast for distance learning.

ISBN 13: 978-0-07-719095-8 (Student Book with Audio Highlights)
ISBN 10: 0-07-719095-5
1 2 3 4 5 6 7 8 9 10 QWC 11 10 09 08 07

Editorial director: Tina Carver
Series editor: Annie Sullivan
Senior development editors: Terre Passero, Annie Sullivan
Production manager: Juanita Thompson
Production coordinator: James D. Gwyn
Cover Designer: Wee Design Group
Reading and chart designs: Cynthia Malaran
Interior designer: Nesbitt Graphics, Inc.
Artists: Scott Burroughs, Mona Daly; Nadia Simard
Photo researcher: Photoquick Research

The credits section for this book begins on page 143 and is considered an extension of the copyright page.

Cover photo: © Farinaz Taghavi/Corbis

Hemispheres 2 Components

Student Book with Audio Highlights
Workbook
Teacher's Manual
Audio CDs
DVD
DVD Workbook
Online Learning Center
EZ Test® CD-ROM Test Generator
Teacher Training DVD

McGraw-Hill ELT

www.esl.mcgraw-hill.com

The McGraw-Hill Companies

ACKNOWLEDGMENTS

The authors and publisher would like thank the following teachers, program directors, and teacher trainers, who reviewed the Hemispheres program at various stages of development and whose comments, reviews, and field-testing were instrumental in helping us shape the series:

Dee Parker, Jeffrey Taschner, **American University Alumni Language Center,** Bangkok, Thailand
David Scholz, **AUA- Rajadamri Branch,** Bangkok, Thailand
Snow White O. Smelser, **AUA- Ratchayothin,** Bangkok, Thailand
Anthony Pavia, Dr. Joseph W. Southern, **AUA-Srinikarin,** Bangkok, Thailand
Maria Adele Ryan, Maria Teresa de la Torre Aranda, **Associação Alumni,** São Paulo, Brazil
Lúcia Catharina Bodeman Campos, **Associação Brasil-América (ABA),** Pernambuco, Brazil
Marissa Araquistain, Gabriel Areas, Douglas Arroliga, Francisco Hodgson, Maria Mora, Aleyda Reyes, Jairo Rivar, Gloria Tunnerman, Sarah Walsh, **Ave Maria College of the Americas,** Managua, Nicaragua
Bruce Avasadanand, **Bangkok School of Management,** Bangkok, Thailand
Yanan Une-aree, **Bangkok University,** Bangkok, Thailand
Suchada Rattanawanitpun, **Burapha University,** Chon Buri, Thailand
Isabela de Freitas Villas Boas, Catherine Taliaferro Cox, **Casa Thomas Jefferson,** Brasilia, Brazil
Fernando Trevino, **Centro de Idiomas,** Monterrey, Mexico
Maria Zavala, **Centro Educativo los Pinos,** Guadalajara, Mexico
Karen Pereira Meneses, **Centro Educativo Yurusti,** Costa Rica
Wuyen Wayne Ni, **Chung Kuo Institute of Technology and Commerce,** Taipei, Taiwan
Mónica González, **Colegio InterCanadiense de Puebla,** A.C, Puebla, Mexico
Rosa Ma. Chacon, Henry Angulo Jiménez, Johannia Piedra, **Colegio Saleciano Don Bosco,** San Jose, Costa Rica
Marjorie Friedman, **ELS Language Centers,** Florida, United States
Joseph Dziver, **Florida State University** - English Language Program, Panama
Raymond Kao, **Fu Hsing Kang College,** Taipei, Taiwan
Marie J. Guilloteaux, **Gyeongsang National University,** Jinju, Korea
Jana Opicic, **Harvest English Institute,** New Jersey, United States
Wilma Luth, **Hokusei Gakuen University,** Sapporo, Japan
Daniela Alves Meyer, José Manuel da Silva, Maria do Socorro Guimarães, **Instituto Brasil-Estados Unidos (IBEU),** Rio de Janeiro, Brazil
Rosario Garcia Alfonso, **Instituto Copernico,** Guadalajara, Mexico
Nefertiti Gonzales, **Instituto Mexicano Madero,** Puebla, Mexico
Rosa Isabel de la Garza, Elvira Marroquin Medina, **Instituto Regiomontano,** Monterrey, Mexico
Robert van Trieste, **Inter American University of Puerto Rico,** San Juan, Puerto Rico
Elisabeth Lindgren, Annetta Stroud, **Intrax International Institute,** California, United States
Tracy Cramer, **Kansai Gaidai University,** Osaska, Japan
Lilliam Quesada Solano, **Licco Experimental Bilingue Jose Figueres,** Cartago, Costa Rica
Paul Cameron, **National Chengchi University,** Taipei, Taiwan

Elsa Fan, **National Chiao Tung University,** Taipei, Taiwan
Jessie Huang, **National Central University,** Taipei, Taiwan
Marcia Monica A. Saiz, **Naval Academy,** Brazil
Pamela Vittorio, **New School University,** New York, United States
Steve Cornwell, **Osaka Jogakuin College,** Osaska, Japan
Kathryn Aparicio, Inda Shirley, **San Francisco Institute of English,** California, United States
Dan Neal, **Shih Chien University,** Taipei, Taiwan
Kevin Miller, **Shikoku University,** Tokushima, Japan
Mark Brown, Linda Sky Emerson, Jinyoung Hong, Young-Ok Kim, **Sogang University,** Seoul, Korea
Colin Gullberg, **Soochow University,** Taipei, Taiwan
Michael Martin, Juthumas Sukontha, **Sripatum University,** Bangkok, Thailand
Damian Benstead, Roy Langdon, **Sungkyunkwan University,** Seoul, Korea
Cheryl Magnant, Jeff Moore, Devon Scoble, **Sungkyunkwan University,** Seoul, Korea
Raymond Kao, Taiwan **Military University,** Taipei, Taiwan
Dr. Saneh Thongrin, **Thammasat University,** Bangkok, Thailand
Patrick Kiernan, **Tokyo Denki University,** Tokyo, Japan
Yoshiko Matsubayashi, **Tokyo International University,** Saitama, Japan
Mike Hood, Patrick McCoy, **Tokyo University,** Tokyo, Japan
Rafael Cárdenas, Victoria Peralta, Isaac Secaida, Roy Tejeira, **UDELAS - Centro Inteligente de Lenguas de Las Américas,** Panama
Olga Chaves Carballo, **ULACIT,** San Jose, Costa Rica
Adela de Maria y Campos, **Unidades Básicas UPAEP,** Puebla, Mexico
Olda C. de Arauz, **Universidad Autonoma de Chiriqui,** Panama
Ignacio Yepez, **Universidad Autonoma de Guadalajara,** Guadalajara, Mexico
Yohanna Abarca Amador, Cesar Navas Brenes, Gabriela Cerdas, Elisa Li Chan, Ligia de Coto, Maria Eugenia Flores, Carlos Navarro, Johanna Piedra, Allen Quesada-Pacheco, Mary Scholl, Karen Solis, Alonso Canales Viquez, **Universidad de Costa Rica,** San Jose, Costa Rica
John Ball, Geraldine Torack-Durán, **Universidad de las Americas, A.C.,** Mexico City, Mexico
Victoria Lee, **Universidad del Istmo,** Panama
Ramiro Padilla Muñoz, Sandra Hernandez Salazar, **Universidad del Valle de Atemajac (UNIVA),** Guadalajara, Mexico
Alan Heaberlin, Sophia Holder, **Universidad Interamericana,** San Jose, Costa Rica
Fraser Smith, Michael Werner, **Universidad Latina,** Costa Rica
Gilberto Hernàndez, **Universidad Metropolitana Castro Carazo,** Alajuela, Costa Rica
Angela Calderon, **Universidad Santa Maria La Antigua,** Panama
Edith Espino, **Universidad Tecnológica de Panamá,** Panama
Thomas Riedmiller, **University of Northern Iowa,** Iowa, United States
Stella M. Aneiro, Ivette Delgado, Prof. Marisol Santiago Pérez, Ida Roman, **University of Puerto Rico - Arecibo,** Puerto Rico
Aida Caceres, **University of Puerto Rico - Humacao,** Humacao, Puerto Rico
Regino Megill, **University of Puerto Rico - Ponce,** Ponce, Puerto Rico
Dr. Emily Krasinski, **University of Puerto Rico,** San Juan, Puerto Rico

iii

WELCOME TO HEMISPHERES

Hemispheres puts skills-building back into integrated skills. Hemispheres is a four-level integrated skills series for adults and young adults that takes students from high beginning to high intermediate level. The course is uniquely suitable for students studying general English language and those studying English with a view toward more academic work. The series strategically develops both language skills and critical thinking skills. The thought-provoking topics and appealing, user-friendly design invite learners into the skills development without hesitation.

FEATURES

- **Balance of language areas:** Reading, listening, speaking, writing, and grammar are balanced and integrated throughout the unit.

- **Academic skills:** A variety of activities ensures the purposeful development of academic skills, such as summarizing, paraphrasing, making predictions, identifying gist, and using graphs to aid comprehension.

- **Critical thinking skills:** The consistent focus on essential critical thinking skills, such as analyzing, synthesizing, making inferences, understanding organization, and drawing conclusions, encourages independent thinking and learning.

- **TOEFL® iBT:** Each unit helps to build readiness for the TOEFL® iBT. This section includes a new reading and listening and TOEFL® iBT type questions that include personal interpretation, independent speaking and writing, and integrated speaking and writing.

- **Vocabulary expansion activities:** Additional vocabulary practice activities for each unit reinforce learning.

- **High interest content:** Unusual, attention-grabbing topics generate discussion and personalization.

- **DVD and DVD Workbook:** The DVD illustrates conversation strategies and critical thinking skills in an engaging storyline, and the accompanying DVD Workbook ensures comprehension and encourages more open-ended application of the critical thinking skills.

- **Student book with audio highlights:** Students can listen to dialogues multiple times with the audio for additional individual practice.

- **Recycling:** Content and language are continuously and consistently recycled with variations to lead the learner from receptive to creative language production.

COMPONENTS FOR LEVEL 2

- **Student Book with audio highlights**
- **Interleaved Teacher's Book**
- **Workbook**
- **Audio CDs**
- **DVD**
- **DVD Workbook**
- **Online Learning Center**
- **EZ Test® CD-ROM with Test Generator**
- **Teacher Training DVD**

*TOEFL is a registered trademark of Educational Testing Service (ETS).
This publication is not endorsed or approved by ETS.

PUTTING THE SKILLS BACK INTO THE FOUR-SKILLS COURSE

Hemispheres has put the skills-building back into the four-skills course. It supports students in the development of language skills, while at the same time emphasizing critical thinking skills. Reading, listening, speaking, and writing skills are purposefully developed in ways that are similar to single skill books. Helpful skill focus boxes make the skills development information manageable and give students practical guidance that they can use throughout the book or as a reference.

Critical Thinking Skills

Hemispheres features critical thinking skills development together with language skills development. Students are encouraged to take charge of their learning and to become independent thinkers. Activities ask students to make inferences, analyze, synthesize, and understand the relationships between ideas.

Integrating the Skills

Hemispheres carefully integrates skills in both presentations and practice. Meaningful speaking activities and role-plays are integrated with reading and listening. Relevant reading models are integrated with writing. Grammar is practiced through thematically related reading, listening, speaking, and writing. Natural personalization opportunities feature throughout the series.

Putting It Together and TOEFL® iBT

Hemispheres builds valuable test taking skills while recycling critical thinking skills in the Putting It Together section of each unit. A strategic pairing of reading and listening requires students analyze or synthesize information to understand how the two are related. The reading may present a theory, while the listening provides examples supporting that theory; the reading may explain a problem, while the listening provides a solution to the problem; the reading may present an argument, while the listening presents a counterargument; or the reading and listening may present different points of view. The readings and listenings are short and thematically related to the unit, and they are followed by comprehension checkpoints. Students are asked non-intimidating TOEFL® iBT style questions to identify the relationship between the ideas in the reading and those in the listening. They then have an opportunity to discuss and personalize the topic in this section.

DVD

Shot in high-definition, the DVD features six young adults who work at the *Hemispheres* internet café. In addition to showing conversation strategies and critical thinking skills in real-life contexts, the DVD recycles the vocabulary and grammar presented in the student books.

Correlations

Hemispheres is correlated to the TOEFL®iBT, TOEIC® examination, and CEF. It is solid preparation for students whose instructional needs are linked to any of these instruments.

SCOPE AND SEQUENCE

★ Critical thinking skill

vi

Vocabulary	Conversation Strategy	Writing	TOEFL® iBT Focus
■ Identifying word forms *accurate, appear,* *assumptions,* *impression,* *judgments,* *misconception,* *presume, superficial*	■ Starting conversations	■ Understanding the parts of a paragraph ■ Writing about a place	■ Recognizing examples
■ Synonyms *contributions,* *donations, fans,* *journey, original,* *supporters, travels, trip,* *unique, voyage*	■ Asking about and expressing preferences	■ Describing a place using sensory details ■ Organizing ideas with a chart	■ Identifying advantages and disadvantages
■ Phrasal verbs *get along, give up on* *(someone / something),* *grow apart, hang out,* *let (someone) down,* *mess up, put* *(someone) down,* *speak up*	■ Agreeing and disagreeing	■ Writing about problems and solutions ■ Organizing ideas with a mind map	■ Identifying support for a theory
■ Reality shows *alter, catch on, come* *up with, instant,* *redecorate, script*	■ Doing a survey about preferences	■ Giving advice or making suggestions ■ Writing a letter	
■ Identifying positive and negative connotations *balance, conflicts,* *overwhelmed,* *pressed for time,* *refreshing, running* *behind, rushing, take* *time off*	■ Offering, accepting, and declining invitations	■ Categorizing information and ideas ■ Organizing ideas with a mind map	■ Categorizing
■ Understanding words from context *artificial, boulder,* *escape, remote,* *struggled, supplies,* *survive, trapped*	■ Expressing sympathy and concern	■ Supporting predictions with reasons	■ Comparing and contrasting
■ Phrasal verbs *cut back on, do* *without, get rid of,* *give up, kick out, rip* *off, save up for, sell* *out of, show off,* *wind up*	■ Hesitating and refusing politely	■ Using direct quotations ■ Writing about classmates' spending habits	■ Identifying alternatives
■ Expressions *go broke, hit the* *jackpot, put to good* *use, set up, show up,* *turn out*	■ Asking for reasons	■ Writing and supporting predictions	

SCOPE AND SEQUENCE

Unit	Reading	Listening	Grammar
Unit 7 Make Up Your Mind! page 58	■ Reading for specific information ★ Identifying examples (of solutions)	■ Listening to identify decisions and reasons ★ Listening to infer speaker's attitude	■ The past continuous and the simple past
Unit 8 On the Edge page 66	■ Scanning for specific information ★ Categorizing	■ Listening for specific information ★ Making inferences	■ Using gerunds and infinitives to talk about activities
Unit 9 Makeovers page 74	■ Skimming for main ideas ★ Summarizing	■ Listening for specific information ★ Comparing and contrasting	■ Present unreal conditional (the 2nd conditional)
Expansion Units 7–9 page 82	■ Reading for main idea ★ Categorizing	■ Listening for specific information ★ Identifying similarities and differences	
Unit 10 Staying in Touch page 86	★ Previewing a reading ★ Making inferences	■ Identifying problems and solutions ■ Sequencing	■ The passive verb form in the present, past, and future
Unit 11 Making a Difference page 94	■ Making predictions ★ Paraphrasing	■ Listening for specific information ★ Distinguishing between facts and opinions	■ The present perfect versus the simple past
Unit 12 Memories page 102	★ Understanding internal definitions ■ Identifying cause and effect	★ Listening for gist ■ Listening for specific information	■ The present perfect continuous versus the present perfect
Expansion Units 10–12 page 110	■ Reading for specific information ★ Identifying facts and opinions	★ Listening for gist ■ Listening for specific information	

★ Critical thinking skill

Vocabulary	Conversation Strategy	Writing	TOEFL® iBT Focus
■ Idioms *at the last minute, be on the fence, call off, down the road, get cold feet, make up your mind, see eye-to-eye, tie the knot*	■ Helping people make decisions	■ Sequencing steps in a process ■ Organizing information with a chart	■ Identifying information that refutes an opinion
■ Compound words *adventure tour, amusement parks, extreme sports, leisure-time activities, risk tolerance, risk-takers, safety equipment, thrill-seeker*	■ Using exclamations to express opinions	■ Beginning a writing with a "hook" ■ Writing about a leisure-time activity	■ Making inferences to draw an analogy
■ Synonyms *achieve, ambition, appearance, audition, makeover, mentor, motivation, obstacle*	■ Asking for and giving clarification	■ Comparing two things ■ Organizing information with a Venn diagram	■ Identifying effects
■ Nature versus nurture *environment, factors, genetic, influence, interaction, long-standing, trait*	■ Discussing advantages and disadvantages	■ Organizing information with a Venn diagram ■ Comparing and contrasting two people	
■ Internet terminology *board, browse, chat room, hit, link, post (a message), server, text message*	■ Keeping in touch	■ Summarizing	■ Identifying information that supports or challenges a theory
■ Persuasive language *argue, believe, controversial, oppose, protest, refuse, support, urge*	■ Discussing opinions	■ Using details to support an opinion	■ Categorizing
■ About memory loss *condition, cure, deal with, examine, memoir, permanent, recall, recognize*	■ Correcting and admitting mistakes	■ Writing descriptive paragraphs ■ Writing a description of difficulties and challenges	■ Making inferences
■ Campus concerns *consider, drop, equip, get across, grave, opt, undergraduates*	■ Interviewing and sharing results	■ Organizing ideas with a mind map ■ Writing an opinion letter to a newspaper	

6 Why People Buy

READING AND SPEAKING

A ▸ **Warm up.** How often do you buy these items? Frequently, sometimes, rarely, or never? Add your own idea to the last frame.

Your idea:
_____
_____

∩ B ▸ **Read.** What are two types of buyers?

Let's Shop!

Julia Choi, 22, loves Hello Kitty. She **shows off** the popular Japanese cartoon character—a white kitten with a pink hair bow—everywhere in her apartment. She has pens and pencils, clothing, towels, a shower curtain, dishes, clocks, a TV/DVD player, a computer, and over 300
5 stuffed animals. She picks up a pink guitar. "I **saved up for** a year to buy this. The store **sold out of** them in two hours. I bought it online." Will she ever quit collecting? "Probably not," she admits. "If I get married, I'll spend less money on Hello Kitty. But I won't **give** her **up**. I can't **do without** her. If someone marries me, he'll marry my collection, too."
10   Matt Anderson, 21, doesn't just collect one thing. He'll buy anything if he likes it. His apartment is filled with his purchases. "If I'm in a store, and I see a cool watch, I'll buy it. Last week, I bought a backpack over the Internet. I know the company **ripped me off**—it was an expensive bag and poor quality. But I liked the color, so I kept it." He worries, though.
15 "I can spend my whole paycheck in a week. I worry I'll **wind up** broke. I'd like to **cut back on** buying things. And my roommate might **kick me out** if I don't **get rid of** some stuff."
    Julia and Matt have different spending personalities. "Self-expressive buyers" like Julia, collect things that reflect their personality. "Impulsive buyers" like
20 Matt, don't plan their purchases, and they shop without self-control.

▸ **WARM UP** activates prior knowledge of the unit theme and introduces the reading context.

▸ **ENGAGING CONTENT** about real people, places, and ideas captures student interest.

▸ **ACADEMIC AND CRITICAL THINKING SKILLS** encourage independent thinking and learning. Skills include comparing and contrasting, making inferences, summarizing, analyzing, and categorizing.

▸ **VOCABULARY** is presented and practiced in the opening reading of each unit and in expansion activities at the end of the book.

▸ **SKILL FOCUS BOXES** give students practical guidance that they can use throughout the book or as a reference.

C ▸ **Read again.** Check (✓) the information that is true about Julia, Matt, or both.

Information	Julia	Matt
1. likes to buy things		
2. has a home filled with many purchases		
3. plans to buy things		
4. does not always plan to buy things		
5. sometimes buys things online		

Skill Focus Comparing and Contrasting
When we compare, we look for similarities. When we contrast, we look for differences. Usually we compare and contrast at the same time.

D ▸ **Discuss.** Discuss these questions with your classmates.
1. Do Julia and Matt think their shopping is a problem? How do you know?
2. Could you live with someone like Julia or Matt? Why or why not?
3. Are you a "self-expressive buyer" or an "impulsive buyer"? Describe your shopping habits.

VOCABULARY Phrasal Verbs

A ▸ **Identify.** Look at these phrasal verbs from the article. Use the contexts in the article to help you match them to their meanings.

1. ___ show off (something) / show (something) off
2. ___ save up for (something)
3. ___ give up (something) / give (something) up
4. ___ do without (something)
5. ___ sell out of (something)
6. ___ rip off (someone) / rip (someone) off
7. ___ cut back on (something)
8. ___ get rid of (something)
9. ___ kick out (someone) / kick (someone) out
10. ___ wind up

a. eliminate
b. live without something you want
c. make someone leave a place
d. reduce the quantity
e. display something you're proud of
f. result in
g. quit, stop doing
h. sell everything in stock
i. make someone pay more than something is worth
j. accumulate money for a reason

B ▸ **Pair work.** Complete the questions with the correct word. Then discuss them with a partner.
1. What are you saving _____ for right now?
2. What do you like to show _____ in your room?
3. What is one thing you cannot do _____?
4. What do you think you should cut back _____, get rid _____, or give _____? Why?
5. When you're older, do you think you'll wind _____ rich? Why or why not?
6. Did a store or a salesperson ever rip you _____? What happened?
7. Why do managers sometimes kick people _____ of a store or a restaurant?

GRAMMAR explanation and examples serve as a reference for students.

GUIDED PRACTICE includes controlled practice of the grammar or an error correction exercise.

INTEGRATED LISTENING AND GRAMMAR ACTIVITIES allow students to experience the grammar in real language through meaningful, thematically related listening activities.

GETTING INTO GRAMMAR

Using Gerunds and Infinitives to Talk about Activities

Gerunds (verb + *ing*) and infinitives (*to* + verb) are verb forms used as nouns.
Gerunds can be used as subjects and can begin a sentence.

"**Taking risks** is my way of life," says Alain Robert.

Gerunds can also be used as objects after certain verbs: *discuss, enjoy, practice, quit.*

Alain Robert **practiced climbing** rocks and mountains.

Gerunds can also come after a verb + preposition: *apologize for, argue about, believe in, insist on, look forward to, plan on, talk about, think about, worry about.*

Alain Robert doesn't **worry about falling.**

Infinitives are usually used as objects of certain verbs: *agree, appear, can't wait, decide, expect, forget, hope, intend, learn, love, need, offer, plan, refuse, want, would like / love.*

One day, he **forgot to take** the key to his family's eighth-floor apartment.

Some verbs can be followed by either a gerund or an infinitive: *begin, can't stand, continue, hate, like, love, prefer, start, try.*

"I **like taking** risks," says Robert.   "I **like to take** risks," says Robert.

A ▸ **Practice.** Eight of the ten underlined words and phrases are in the wrong form. Correct them.

If you decide <u>try</u> skateboarding, here is some advice. You need to <u>buy</u> some safety equipment. You should definitely get a helmet. <u>Protect</u> your head is the most important thing. <u>Taking</u> a few lessons can also help. If you learn <u>using</u> your skateboard correctly, you can avoid <u>to have</u> painful falls. If you want <u>learning</u> turns and jumps, an instructor or coach can help. Then you must think about <u>to buy</u> the right skateboard. Some people buy inexpensive boards; they plan on <u>use</u> them only on sidewalks and streets. Above all, practice <u>ride</u> every day, and you will see improvements in no time!

Ω B ▸ **Listen.** Complete the questions and answers using the gerund form of the words in the box.

1. What does the man love doing? He loves _____.
2. Why does the woman hate _____? She doesn't like _____.
3. What does the man look forward to _____ the next time he goes to Seven Hills?
   does the man plan on _____ there? He'll next weekend.
   es the man think the woman should try the Death Drop ride?
   _____ is the first step toward overcoming them.

get dizzy
go back
face one's fears
ride roller coasters
spin around
try again

ACTIVATING GRAMMAR

A ▸ **Read and role-play.**

1. Read the obituary of a mountain climber. Underline the gerunds and infinitives.

Ulrich Inderbinen

December 3, 1900 – June 14, 2004

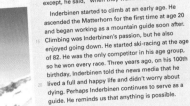

On June 14, 2004, the Swiss mountain climber Ulrich Inderbinen died at the age of 103. Inderbinen rarely left his small mountain village of Zermatt, except to climb in the Swiss Alps. He did that until he was 95. He worked as a mountain guide for 70 years. He always looked forward to taking tourists up the Matterhorn, one of the world's most dangerous and challenging mountain peaks. He climbed the 14,700-foot tall mountain more than 370 times. He never got bored leading tourists up the mountain, except, he said, "when they walked too slowly."

Inderbinen started to climb at an early age. He ascended the Matterhorn for the first time at age 20 and began working as a mountain guide soon after. Climbing was Inderbinen's passion, but he also enjoyed going down. He started ski-racing at the age of 82. He was the only competitor in his age group, so he won every race. Three years ago, on his 100th birthday, Inderbinen told the news media that he lived a full and happy life and didn't worry about dying. Perhaps Inderbinen continues to serve as a guide. He reminds us that anything is possible.

2. **Role-play.** Role-play the last interview with Inderbinen. One of you is a news reporter. The other person is Inderbinen. Ask and answer questions about his life using gerunds and infinitives. Use information from the article and your own ideas.

Example: Reporter: Do you think you'll ever quit mountain climbing?
Inderbinen: I hope not. I'll keep on climbing as long as I can. I don't plan to stop anytime soon.

B ▸ **Group work.**

1. Think of an inspirational person that you know about. You can choose a famous person or someone you know. Write notes about his or her activities and accomplishments.

Example: Joanna:
   • bad knee, but ice skates every day
   • hopes to compete in the Olympics

2. Tell your classmates about this person using gerunds and infinitives. Then answer any questions and give more information.

Example: My friend Joanna is an ice skater. She has a bad knee, but she practices skating every day. She needs to practice because she hopes to compete in the Olympics.

INTEGRATED READING AND GRAMMAR ACTIVITIES encourage students to actively apply their understanding of the grammar to aid in reading comprehension.

FOLLOW UP ACTIVITIES include pair work and writing to ensure students are confident applying the grammar in all language areas—reading, writing, listening, and speaking.

INTERVIEWS AND GROUP WORK expand students' skills through personalized, communicative activities.

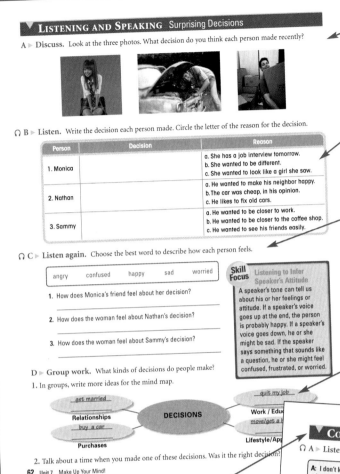

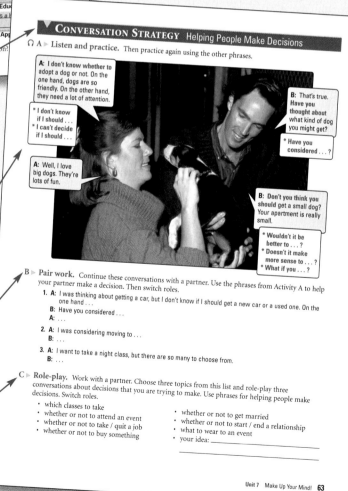

PREDICTION and INFERENCING activities encourage students to anticipate content in the listenings and readings.

A VARIETY OF LISTENING COMPREHENSION ACTIVITIES establishes a solid base of listening competency in students.

CRITICAL LISTENING SKILLS build students' comprehension ability with more challenging listening experiences. Skills include listening for gist, identifying tone, distinguishing between pros and cons, identifying cause and effect relationships, and sequencing.

GRAPHIC ORGANIZERS illustrate the relationships between ideas in reading, listening, and writing.

CONVERSATION STRATEGIES include useful strategies such as showing interest, expressing disbelief, asking for additional information, and asking for and giving opinions.

CALLOUT BOXES allow students to substitute additional expressions directly into the conversation model for controlled practice.

PAIR WORK uses scaffolded dialogues to bolster students' confidence.

ROLE-PLAYS build fluency through interactive, open-ended practice.

► **STUDY IT** highlights the writing skill in a realistic model.

► **WRITE IT** implements the writing skill in a step-by-step process.

► **PREWRITING GRAPHIC ORGANIZERS**, such as mind maps and charts, help students organize their thoughts before writing.

► **EDITING CHECKS** encourage students to share their writing with classmates for peer review.

▼ WRITING Comparing Two Things

A ► Study it. Read the paragraph comparing two laptops and answer these questions.

1. What are the three similarities? _____, _____, and _____

2. Underline the phrases that introduce each similarity.

3. What are the three differences? _____, _____, and _____

4. Highlight the phrases that introduce each difference.

> **TIP** Transition phrases introduce similarities and differences:
> • One similarity / difference is . . .
> • Another similarity / difference is . . .
> • Another thing they have in common is . . .
> • The biggest difference is . . .

Which Laptop Should I Buy?

I can't decide between two laptop computers. They are both the same brand, but one is used and one is new. They have some similarities. One similarity is weight. They both weigh about nine pounds. Another similarity is software. They each come with the basic programs. Another thing they have in common is memory. If I bought either one, I would have no trouble storing all my papers, photos, and music. However, there are some differences. One difference is screen size. The used computer has a small screen. The new one has a bigger screen. If I wrote my papers on the new one, they would be easier to see. Another difference is keyboard size. The used keyboard might be hard to use because it's small. The keyboard on the new computer is more comfortable. The biggest difference is cost. The new computer costs $1,100. The used one costs $800. Which would you choose if you were me?

B ► Write it. Write a paragraph comparing two items.

1. Choose one of these items. Think of two types or brands of these items. Then complete the Venn diagram with information about each item.

| a car | a computer | your idea: _____ |
| a cell phone | an MP3 player | |

Item 1: _____   Similarities   Item 2: _____

2. Write your paragraph. Use ideas from the Venn diagram. In the last sentence, state which item you prefer, or ask for advice about which item to buy.

3. Edit your paragraph.
   • Do you discuss both similarities and differences?
   • Do you use transition phrases to introduce them?

80 Unit 9 Makeovers

PUTTING IT TOGETHER Trash or Treas[...]

A ► Read.

1. Where do these artists create their artwork?

2. **Checkpoint.** Answer these questions.

   1. What must artists do if they are chosen for this program?
   _____
   _____

   2. What are the advantages of working there?
   _____
   _____

   3. Can you think of any disadvantages of working there?
   _____
   _____

If you were an artist, where would you [...] At a studio in New York? At an apartment in Paris? How about at a garbage dump in San Francisco? San Francisco Recycling and Disposal, Inc., sponsors a unique artist-in-residence program. Artists work on projects there for three to six months. They receive 24-hour access to a studio, a small amount of money for expenses, and a public exhibit.

In exchange, artists must create art out of the city's garbage. They must also talk to tour groups about what it is like to transform trash into art. "If I were working at home, I wouldn't get anything done," says one artist-in-residence, Kara Allen. "But what I really love is all the great material I can use. I made this sculpture of a woman from old coat hangers and broken TV sets."

The program started in 1990, when an artist asked to look around for materials. The company saw an opportunity to educate people about recycling, and they opened their doors to more artists. They hoped that the public exhibits would inspire people to think about recycling.

B ► Listen.

1. What is going on right now at the San Francisco dump? _____

2. **Checkpoint.** Discuss these questions.

   1. What did the artist Gabriel Moura create?
   2. Is the public response to the exhibit mostly positive or negative? Why?
   3. If you saw this art exhibit, do you think it would change you? Why or why not?

C ► Wrap it up.

1. TOEFL® iBT Write the effects of the program and exhibition on each person in the chart. Which two people show the effects that the company hoped for? Circle their names.

Gabriel Moura	Woman at the exhibit	Man at the exhibit

2. Can you think of other examples of "transformed trash" in society?

3. Think of other ways to educate people about the importance of recycling. Present one idea to the class. Vote on the best idea.

Unit 9 Makeovers **81**

► **THE STRATEGIC PAIRING OF READING AND LISTENING IN PUTTING IT TOGETHER** requires students analyze or synthesize information. This builds valuable test-taking skills while recycling critical thinking skills.

► **CHECKPOINTS** after the reading and the listening ensure comprehension.

► **WRAP IT UP** provides a non-intimidating TOEFL® iBT style question, which asks students to identify the relationship between the ideas in the reading and those in the listening. It also provides the opportunity for students to discuss and personalize the topic.

First Impressions

▼ READING AND SPEAKING

A ▶ Warm up. Describe five things about the people in the photos. Who do you want to get to know? Why?

○ B ▶ Read. Skim the article. What is the main idea? Circle a, b, or c.

   a. First impressions happen in seconds.
   b. It takes eight minutes to make a first impression.
   c. Speed dating is a good way to meet people.

> **Skill Focus** **Skimming for the Main Idea**
> Skimming is reading a text quickly to identify the topic and find the main idea. Read the title and look at any photos or diagrams when you skim. Because main ideas are often found in the first or last sentences of paragraphs, we pay more attention to these when we skim.

In the Blink of an Eye

It's Friday night in a Chicago restaurant. Seventy men and women are talking in pairs at tables. They **appear** happy – they are smiling and laughing. After eight minutes, a bell rings. Everyone stands up and
5 finds a new partner. This is the world of speed dating, where singles go on eight "dates" in one evening. Each date lasts only eight minutes. But can you really get to know someone in eight minutes? "Of course," says Kim Daniels, 23. "I don't even need
10 that long to get all the information I need."

She may be right. Experts say we form our opinion of strangers in seven to seventeen seconds. And, according to Malcolm Gladwell, the author of *Blink*, it takes even less time to make a first **impression**. He
15 says that humans make **judgments** and **assumptions**
about other people in the blink of an eye: just two seconds. We naturally look for "surface clues" about someone. These include appearance, clothing, and
20 body language.

So are first impressions always **accurate**? Some speed daters say no. "I'm quiet, so women usually think I'm shy," one man complains. "But I'm not shy. People who judge other people quickly are so **superficial**." Similarly, an attractive woman says
25 that some people **presume** she's not smart. But in fact, that's a big **misconception**: she's a doctor.

Gladwell says first impressions may be wrong, but they're almost impossible to reverse. The saying "You never get a second chance to make a first
30 impression" is true.

C ▶ Read again. Find these excerpts in the article. Write the nouns the pronouns refer to.

1. They appear happy . . .

   They = _____. (Paragraph 1)

2. She may be right.

   She = _____. (Paragraph 2)

3. He says that humans make judgments . . .

   He = _____. (Paragraph 2)

4. These include appearance, clothing, and body language.

   These = _____. (Paragraph 2)

Skill Focus Identifying Pronoun References
A pronoun often refers to a specific noun that comes before it. Writers use pronouns to avoid repeating words. Identifying the nouns the pronouns refer to helps us understand what we read. **Example:** *The woman* is happy. *She* is smiling. She = The woman.

D ▶ Discuss. Discuss these questions with your classmates.

1. According to most experts, how long does it take to form an opinion about someone? According to Gladwell, how long does it really take? What do you think?
2. What "surface clues" does Gladwell mention? Can you think of other surface clues?
3. The article refers to this saying: "You never get a second chance to make a first impression." What do you think this means? Do you agree? Why or why not?

VOCABULARY Identifying Word Forms

A ▶ Identify. Use a dictionary to find other forms of these words from the article on page 2.

	Noun	Verb	Adjective	Adverb
1.		appear	apparent	
2.	impression			(none)
3.	judgments		judgmental	judgmentally
4.	assumptions		(none)	(none)
5.		(none)	accurate	
6.		(none)	superficial	
7.		presume	presumptuous	
8.	misconception		(none)	(none)

B ▶ Practice. Choose the best two words to complete each sentence. Write the correct form of the word.

1. James is concerned about his ___appearance___. He spends all his money on clothes. Some people think he's _____. (appear, superficiality, assume)

2. I'm _____ by how open-minded Su Kyung is. She never _____ other people. (superficial, judge, impress)

3. People _____ Rachel is quiet, but this is a _____. She loves to talk and laugh with her friends. (presume, accurate, misconceive)

4. People _____ that Jason is good at sports because his brother is. This impression is _____; he loves sports. (misconceive, assume, accuracy)

GETTING INTO GRAMMAR

The Simple Present and Present Continuous

We use the simple present to talk about facts (things that are always true), habits, and routines. If the subject is a noun that can be replaced with *he, she,* or *it,* add *-s* or *-es* to the verb.

We **form** our opinion of strangers within seven to seventeen seconds.	fact
Kim **goes** to speed dating events regularly to meet people.	routine
Are first impressions always accurate? → Some people say they **aren't**.	fact
Do you **like** speed dating? → No, I **don't** really **like** it.	fact

We use the present continuous to talk about things that are happening right now or at this general time. We use a form of *be (is / are)* and the base verb + *-ing*.

Most couples **are smiling**. → Some **aren't having** fun.	now
Is the woman **smiling**? (now)	
How **is** Kim **meeting** people these days? → She **is trying** speed dating.	at this general time

A ▶ **Practice.** Circle the correct verb form. Then write the questions to complete the conversations.

> **TIP** There are some verbs that you don't usually find in the present continuous. These include *appear, be, forget, hate, hear, like, look, love, prefer, remember, see, seem, smell, taste,* and *want.*

1. **A:** You (seem / are seeming) tired today. _Do you feel OK_ ?
   B: No, I don't feel very well. I (don't sleep / am not sleeping) much these days. We have a new baby at home, and she (is crying / cries) every two hours.

2. **A:** I love your sweater. It (looks / is looking) nice with your hat. _____?
   B: Thanks! Yes, it's new. It's from Christy's Clothes.

   A: You always (find / are finding) great clothes at that store. _____?
   B: Yes, I shop there a lot. I (am buying / buy) clothes there almost every week.

3. **A:** Something (smells / is smelling) great! What _____?
   B: I (make / am making) pasta. There's garlic in the sauce. _____ garlic?
   A: Yes! I (love / am loving) garlic! I (cook / am cooking) with it all the time.

B ▶ **Listen.** Listen to people talk about their interests. Is each activity a routine or an activity happening right now? Write *R* for *routine* or *N* for *now* in each blank.

Conversation 1	Conversation 2
a. _____ listen to a new Black Eyed Peas CD	a. _____ read *Rich Dad, Poor Dad*
b. _____ practice some new dance moves	b. _____ read novels
c. _____ take a hip-hop dance class	c. _____ learn about finance
d. _____ listen to jazz	d. _____ manage money
e. _____ listen to hip hop	e. _____ spend money when going out
	f. _____ have money in the bank

4 Unit 1 First Impressions

▼ ACTIVATING GRAMMAR

A ▶ Read and write.

1. Read these personal profiles on a website about dating. Then answer the questions.

    1. Who is spending a lot of time in New York these days?

    2. How old is Miguel?

    3. What is Sang's favorite video game?

    4. Which three people like sports?

    5. Which two people have jobs related to art and design?

    6. Where does Isabelle live?

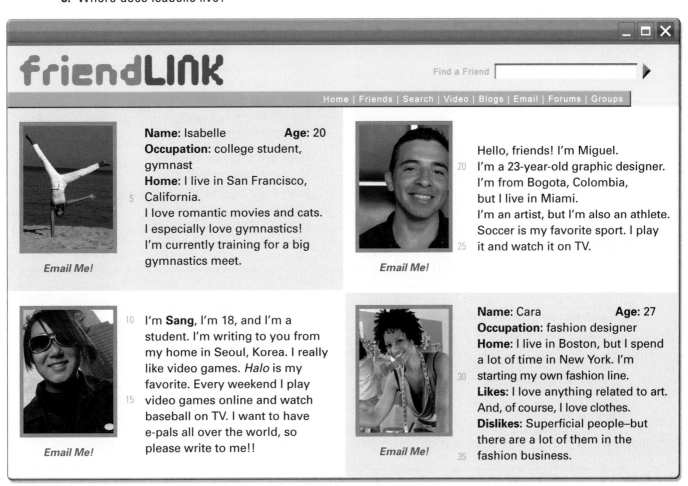

friendLINK

Find a Friend ▶

Home | Friends | Search | Video | Blogs | Email | Forums | Groups

Name: Isabelle   **Age:** 20
Occupation: college student, gymnast
Home: I live in San Francisco,
5 California.
I love romantic movies and cats.
I especially love gymnastics!
I'm currently training for a big gymnastics meet.

Email Me!

20 Hello, friends! I'm Miguel.
I'm a 23-year-old graphic designer.
I'm from Bogota, Colombia,
but I live in Miami.
I'm an artist, but I'm also an athlete.
Soccer is my favorite sport. I play
25 it and watch it on TV.

Email Me!

10 I'm **Sang**, I'm 18, and I'm a
student. I'm writing to you from
my home in Seoul, Korea. I really
like video games. *Halo* is my
favorite. Every weekend I play
15 video games online and watch
baseball on TV. I want to have
e-pals all over the world, so
please write to me!!

Email Me!

Name: Cara   **Age:** 27
Occupation: fashion designer
Home: I live in Boston, but I spend
a lot of time in New York. I'm
30 starting my own fashion line.
Likes: I love anything related to art.
And, of course, I love clothes.
Dislikes: Superficial people–but
there are a lot of them in the
35 fashion business.

Email Me!

2. Write an email to one of these people. Describe your interests and what you're doing these days. Ask at least two questions about them.

    Example: Hi, Sang! Your profile is interesting. It looks like we have something in common. I'm a student, too.
             I also play video games, usually with my brother. He's playing Halo right now! I like baseball, too.
             My favorite American team is the New York Yankees. What is your favorite team? Write back soon!

B ▶ Group work.
Talk about positive first impressions of your school or language program. Give reasons. Are your impressions accurate, or are they misconceptions?

    Example: A: What's your impression of this school?

               B: So far so good. It seems well-organized. But it also feels challenging.

               A: Oh, really? Why do you say that?

               B: My teachers are assigning a lot of homework these days. What's your impression?

A ▶ Discuss. Look at the photos. What do you think is happening in each situation?

🎧 **B ▶ Listen.** For each situation, circle the details that give the woman her first impression.

First Impression	Details
1. The car is unsafe to drive.	a. There is no back bumper. b. The car looks old. c. The engine doesn't sound healthy. d. The left mirror is missing. e. The seatbelts are missing.
2. The restaurant has good food.	a. There is a long line to get in. b. The menu has many choices. c. Many people ordered the chicken special. d. The food is not expensive. e. The food looks good.

🎧 **C ▶ Listen again.** Circle the words that best describe the person's first impression.

a: Conversation 1, female's impression:
   accurate assumption   misconception

b: Conversation 2, male's impression:
   accurate assumption   misconception

Skill Focus Making Inferences
We often guess, or infer something, based on information that we read or hear. A writer or speaker may not give all of the details, but we can logically infer something based on the details that they do give. Inferences may be accurate or inaccurate.

D ▶ Interview.

1. Complete the chart with information about yourself. Use some of the adjectives in your answers.

boring	confusing	exciting	fascinating	frightening	interesting	tiring

Questions	Your answers	Your partner's answers
1. What classes are you taking right now?		
2. Which class is your favorite? What's your impression of it?		
3. What musical groups or singers are you listening to these days?		
4. Your question:		

2. Interview a classmate and complete the chart with your partner's answers.

🎧 **A ▶ Listen and practice.** Then practice again using the other phrases.

A: It seems like this party's a big success. Look at all the people here!
* It looks like . . .
* Apparently, . . .

* Wow, there are lots of . . .
* There are so many . . .

B: Yeah, Lisa always throws a good party.

A: So tell me, how do you know Lisa?
* Let me ask you something.
* I'm just curious.
* So . . .

B: We're taking an art class together. How do you know her?

B ▶ Pair work. Continue these conversations with a partner. Use the phrases from Activity A to start the conversations.

    1. (*watching a soccer match*)
      A: It seems like our team's getting better. There are so many great new players this year!
      B: . . .
      A: So tell me, . . . ?
      B: . . .

    2. (*standing in line at a DVD rental store*)
      A: It looks like this line isn't moving. . . .
      B: . . .

    3. (*waiting for a bus*)
      A: Apparently the bus is running late. . . .
      B: . . .

C ▶ Role-play. Use these situations to role-play a conversation. Be sure to use expressions for starting a conversation.

    • Shopping in a music store
    • Sharing a table in a café
    • Standing in line to buy tickets for a movie or sports event

A ▶ Study it. Read the paragraph.

1. The topic sentence gives us the main idea of a paragraph. Underline the topic sentence.

2. What are the three points that support the main idea?

a. _____

b. _____

c. _____

3. How does the paragraph end? Circle the concluding sentence.

People usually assume that my city is boring. The main reason for this assumption is the name of my city:

Boring!

5 I live in Boring, Oregon. Yes, that's its real name! Another reason is the small size of the town. It has only two main streets and two intersections. A third reason is the location. 10 The town is next to a highway, and it doesn't seem to be near anything important. For these reasons, most people don't stop in Boring when they are traveling in Oregon.

B ▶ Write it. Write a paragraph about a place you know.

1. List the assumptions people make about a place you know. Choose one assumption and list three reasons for this assumption.

2. Complete the paragraph about the place you know. Be sure to write a concluding sentence.

People usually assume that _____ is _____. The main reason
is _____. Another reason is _____.
A third reason is _____. For these reasons, _____
_____.

3. Edit your paragraph.
- Do you use correct word forms?
- Do you use simple present and present continuous correctly?

PUTTING IT TOGETHER Spirit in Motion

A ▶ Read.

1. What are the Paralympic Games?

THE PARALYMPIC GAMES

Everyone knows that the largest sporting event in the world is the Olympic Games. Not everyone knows that the second largest sporting event, which takes place after the Olympics but at the same place, is the Paralympic Games.

The Paralympics are for athletes with disabilities, and they challenge assumptions
5   about sports and athletes in general. Do you assume that people who are physically challenged can't play sports at an elite level? Well, your assumption is wrong! Athletes from 136 countries compete in four winter sports and 20 summer sports.

The Paralympic movement is growing fast. Around 4,000 physically and intellectually challenged athletes compete in over 300 international competitions every year. Skiing,
10 basketball, tennis, and cycling are very popular. Each athlete's performance is inspirational and reflects the Paralympic motto: spirit in motion.

2. Checkpoint. Answer these questions.

1. Where and when do the Paralympics take place? _____

2. Name at least three sports in the Paralympics. _____

3. What assumptions do some people have about people with disabilities? Do the Paralympics challenge those assumptions? _____

B ▶ Listen.

1. Which two Paralympic sports does Sandy Dukat compete in? _____

2. Checkpoint. Answer these questions.

1. Who did Dukat compete against before the late 1990s? _____

2. What other sports and activities does Dukat participate in? _____

   _____

3. What assumptions do you think some people could make about someone with only one leg? How does Sandy challenge those assumptions? _____

   _____

C ▶ Wrap it up.

1. [TOEFL® iBT] How does the listening about Dukat relate to the reading about the Paralympics? Circle a, b, c, or d.
   a. The listening gives more information about the Paralympics.
   b. The listening explains the difference between the Paralympics and the Olympics.
   c. The listening presents a specific example of a Paralympic athlete.
   d. The listening provides a solution to the problem mentioned in the reading.

2. Do you ever watch the Paralympics or disabled athletes on TV? Why or why not?

3. How could more people learn about Paralympic athletes? Give your suggestions.

2 On the Road

▼ READING AND SPEAKING

A ▶ Warm up. Why do you usually travel? Check all your reasons.

____ to visit family

____ to visit friends

____ to work

____ to meet new people

____ to learn about new things (cultures, languages, etc.)

____ to relax and "get away from it all"

____ to participate in sports or other activities

____ other: _____

🎧 **B ▶ Read.** Scan the article. How many countries did Smith visit?

> **Skill Focus** **Scanning for Specific Information**
> To scan for specific information, move your eyes quickly across the text until you find the information you need. Don't read every word.

Coffee to Go, and Go, and Go...

How far would you go for a cup of coffee? Probably not as far as John "Winter" Smith. Smith, known as "Winter," plans to buy coffee at every Starbucks in the world.

5 When did he start this **voyage**? In 1997, he worked as a freelance computer programmer in Texas. He used to spend many hours at his local Starbucks. He would drink coffee while he worked on his laptop. He was interested in the growing coffee chain, and decided to
10 visit all of the cafés. He started with every Starbucks in Dallas. The next year, he continued his **travels** across the United States and then to other countries. He bought coffee at over 4,500 North American and 213 overseas Starbucks.

15 At each café, he asks the manager for a free sample and explains his project. He takes photos. He drinks around ten cups of coffee a day.

Starbucks didn't pay him to do this. He uses his own money. He also accepts **donations** on his website.
20 Many **fans** and **supporters** follow his progress, and some give him **contributions**.

Some people think Winter is doing this to get attention. Winter insists that's not true. So why did he start this **journey**? "I wanted to do something **unique**,
25 something **original**," he says. "I'm investing a lot of time and money. This isn't a silly little **trip**."

Winter still works as a computer programmer, but he spends most of his spare time on the road. When he's not traveling, Winter enjoys drinking coffee... at
30 Starbucks!

C ▶ Read again. Why did Smith decide to go on this trip?
Check the reasons.

1. ____ He didn't have a job, so he had a lot of time.

2. ____ He was a Starbucks employee.

3. ____ He spent a lot of time in cafés and was interested in the
coffee business.

4. ____ He wanted to get attention.

5. ____ Starbucks paid him to do this.

6. ____ It was an unusual idea for a trip.

Skill Focus **Identifying Reasons**
Reasons answer a *why* question. This specific information is usually found in the middle of a paragraph. **Example:** I want to move to New York. ➝ *Why?* I like big cities and lots of action.

D ▶ Discuss. Discuss these questions with your classmates.

1. Is Smith's trip a good idea? Why or why not?
2. Do you think people should send money to Smith for his trip? Should Starbucks pay him? Why or why not?
3. What was your most unusual travel experience? Describe it.

VOCABULARY Synonyms

A ▶ Identify. Decide which words from the article are synonyms. Write them under the correct picture.

TIP Synonyms are words that have the same or a similar meaning, for example, *money* and *cash*.

contributions	fans	original	travels	unique
donations	journey	supporters	trip	voyage

_____ _____ _____ _____

_____ _____ _____ _____

_____

_____

B ▶ Pair work. Discuss these questions with a partner. Use vocabulary from Activity A.

1. Where do you want to go on your next trip? Why?
2. Describe something unique that you did, made, or bought.
3. Describe something or someone that you're a fan or supporter of.
4. Describe something you did or didn't make a donation to.

The Simple Past

We use the simple past to talk about past completed events. We add *-d* or *-ed* to form the past tense of regular verbs. Many verbs are irregular.

> He **noticed** the coffee chain was growing fast.
> He **worked** as a freelance computer programmer.
> He **was** interested in the coffee chain.

For questions with the verb *be*, we put the verb (*was* or *were*) before the subject. For negative statements, we use *not* after the verb, or contractions: *wasn't, weren't*.

> **Were** the Starbucks managers interested in his project? → Yes, they **were**.
> **Was** Winter a Starbucks employee? → No, he **wasn't**.

For verbs other than *be*, use the past tense of *do* to form questions and negative statements in the past. The base verb remains the same.

> When **did** he **start** this unusual voyage? Starbucks **didn't pay** him to do this.

We use *used to* or *would* to talk about past habits or routines that are no longer true.

> He **used to spend** many hours at Starbucks. He **would work** on his laptop there.

A ▸ Practice. Complete the sentences with the correct simple past forms of the verbs in parentheses.

Three days ago, I (finish) _____ my journey to all 88 temples on the Japanese island of
₁
Shikoku. I'm sorry I (write, not) _____ to you earlier, but there (be, not) _____ any
₂ ₃
Internet cafés. Every day, for the past 60 days, I (hike, would) _____ up and down mountains and
₄
past beautiful beaches. Almost every morning, I (buy, would) _____ breakfast at village markets.
₅
Once or twice, I (meet) _____ Japanese travelers. They (seem) _____ surprised to see an
₆ ₇
American woman there. At the end of my trip, one person (ask) _____ me: "Why
₈
(travel) _____ you _____ on foot? It takes only one week to visit the temples by bus or
₉ ₁₀
taxi!" But I'm glad I (go) _____ on foot. I (be, used to) _____ afraid of traveling alone,
₁₁ ₁₂
but now I'm not!

🎧 **B ▸ Listen.** Listen to the conversation about someone's vacation. Listen for the verbs and decide if each action is a completed event or a past routine.

	Completed event	Past routine
a. go to the Caribbean	☐	☐
b. build a house	☐	☐
c. go to the beach and relax	☐	☐
d. eat too much and feel lazy	☐	☐
e. volunteer with Habitat for Humanity	☐	☐

ACTIVATING GRAMMAR

A ▶ Read and role-play.

1. Read the blog. Then check True or False for the statements.

Posted by: travel_love
Thu 27 Aug 2007 4:46pm

The Friendly Youth Hostel in London—Not Friendly!
Warning to travelers: Do not go to the Friendly Youth Hostel in London! I stayed there for three nights, and it was terrible. I didn't get any sleep. People had parties all night long, and they would play loud music. The beds were very uncomfortable. The bathrooms were dirty,
5 and they didn't have hot water. And on the last day, somebody stole my camera. My sister and I used to stay at this hostel every summer, and it was never this bad. Stay away!

	True	False
1. You can get a good night's sleep at this place.	....	....
2. The beds are not comfortable.	....	....
3. You can't get a hot shower there.	....	....
4. People might steal your things.	....	....
5. This is the first time the writer stayed at the Friendly Youth Hostel.	....	....

TIP ▶ We often use time words and expressions with the past: *Last year/month/week; yesterday; the day before yesterday; the other day; when I was 10; when I was a child; last night; yesterday morning/afternoon; a long time ago; for a long time; eventually*

2. Role-play. Role-play a conversation with the blogger above. With a partner, ask and answer questions using the simple past, *used to*, and *would*.

> **Example: A:** Where did you stay in London?
> **B:** I stayed at the Friendly Youth Hostel. It used to be . . .

B ▶ Interview.
Ask classmates about trips where things went wrong. Talk about yourself or someone you know. Why did things go wrong? Put a check (✔) by the reasons you hear.

Reasons why trips went wrong	
_____ had transportation problems	_____ didn't get along with traveling companions
_____ had problems with luggage	_____ got sick
_____ had communication problems	_____ got lost
_____ other:_____	_____ other:_____

> **Example: A:** I went to see my grandparents in Miami last week.
> **B:** How nice! Did you have a good trip?
> **A:** Well, no. Everything went wrong. My flight to New York was delayed, so . . .

A ▶ Discuss. Where do you think these places are? What activities can people do at each place?

⌒ B ▶ Listen. Check the activities each person wanted to do on vacation.

Conversation 1	Man	Woman	Conversation 2	Man	Woman
a. run on the beach	☐	☐	a. be somewhere cold	☐	☐
b. sail a boat	☐	☐	b. travel far from home	☐	☐
c. swim in the sea	☐	☐	c. ski	☐	☐
d. dance at nightclubs	☐	☐	d. walk in the woods	☐	☐
e. visit museums	☐	☐	e. stay inside, watch TV	☐	☐
f. water ski	☐	☐	f. visit museums	☐	☐
g. read a book on the beach	☐	☐	g. see historical sites	☐	☐
h. eat in nice restaurants	☐	☐	h. learn new things	☐	☐

⌒ C ▶ Listen again. Circle the letter of the statement that best describes the different opinions in each conversation.

Conversation 1:
    a. The woman likes fun vacations. The man doesn't.
    b. The woman likes active vacations. The man likes relaxing ones.

Conversation 2:
    a. The man likes to vacation in nature. The woman prefers cities.
    b. The man likes to play sports on vacation. The woman doesn't.

> **Skill Focus**   Making Inferences about Opinions
>
> We can infer a person's opinion by listening to, or reading about, specific information that a person gives. When we make inferences, we make guesses about things that are not stated directly.

D ▶ Group work.

1. Check the vacations that sound fun or interesting to you.

    ____ doing environmental work in a rainforest
    ____ relaxing on a beach with a book
    ____ scuba diving in Australia
    ____ visiting a big city

    ____ digging for dinosaur bones
    ____ picking grapes in a vineyard
    ____ taking a road trip in a car
    ____ going to an amusement park

2. Interview. Imagine you went on one of the vacations that you checked. With a partner, ask and answer questions about the vacations.

    Example: A: Where did you go on your last vacation?
                  B: I did environmental work in a rainforest. I planted trees and tested soil.
                  A: Really? Why did you do that? . . .

⌒ **A** ▶ **Listen and practice.** Then practice again using the other phrases.

A: Do you prefer the window seat or the aisle?

* Would you rather (have) . . . ?
* What's your preference: . . .?
* What do you prefer: . . .?

B: I definitely prefer the aisle seat. The last time I flew, the person next to me fell asleep. I couldn't get out!

* I prefer . . .
* I'd rather (have) . . .
* I'd much rather (have) . . .
* My preference is . . .

A: I'm the opposite. **I'm not crazy about** the aisle seat. On my last trip, every time the serving cart went by, it hit my arm.

* I'm not big on . . .
* I'm not wild about . . .
* I'd rather not (have) . . .
* I'd prefer not to (have) . . .

B ▶ **Pair work.** Continue these conversations with a partner. Use the phrases from Activity A to ask about and express preferences.

    1. A: Would you rather travel alone or with other people?
       B: . . .

    2. A: What's your preference: cold or warm weather?
       B: . . .

    3. A: Do you prefer to travel by plane, car, bus, or train?
       B: . . .

C ▶ **Group work.** Ask classmates about their travel preferences. Write notes in the chart. Use this information to plan a trip together. Choose the best destination for your group.

Do you like . . .	Classmate 1	Classmate 2	Classmate 3
rest and relaxation, or adventure?			
to be in nature or be in the city?			
to travel where you know the language, or where you don't?			
Your idea:			

A ▶ Study it. Read the paragraph.

1. Underline the topic sentence and the concluding sentences.

2. Circle the nouns or adjectives that give sensory details: descriptions of what the writer saw, heard, smelled, touched, and tasted (the five senses).

3. Does the writer have mostly positive or negative feelings about this place? How do you know?

My Trip to Japan

On my last vacation, my friend and I went to an amazing city: Tokyo! It was exciting to walk around at night and see all the bright signs on the buildings. Some days, we would walk through
5 beautiful green parks and smell the colorful, fragrant flowers. I shopped a lot and spent too much money. I never used to like shopping, but in Japan, I found some stylish clothes and unique gifts. We also ate delicious Japanese food every
10 day, and I tried sushi. It felt slippery and smooth, and it tasted almost like candy. On our last night, we went to a Tokyo Giants baseball game. We listened to the excited fans cheer and sing songs. It was interesting to see a baseball game in another
15 country. We saw a lot in Tokyo, but we didn't see everything. I can't wait to go back!

B ▶ Write it.

1. Complete the chart with nouns and adjectives about a place you visited in the past.

sights —	What did you see there?
sounds —	What did you hear?
smells —	What did you smell?
tastes —	What food did you eat?
textures —	What did you touch?

2. Write your paragraph.

3. Edit your paragraph.
   • Do you have a topic sentence?
   • Do your details use each of the five senses?
   • Do you have a concluding sentence?

> **TIP** Use adjectives with *-ing* endings to describe a person, thing, or place. Use adjectives with *-ed* endings to describe how someone feels about a person, thing, or place. **Examples:** Our train journey through Europe was *tiring*. We were *tired* of sitting in our seats for so many hours.
>
> Other adjectives: *boring / bored; surprising / surprised; disappointing / disappointed; annoying / annoyed; confusing / confused; exciting / excited; relaxing / relaxed.*

A ▸ Read.

1. Which of the flight attendants in the article quit his or her job? Why?

2. Checkpoint. Answer these questions.

    1. What are some benefits of a flight attendant's job?

    _____

    _____

    _____

    2. What do Olivia and Simon dislike about being a flight attendant?

    _____

    _____

    _____

    3. Do you think Simon is satisfied with his job? Why or why not?

    _____

    _____

    _____

Flight Attendants Speak Out

Do you like shopping in Paris and London and free airplane tickets to anywhere in the world? These are some travel benefits flight attendants receive. Sound exciting? Maybe not! A recent survey of flight attendants showed that
5 many are unhappy. Rude customers, long working hours, and unpredictable schedules all contribute to job dissatisfaction.

  "Sure, free travel is great. But it wasn't worth it," says Olivia Martin, a former flight attendant. (She now works as a corporate travel agent.) "I spent most of my time in the sky
10 on long international flights. I went to great cities, but I was too tired to enjoy them. I used to stay in the hotel room trying to catch up on my sleep. I would also get sick from the bad air in the planes. And I spent a lot of time away from my family. Ten years was enough for me."

15 Simon Vasquez, who still works as a flight attendant, says that rude customers make the job difficult. "Some people think that flight attendants are just waiters in the sky. But that's not true. We work hard to make sure travelers are safe. It's a serious job!"

B ▸ Listen.

1. Listen to two people at an airport. Which one would prefer not to travel for work?

2. Checkpoint. Answer these questions.

    1. Why is the woman traveling to Seattle? _____

    Why is the man traveling there? _____

    2. Why does the man feel that he can't see or do anything in the city? _____
    has time to see anything.

    3. What did the woman like about traveling for work? _____

    _____

C ▸ Wrap it up.

1. **TOEFL® iBT** Write advantages and disadvantages of traveling for work in the T-chart.

Advantages	Disadvantages

2. What other jobs involve a lot of travel? Name at least five.

3. Would you like a job that required a lot of travel? Why or why not?

3 Friends

READING AND SPEAKING

A ▶ Warm up. Rank the qualities you value most in a friend. Number 1 is the most important.

A friend _____.

____ is fun to be around   ____ is a good listener   ____ is funny

____ has a lot in common with me   ____ loves to talk   ____ is honest

____ is very different from me   ____ is attractive   ____ other: _____

B ▶ Read. What problem does the writer "Bad Haircut" have with her friend? What problem does the writer "Not with the Band" have with his friend?

Friendship Advice: ask Dr. Ann!

Dear Dr. Ann,

I like my friend Liz because she's outgoing and I'm shy, but now we're having problems. Last weekend, she criticized the clothes that I wore to a party. Then she laughed at my new haircut and said I ought to
5   wear a hat! She says things like this every time we get together. Should I **give up on** this friendship? I don't really want to end it.

—Bad Haircut

Dear Bad Haircut,

With friends like this, who needs enemies? You must **speak up**. Tell her that these comments hurt your feelings. Maybe she has to
10   **put** you **down** to feel good about herself, or maybe she is jealous. Your friends should help you feel good about yourself. It's time to find a new friend.

Dear Dr. Ann,

After we finished high school, my friend Jason joined a band. Now he
15   **hangs out** with his new friends. We make plans, and he doesn't show up. He never used to **let** me **down** like that. Worse, last week, he got into trouble for drinking and driving. We didn't use to argue, but now we never **get along**. We fight all the time. I hate to see him **mess up** and get into trouble. He says I shouldn't tell him what to do. Can I
20   save this friendship? —Not with the Band

Dear Not with the Band,

Sometimes friends **grow apart** when one person discovers new interests. You could talk to Jason. Tell him why you're worried. Unfortunately, some of Jason's new interests aren't healthy, and
25   you should not get involved in them.

C ▶ **Read again.** Find these phrases in the reading. Choose the context clue that helps define each phrase. Circle a, b, or c.

1. give up on
   a. we get together
   b. I don't really want to end it.
   c. both
2. speak up
   a. hurt your feelings
   b. tell her
   c. both
3. get along
   a. didn't use to argue
   b. fight all the time
   c. both
4. mess up
   a. get into trouble
   b. fight all the time
   c. both

Do they get along?

D ▶ **Discuss.** Discuss these questions with your classmates.

1. Did Dr. Ann give good advice? Explain. What are some other ways to solve the writers' problems?
2. "With friends like this, who needs enemies?" What do you think this expression means?
3. Have you ever had a friend like Liz or Jason, or any problem with a friend? Or do you know someone who has? What happened?

VOCABULARY Phrasal Verbs

A ▶ **Identify.** Match each phrasal verb with its meaning. Write the letter on the line.

1. ____ give up on (someone/something)
2. ____ speak up
3. ____ put (someone) down
4. ____ hang out
5. ____ mess up
6. ____ let (someone) down
7. ____ get along
8. ____ grow apart

a. express your opinion
b. have a good relationship
c. make mistakes
d. see each other less and less often
e. criticize
f. end or quit
g. disappoint
h. spend time with someone

TIP ▶ Phrasal verbs are composed of a verb and a small word—a preposition or an adverb. The phrase they make has a special meaning. Some phrasal verbs can be separated by an object, others cannot.

B ▶ **Pair work.** Work with a partner. Describe an action or situation that fits a phrasal verb in Activity A. Your partner should ask you a question or make a comment about the situation, using a phrasal verb. Repeat the process with four other phrasal verbs.

Example: **A:** I went to meet my friend for dinner. I waited for over an hour, but she never came.
    B: Did she let you down? / Did you give up on her? / Did you grow apart?

GETTING INTO GRAMMAR

Modals for Suggestions, Advice, and Necessity

	could	should	ought to	have to	must	
weak ◄——————————————————————————————————► strong						
		suggestion, advice		necessity		

We use *could*, *should*, and *ought to* to give advice.

I have an idea. You **could try** talking to Jason.	*suggestion or advice*
You **should start** looking for new friends.	*advice*
Should I **end** the friendship? ——► No, you **shouldn't**.	*advice*
You **ought to wear** a hat.	*suggestion or advice*

We use *have to* and *must* to give very strong advice or to say that something is necessary.

Maybe **she has to** work late. You **must tell** her how you feel. *necessity*

In the negative form, *must* and *have to* have different meanings. *Must not* expresses necessity ("it's very important not to ..."). But *don't have to* means "it's not necessary to."

You **must not get** involved in Jason's unhealthy interests. They're not good for you.
You **don't have to end** the friendship. You can remain friends.

A ▶ Practice. Correct the eight errors in these conversations.

1. Q: My friend wants to eat in expensive restaurants all the time. I don't want to let her down, but I can't spend so much. What I should do?

A: You haven't to spend a lot of money to have fun. You could exercise together for free. You could to also limit your friend to one expensive activity a month.

2. Q: Help! I only have two friends! We are close, but I should to have more.

A: Many people feel like they must to have many friends. To meet friends, you has to talk to people. However, you no should feel like this is a problem. You ought feel happy that you have two great friends!

⌒ B ▶ Listen. Check (✓) if you hear suggestions / advice or a necessity. Write the clue(s).

Conversation 1	Suggestion / Advice ☐ Necessity ☐	Clues: You ought to call her.
Conversation 2	Suggestion / Advice ☐ Necessity ☐	Clue(s):
Conversation 3	Suggestion / Advice ☐ Necessity ☐	Clue(s):

A ▶ Read and role-play.

1. Read the magazine article. Then match the types of friends to the definitions.

1. ____ Fault Finder   a. is not reliable

2. ____ Discloser   b. always decides what to do

3. ____ Promise Breaker   c. is only interested in himself / herself

4. ____ Self-Absorbed   d. views your friendship as a contest

5. ____ Competitor   e. shares your secrets with other people

6. ____ Controller   f. makes comments that make you feel bad

Toxic Friends

Are your friendships healthy? In her book *When Friendship Hurts*, Dr. Jan Yager identifies toxic (or negative) types of friends. One is the Promise Breaker. This friend constantly
5 disappoints you: he or she cancels meetings or shows up late. Another is the Discloser. This person tells your secrets to other people. A third type is the Competitor. This friend competes with you at work, at school, or in romance. A
10 fourth is the Fault Finder. This person criticizes everything from your clothes to your behavior. A fifth type, the Controller, makes all the decisions. The Self-Absorbed, the sixth type, talks about himself or herself all the time and
15 never takes time to listen to you. Yager describes 15 other types. With each type of friend, you must decide if you want to save the friendship. In some cases, the friendship may be so unhealthy that you ought to end it instead.

2. Role-play. With a partner, role-play a conversation between friends in an unhealthy relationship. Have your classmates make guesses about the types of toxic friends. Use modals of advice and necessity.

Example: A: Where were you? You're 30 minutes late. The movie already started!
   B: Oh, sorry. I decided to get my hair cut. Then I ate some lunch.
   A: You should call my cell phone when you're late. And you ought to plan your time better.

B ▶ Discuss. Do you have a toxic friend, or do you know someone who does? Tell your classmates about your friend and ask for advice.

Example: A: I think my friend Gina is a promise breaker. I waited for her at the mall for two hours. Finally, I gave up. Later, she said that her boyfriend came over, so she forgot.
   B: She shouldn't put her boyfriend before you. Friends should come first.
   C: I think you ought to speak up. Tell her you were angry.

A ▶ Discuss. Look at the photos. What kinds of problems do you think these friends have?

⌒ B ▶ Listen. What problems do these friends have? Circle two true statements about each conversation.

Friends	Problems
1. Mike and Jim	a. Jim does not want to be roommates with Mike. b. Jim wants to be roommates but not friends. c. Mike doesn't put away his things. d. Mike paid Jim money for rent but not the phone bill.
2. Angela and Sandra	a. Sandra always puts Angela down. b. Sandra criticizes Angela's new boyfriend, Joe. c. Sandra and Angela don't see each other very often anymore. d. Sandra always decides what she and Angela should do.
3. Stephanie and Nick	a. Stephanie and Nick are having car problems. b. Stephanie always talks about herself. c. Stephanie always listens to Nick. d. Stephanie doesn't always listen to Nick.

⌒ C ▶ Listen again. Which type of toxic friend is each person? Choose one of these categories: Fault Finder, Promise Breaker, Self-Absorbed, or Controller.

> **Skill Focus** Categorizing
> When we categorize, we put people or things into groups according to what type or kind they are.

1. Mike: _____

2. Angela's boyfriend, Joe: _____ and _____

3. Stephanie: _____

D ▶ Pair work.

1. Work with a partner and complete the sentences with your advice about friendships.

   1. You should always _____.

   2. You should never _____.

   3. You ought to _____.

   4. You must not _____.

   5. You have to _____.

2. Present your advice to your classmates. Ask which statements they agree or disagree with and why.

∩ **A** ▶ **Listen and practice.** Then practice again using the other expressions.

A: I think this writer makes a good point. He says that respect is the key to a true friendship.

B: I'm not so sure about that. I think that honesty is the most important thing in a friendship.

* I disagree.
* I completely disagree.
* I don't think so.
* I doubt that.

A: You may be right. You can't have a good friendship without honesty!

* I agree.
* I think you're right.
* That's a good point.
* I couldn't agree more.

B ▶ **Pair work.** Continue these conversations with a partner. Ask the question. Your partner should answer with an opinion and reason for the opinion. Then use the expressions from Activity A to agree or disagree.

    1. A: Do you think your brother or sister can be your best friend?
       B: . . .
    2. A: Do you think your mother or father can be your best friend?
       B: . . .
    3. A: Do you think pets make better friends than people?
       B: . . .

C ▶ **Group work.** Read the proverbs about friendship. Discuss what you think each proverb means. Then say whether you agree or disagree and give reasons.

- "The only way to have a friend is to be a friend."
- "The best mirror is an old friend."
- "Love is blind; friendship closes its eyes."
- "A friend is easier lost than found."
- "A friend to everybody is a friend to nobody."
- "False friends are worse than open enemies."
- "The best of friends must sometimes part."

A ▶ Study it. Read the paragraph.

1. Underline the main problem that the writer mentions.

2. Circle words or phrases that introduce specific examples of the problem.

3. Highlight the solutions that the writer suggests.

PROBLEMS WITH THE STUDENT CENTER

The student center at our school is not a convenient or comfortable place for students to hang out. First of all, the center is only open from 9:00 a.m. to 4:00 p.m., when most students are in classes. Many students want to relax there before or after class, but the door is locked. Second, the snack bar does not have enough employees. The lines to get food or coffee are very long. Most importantly, the center is usually a mess, with papers and garbage everywhere. In my opinion, the school administrators could make several basic improvements. They could keep the center open longer, hire more staff, and provide more garbage and recycling bins. Our school really must have a clean, comfortable place where students can relax and make friends.

B ▶ Write it.

1. Complete the mind map with two more problems affecting your school or community. Give two examples of each problem. Then choose one problem to write about.

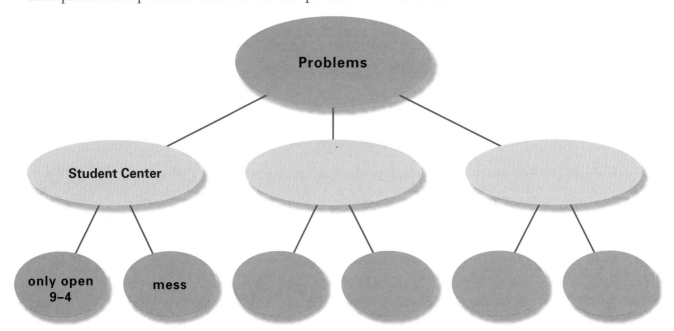

2. Write your paragraph.

3. Edit your paragraph.
- Do you clearly identify the problem? Do you give examples of the problem?
- Do you suggest a solution?

PUTTING IT TOGETHER   Friends Forever?

A ▸ Read.

1. Why did each of these friendships end?

Why Did Your Friendship End?

Ji Youn: My friend Amy and I used to live next door to each other. We did *everything* together. Then she moved. At first we emailed each other every day . . . then once every two days . . . and eventually, just once a week. Then I stopped hearing from her.

Will: Last year, I found out that my buddy Ethan was dating my girlfriend behind my back. I saw them at a restaurant. When I asked him about it, he said they were just friends. But I didn't believe him. So I lost my friend and my girlfriend at the same time.

Pat: My friend Emma and I grew apart when Emma got married. All she wanted to talk about was her wedding, her husband, and her new house. I just couldn't relate. And she wasn't free on the weekends anymore. She did things with her husband instead.

2. Checkpoint. Answer these questions.

1. In your opinion, why did Amy stop emailing Ji Youn? _____

_____

2. How was the end of Will and Ethan's friendship similar to that of Pat and Emma's? _____

_____

3. Do you think any of these people could be close friends again? Why or why not? _____

_____

B ▸ Listen.

1. Why do many people think friendships end?

2. Checkpoint. Answer these questions.

1. According to Dr. Allen, what is the main reason friendships end?

_____

2. According to Dr. Allen, how can people try to save their friendships? _____

_____

3. Do you agree with his theory and solution? Why or why not? What are some other ways friends can work to keep their friendships alive? _____

_____

C ▸ Wrap it up.

1. TOEFL® iBT Put a check by the friendship endings that support Dr. Allen's theory.

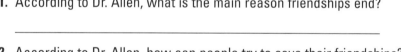

____ Ji Youn and Amy   ____ Will and Ethan   ____ Pat and Emma

2. When you need advice about a problem with a friend, who do you talk to? Why?

3. Do you agree that sometimes friendships have to end? Give examples from your own experience or observations to support your opinion.

Expansion Units 1–3

A ▶ **Warm up.** Check the ways you commute to work or school. Circle the ways you would prefer to commute. What do you like or dislike about these ways of commuting?

____ by car   ____ by bus   ____ by bicycle

____ on a skateboard   ____ by train   ____ on foot

🎧 **B** ▶ **Listen.** Listen to the TV newscast. How does each person travel to work or school now? Write your answers in the chart.

	How they travel now
Interview 1	
Interview 2	
Interview 3	

C ▶ **Discuss.** Discuss these questions with a partner.

1. What are some things people in the interviews used to do on the bus? What are some things they usually do now when they are commuting? Do you think these activities are a good way for people to use their time while they are commuting? Explain.

2. How do people in your city commute? Look at the photos in Activity A. Rank them from 1 (most common) to 6 (least common).

3. What do you usually do while you are traveling to work or to school? Is it a good way to use your time? Why or why not?

∩ **D ▶ Listen again.** What way of commuting does each person prefer? What reasons do they give ∟ their preferences? Complete the chart.

	Preference	Reason for preference
Interview 1		
Interview 2		
Interview 3		

E ▶ Interview. Find out how four of your classmates commute and what they usually do while they are commuting. Then ask how they would prefer to commute and why. Complete the chart.

	How they commute	What they do while commuting	How they prefer to commute	Reason for preference
Student 1				
Student 2				
Student 3				
Student 4				

A ▶ Vocabulary boost! Read each sentence. Circle the correct definition of the words in bold.

1. Everyone knew exactly what to say in the presentation because we prepared a detailed **script** for them.
   a. a written text of a performance or presentation
   b. instructions for using a piece of equipment
   c. letter about what to say

2. This computer program is so fast! It saves a lot of time. When you enter the data, you get **instant** results.
   a. interesting; fascinating   b. reliable; trustworthy   c. immediate; extremely quick

3. We expected many people to like this TV program, but it didn't **catch on.** It was cancelled after the third show because no one was watching it.
   a. become popular   b. make money   c. attract young people

4. This restaurant looks so much better since they **redecorated**. It's completely different now—more open space and much brighter.
   a. got a new chef   b. changed the furniture and lighting   c. changed the food

5. Actors use wigs and make-up to **alter** their appearance for the different characters they play. This can make them look much older or younger than they really are.
   a. improve   b. change   c. buy

6. That was a hard meeting! My boss asked each of us to **come up with** three new ways to improve sales this month. But no matter how hard I tried, I couldn't think of one.
   a. review; look at closely   b. experience; try   c. invent; to create

B ▶ Read. Underline the main idea in each paragraph of the article.

Reality TV Shows

There is a new type of TV show, using non-actors without **scripts**. It's called "reality television." British television first introduced a "makeover" show, *Changing Rooms*, in which people **redecorated** other people's houses. American TV soon copied this show with one called *Trading Spaces*. The makeover theme quickly **caught on**. On the program *Extreme Makeover*, people have their personal appearance completely
5   **altered** through diet, exercise, hairstyling, and fashion.

Reality TV is now widespread, and producers continue to **come up with** new ideas. *Survivor* puts a group of strangers together in a remote place and makes them compete in a variety of unusual challenges. At the end of each show, they all vote to eliminate one
10 person from the competition. The last person remaining wins a million dollars. *The Simple Life* shows what happens when a rich and famous celebrity, Paris Hilton, lives and works with ordinary people. Another recent example is *The Osbournes*, which shows how rock singer Ozzy Osbourne and his family live their daily lives
15 at home. Today, the most popular of all American reality shows is *American Idol*. *American Idol* is a different kind of reality show. It's a singing contest that allows the viewers to vote for their favorite contestant using their telephones. *American Idol* was an **instant** hit, and this top-rated show attracts over 30 million viewers every week.

C ▶ Discuss. Discuss these questions with your classmates.

1. What is the main difference between reality TV and traditional TV shows?
2. Have you ever seen any of the shows mentioned in the article? Which of them would you like to see? What are some examples of reality TV that you know?
3. What do you think are three positive aspects of reality TV? What are three negative aspects? Do you think reality TV is a good idea? Explain.

D ▶ Read again. Categorize the TV shows from the box. Write them in the correct column in the chart.

American Idol	The Osbournes	Survivor
Changing Rooms	The Simple Life	Trading Spaces
Extreme Makeover		

Contests	Makeover Shows	Celebrity Shows

E ▶ Write about it.

1. Write a letter to the producer of a reality TV makeover show. Suggest a person for the show and tell what the person should do differently. Use expressions for giving advice or suggestions.

   Example: He needs a new hairstyle. He should cut his hair shorter.

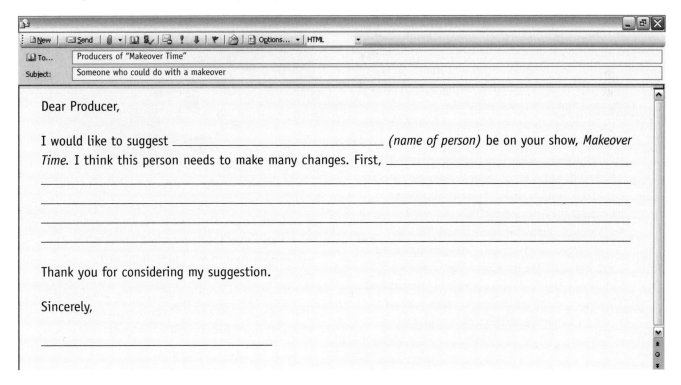

2. Edit your paragraph.
   • Do you use expressions for giving advice or suggestions?

READING AND SPEAKING

A ▶ Warm up. Check the activities that you enjoy in your free time. How often do you do each one?

- ☐ listen to or play music
- ☐ exercise
- ☐ surf the Internet
- ☐ read
- ☐ play video games
- ☐ watch or play sports
- ☐ shop
- ☐ watch TV
- ☐ other: _____

🎧 **B ▶ Read.** Skim the article. What is Take Back Your Time Day? Who started it?

Take Back Your Time

Do you have trouble finding time to relax? Do you feel like you're always **rushing** yet **running behind**? If you answered "yes," you probably suffer from time stress. Many people today are overworked,
5 overscheduled, and **overwhelmed**.

Young adults feel **pressed for time** because they have more responsibilities than ever. It's hard to **balance** them with a social life. Jess Wyman, 21, is a full-time college student with a part-time job.
10 "Most of my friends also work and study," she explains. "With our schedule **conflicts**, it's hard for us to find time to see each other."

Concerned about our fast-paced lifestyle, a group of people in the United States and Canada formed
15 an organization called Take Back Your Time. They believe time pressure is a social problem that damages our health, families, and communities. It's even harmful to the environment. Because we are so busy, we buy more disposable items and recycle less.
20 To address this problem, the organization started a new holiday: Take Back Your Time Day. Every October 24, they encourage people to **take time off**. They recommend **refreshing** activities, such as visiting art galleries, walking, playing games,
25 or reading.

How will Jess take back her time? "One of my professors is canceling his class, so I'm meeting friends for lunch. Then I'm going to take a nap. After that, I'm not sure – maybe I'll walk in the
30 park. But unfortunately, I'm working that evening."

Take Back Your Time publicizes the holiday on its website. The organizers hope more workplaces and schools are going to participate each year.

C ▶ Read again. Match the causes with the effects.

1. ____ Young adults and teens today try to do many things at once.

2. ____ One professor won't make his students come to class on Take Back Your Time Day.

3. ____ The organization Take Back Your Time wants to help stop time pressure.

4. ____ According to Take Back Your Time, society has too many time pressures.

5. ____ Take Back Your Time tells people about the holiday through its website.

a. They started Take Back Your Time Day.

b. Hopefully, more people will participate in the holiday in the future.

c. Jess is going to take back some time in the afternoon on October 24.

d. They feel as much time pressures as older adults.

e. Health, families, communities, and the environment all suffer.

Skill Focus Identifying Causes and Effects

A *cause* explains the reason why things happen. An *effect* explains the result. When you find two ideas that seem to have a cause and effect relationship, try this test: add *because* before the cause, or *as a result* before the effect. *Example:* She opened the window (effect) *because* it was hot (cause).

D ▶ Discuss. Discuss these questions with your classmates.

1. Do you agree that our fast-paced lifestyle is a social problem? Why or why not?
2. Name at least three items that people buy and throw away. Can any be recycled?
3. Name other countries that you think need Take Back Your Time Day. Explain why.

VOCABULARY Identifying Positive and Negative Connotations

A ▶ Identify. Match the words and phrases to their definitions. Label each positive (+) or negative (−).

1. ____ pressed for time   a. late
2. ____ refreshing   b. take a break from something
3. ____ conflicts   c. extremely stressed, pressured
4. ____ running behind   d. energy-giving
5. ____ rushing   e. in a hurry
6. ____ overwhelmed   f. not having enough time
7. ____ balance   g. problems; things that aren't in agreement
8. ____ take time off   h. give two or more things equal time or attention

B ▶ Interview. Interview two classmates. Write their answers in the chart.

Questions	Student 1	Student 2
How often do you feel pressed for time?		
Do you feel overwhelmed, or do you balance things well?		
When do you usually feel like you're running behind?		
How often do you take time out to relax?		
What do you do when you take time off?		

GETTING INTO GRAMMAR

Future Plans with *be going to* and *will*

We use *be going to* and the present continuous to talk about future plans.

> **A:** On October 24, what **is** Jess **going to do**?
> **B:** She**'s going to take** a long nap. She **isn't going to attend** her class.
> The professor **is canceling** his class. Jess and some friends **are meeting** for lunch.

We use *will* to talk about plans that are made at the moment of speaking.

> **A:** Do you want to have lunch with me?
> **B:** Sure, **I'll join** you! That sounds fun.

A ▶ Practice. Complete the conversation. Circle the correct form to talk about the future.

A: Hey, (I'll drive / I'm driving) by your neighborhood after work this evening. Do you want a ride home?

B: No, thanks. (I'll work / I'm going to work) late today. I (am writing / will write) my report this afternoon.

I (am giving / will give) a presentation on it tomorrow morning, so I'm feeling pressed for time right now.

A: I understand. Do you at least have time for lunch? Some of us (are having / will have) lunch at noon.

B: Sure. That sounds great. (I'm going to join / I'll join) you. But I think I need a little more time to work.

So (I'm meeting / I'll meet) you at the restaurant around 12:15.

A: That only gives you 30 minutes for lunch! You work too much. Take a break!

B: Well, (I'll leave / I'm leaving) for my vacation on Friday, and I already know I (am going to relax /

will relax) then.

∩ B ▶ Listen. Decide if the speakers are discussing the present or the future.

Congratulations!

1. Present ☐ Future ☐   5. Present ☐ Future ☐
2. Present ☐ Future ☐   6. Present ☐ Future ☐
3. Present ☐ Future ☐   7. Present ☐ Future ☐
4. Present ☐ Future ☐   8. Present ☐ Future ☐

ACTIVATING GRAMMAR

A ▶ Read and role-play.

1. Read the email Paul wrote to his friends. Then write the phrases in the correct column of the chart.

include a link to the train schedule	email his new phone number	move
be busy with papers and projects	finish his studies	not waste time
	have a whole place to himself	take karate lessons
	leave the city	write his new address

Plans before writing the email	Plans at the time of writing the email

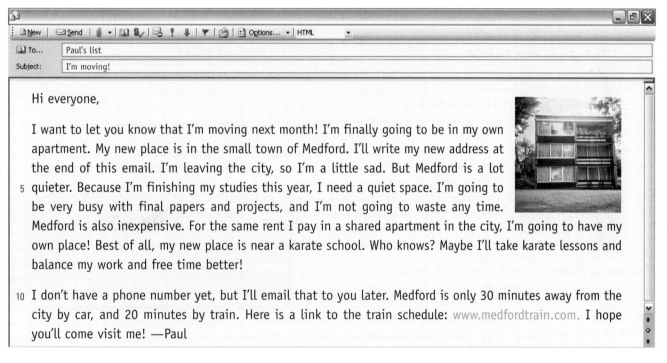

New | Send | Options... | HTML

To... Paul's list
Subject: I'm moving!

Hi everyone,

I want to let you know that I'm moving next month! I'm finally going to be in my own apartment. My new place is in the small town of Medford. I'll write my new address at the end of this email. I'm leaving the city, so I'm a little sad. But Medford is a lot
5 quieter. Because I'm finishing my studies this year, I need a quiet space. I'm going to be very busy with final papers and projects, and I'm not going to waste any time. Medford is also inexpensive. For the same rent I pay in a shared apartment in the city, I'm going to have my own place! Best of all, my new place is near a karate school. Who knows? Maybe I'll take karate lessons and balance my work and free time better!

10 I don't have a phone number yet, but I'll email that to you later. Medford is only 30 minutes away from the city by car, and 20 minutes by train. Here is a link to the train schedule: www.medfordtrain.com. I hope you'll come visit me! —Paul

2. Role-play. Role-play a conversation between Paul and a friend. Paul should explain his plans. Use information from the email and your own ideas. Use *be going to*, the present continuous, and *will*.

> **Example:** **A:** Are you really moving?
> **B:** Yes. I'm going to start packing next week.
> **A:** Are you staying in the city?
> **B:** No, I'm going to rent an apartment in Medford. It's so much cheaper.

B ▶ Interview.
Interview classmates about their living situations. Find out if they plan to move soon, stay where they are, or make any changes at home.

> **Example:** **A:** Are you going to make any changes at home?
> **B:** Yes. I'm getting a roommate next month. I'm going to save so much money on my rent.

A ▶ Discuss. Look at the photos. Why do you think each person feels time pressure?

⌒ B ▶ Listen. Which activities are in Eduardo's and Alison's plans? Check (✓) them on the left.

1. Eduardo	2. Alison
____ tour the city ____	____ eat dinner before dance class ____
____ cook dinner ____	____ take a dance class ____
____ take his parents out to dinner ____	____ teach a class ____
✓ clean his apartment __1__	____ go to a yoga class ____
____ try to get to work on time ____	____ make a Mexican dinner ____
____ go grocery shopping ____	____ work on her French homework ____
____ stay with his parents for one night ____	____ go to a computer lab ____
____ take his parents to the train ____	____ meet with computer class students ____
____ go to work late ____	____ eat dinner at home on Thursday ____

⌒ C ▶ Listen again. Sequence Eduardo's and Alison's plans in the chart above. Write the numbers 1–6 on the lines. Number 1 is marked as an example.

Skill Focus Listening for Sequence
A *sequence* is the order of events from start to finish. When we listen for sequence, we pay attention to words like *first, second, next, then,* and *after that* to help us.

D ▶ Interview.

1. Write your plans for tomorrow afternoon and evening. Leave two boxes empty.

12:00	5:00
1:00	6:00
2:00	7:00
3:00	8:00
4:00	9:00

2. Interview your classmates. Find out when they are free. Make a plan to do something with someone who is free when you are. Write it in the planner.

> **Example: A:** What are you doing at 12:00 on Friday?
> **B:** I'm taking a computer class.
> **A:** What about 6:00? Are you busy then? . . .

🎧 **A** ▶ **Listen and practice.** Then practice again using the other expressions.

A: I'm having some friends over for a barbecue tonight. **Would you guys like to come?**

* Do you want to come?
* Would you care to join us / me?
* Are you free?

B: What time?

A: 6:00.

* I'm afraid I can't.
* I'm not available that night / weekend / day.
* I already have plans.
* Unfortunately, I'm really busy.

B: Oh, I wish I could, but I'm working. **Thanks for asking, though.**

A: That's nice of you to offer, but you don't have to. Just bring your appetite!

C: Sure, I'll come! Can I bring anything? Some salad or bread?

* I'd be delighted to!
* Yes, that sounds fun / great / wonderful!
* Sure!

* That's so nice of you to offer.
* Maybe another time.

B ▶ **Pair work.** Continue these conversations with a partner. Use the expressions from Activity A to offer, accept, or decline the invitations.

1. **A:** Some of us from class are getting together at the library tonight. We're going to review for the English test. Would you like to join us?

   B: What time are you meeting?

   A: . . .

2. **A:** I'm having a party this weekend. . . .

   B: . . .

3. **A:** My friends and I are going to try that new restaurant for lunch. . . .

   B: . . .

C ▶ **Group work.** Invite people in your class to these events. Then accept or decline your classmates' invitations.

- a movie
- a party
- a concert
- a sports event
- *your idea*: _____
- *your idea*: _____

A ▸ Study it.   Study the paragraph.

1. What is the general topic that the writer breaks down into smaller ideas?

2. What three categories (or types) of items are discussed?

3. Underline the topic sentence.

Do you often have schedule conflicts? Do you often put things off until later – or do you forget about them until it's too late? If so, a time management system can help. There are three types of time management systems to consider: calendars, planner books, and handheld computers
5 (PDAs). Calendars are easy to use and inexpensive. They come in all sizes for desks and walls. But some people need to know their schedule wherever they go. For them, a planner book is a good option. It can show a day, a week, or a month on one page. There is room to write information about work, school assignments, and personal plans. In addition, you can take
10 a planner book anywhere. Or you can lose it anywhere! That's why some people prefer handheld computers, or PDAs. You can keep a lot of information in them and connect to a home computer. You can also save your PDA information in your home computer, so it won't get lost. Unfortunately, PDAs are expensive. So now that you know all your
15 options, what are you waiting for?

B ▸ Write it.   Write a paragraph for a student magazine.

1. Choose one of these topics. Complete the mind map. Write two categories related to your topic and two examples of each that you can use in your paragraph.

- types of time-wasting activities
- types of students
- types of teachers
- types of parties
- *your idea:* _____

```
                        ⬭
                      Topic
          ⬭                           ⬭
      Category 1                  Category 2
    ⬭          ⬭              ⬭            ⬭
 Example 1   Example 2     Example 1     Example 2
```

2. Write your paragraph. Include your topic, the two categories related to your topic, and the two examples of each category.

3. Edit your paragraph.
- Do you have a topic sentence stating the main idea?
- Do you have smaller categories?
- Do you have a concluding sentence?

PUTTING IT TOGETHER Not Enough Time

A ▶ Read.

1. What is the general topic of the article? What are the smaller categories?

A Chat with Dr. Sapadin

Dr. Linda Sapadin, a psychologist in private practice, who specializes in helping people overcome self-defeating patterns of behavior, identifies six types of procrastinators: perfectionists, dreamers, worriers, defiers, crisis-makers, and overdoers. Each type has internal conflicts that make them avoid things they need to do. Perfectionists put off their work because they think it has to be perfect.
5 Dreamers fantasize about doing things but don't set realistic goals. Worriers wonder what other people are thinking, or "What if something goes wrong?" Defiers don't like people telling them what to do. Crisis-makers like the feeling of danger that comes with putting things off until the last minute. Finally, overdoers try to do too much; it's hard for them to say "no."

Identifying your procrastination style is the first step toward overcoming the problem. Dr. Sapadin
10 gives advice for each type in her book, *Beat Procrastination and Make the Grade*. If you wish to take a quiz to find out what type of procrastinator you are and for suggestions on how to overcome your style of procrastination, go to www.PsychWisdom.com.

2. Checkpoint. Answer these questions.

1. What is a procrastinator? _____

2. What does the title of Dr. Sapadin's book mean? (Hint: "make the grade" means to succeed.)

_____

3. What kind of people did Dr. Sapadin probably write this book for? _____

B ▶ Listen.

1. What do all of these people have in common?

2. Checkpoint. Answers these questions.

1. What is each person's goal? What is his or her reason for procrastinating?

1. Kim: _____   4. Noah: _____

_____   _____

2. David: _____   5. Caitlin: _____

_____   _____

3. Angela: _____   6. Jeff: _____

_____   _____

2. Which two speakers think they'll complete their tasks? _____

3. Which speaker do you think has the biggest problem? Why? _____

C ▶ Wrap it up.

1. TOEFL® iBT Which type of procrastinator is each person? Write the category next to the name.

a. Kim _____   c. Angela _____   e. Caitlin _____

b. David _____   d. Noah _____   f. Jeff _____

2. Give each person in number 1 advice to overcome procrastination.

5 In the News

READING AND SPEAKING

A ▶ Warm up. Check the items you think an experienced hiker takes on hiking trips.

_____ a compass _____ a cell phone _____ climbing ropes _____ an army knife _____ a headlamp

∩ B ▶ Read.

1. Read the first two paragraphs. Predict what will happen to Aron Ralston.

> **Skill Focus** **Making Predictions**
> The first two paragraphs of a news article give basic information: *who, what, where, when,* and *why.* When we skim the first two paragraphs, we usually have enough information to make predictions, or guesses, about what will happen next. We can read more to confirm the predictions.

> You're hiking alone when you find a **boulder** blocking your path between two canyon walls. You climb across the large rock, but it rolls onto your arm. You're **trapped**. You can't get out. What are you going to do?
>
> Aron Ralston found himself in this situation in April, 2003. Nobody knew where he was since he didn't tell anyone where he was going. He was alone in a **remote** area, far from people. His only **supplies** were climbing
> 5 ropes, food and water for one day, batteries, a video camera, an army knife, and a headlamp. They were not enough for long-term survival.

Predictions: 1. _____ 2. _____

2. Read the rest of the article to confirm your predictions. Were they correct?

> Aron waited for five days, but no one came. His food and water ran out, and he **struggled** to stay alive. He tried very difficult things. He tried cutting the rock with his knife. That didn't work. Then he tried moving the boulder with ropes. This, too, was impossible. He fought to **survive**, but knowing he might not,
> 10 he said goodbye to his family on his video camera.
>
> What Aron did to **escape** was both heroic and horrifying. To free himself, he cut off his arm with his knife. He tied clothing around it to stop the blood. Then he walked six miles and found help.
>
> Aron says he's going to continue to hike, even with his **artificial** arm, but he's also going to change some of his habits. "I'll always tell people *where* I'm going," he explains. "And I'll always take plenty of food and water."
> 15 Will he continue to hike alone? He looks at his human-made arm. "I might," he admits. "But I'll be careful."

C ▶ Read again. Find these excerpts in the article. Write the nouns or phrases that the pronouns refer to.

1. ... but *it* rolls onto your arm. *it* = _____

2. *They* were not enough for long-term survival. *They* = _____

3. *That* didn't work. *That* = _____

4. *This*, too, was impossible. *This* = _____

5. He tied clothing around *it* to stop the blood. *it* = _____

D ▶ Discuss. Discuss these questions with a partner.

1. Ralston's action "was both heroic and horrifying." What does this mean? Do you think Aron Ralston is a hero?

2. What would you do in Ralston's situation? Would you cut off your arm?

3. Do you think it is safe to go hiking alone? Why or why not?

VOCABULARY Understanding Words from Context

A ▶ Identify. Find these words and their meanings in the article. Write a synonym or definition for each word.

1. boulder: _____large rock_____

2. trapped: _____

3. remote: _____

4. supplies: _____

5. struggled: _____

6. survive: _____

7. escape: _____

8. artificial: _____

B ▶ Practice. Complete these sentences with words from Activity A.

1. Ken's backpack is heavy. He packed too many camping _____.

2. I think it's dangerous to walk in _____ places, away from people.

3. People can live up to 15 days without food, but they can't _____ for more than a day or two without water.

4. Several people were _____ in their cars when the bridge collapsed.

5. Two bank robbers tried to _____ to Canada, but the police caught them before they could get away.

6. We were swimming in the ocean when the storm hit. We _____ to get back to shore, but we succeeded.

7. After the earthquake, the main road was blocked by a _____ from the mountain.

8. When patients can't breathe on their own, doctors often use _____ respiration to save their lives.

Future Predictions with *will*, *be going to*, *may*, and *might*

We use *will* and *be going to* for predictions about the future.
      A: Do you really think Aron **will** hike again?
      B: Yes, I think he**'s going to** hike again someday, but he probably **won't** hike alone.

We use *be going to* for predictions about the immediate future based on something we see now.   Oh, look at those clouds! It**'s going to** rain. The sun **isn't going to** stay out long.
We use *may* or *might* when we're less sure about the future.   It **may** be cold on Sunday. It **might** even rain a little, but I don't know.

A ▶ Practice. Find and correct the ten errors.

1. A: I'm giving a speech tomorrow. I'm so nervous!
     B: Don't worry. I'm sure you might do a great job. You no will have any problems.

2. A: Do you think Brazil will win the World Cup?
     B: I don't know. They're going to win. They have some good players.

3. A: Look at all the glass in the road!
     B: We can't ride our bicycles here. We're going ruin our tires.

4. A: I'm certain that people may take vacations on the moon someday.
     B: I agree. But that's not going to happen for a long time.

5. A: Where the next Winter Olympics will be?
     B: I'm not sure. I think Canada might to host the games.

6. A: When the snowstorm is going to arrive, I wonder? It's getting colder and darker. I'm sure it may start snowing within the next hour.
     B: I'm not so sure. The weather report said the storm might hits around 5:00.

B ▶ Read. Circle the correct verb form to complete each sentence.

Earthquake in Alaska

Anchorage, Alaska (is struggling / may struggle) to recover from this morning's earthquake. Many roads are blocked, and the state police are certain that traffic problems and road closings (will continue / might continue) for many more days. Currently, rescue workers (are looking / will look) for survivors. Many people (are trapped / will be trapped) in buildings. One damaged building on State Street (is leaning / will lean) to one side. It looks like it (is going to fall / won't fall) at any moment. Also, firefighters (are working / will work) hard at the moment to put out fires caused by damaged electrical wires. Economists predict that the damage from the earthquake (will cost / is costing) the state billions of dollars over the next few months.

ACTIVATING GRAMMAR

∩ A ▸ Listen and write.

1. Listen to the weather reports. Check (✓) if each prediction is certain or possible.

Event	Certain or Possible?		
1. Heat wave			
a. heat wave to continue all week	.... certain	.... possible	
b. temperature to reach 100° every day	.... certain	.... possible	
c. older people to find the heat exhausting	.... certain	.... possible	
d. thunderstorms to arrive on Saturday	.... certain	.... possible	
2. Tropical storm			
a. storm to hit Palm Beach between 3:00 and 4:00	.... certain	.... possible	
b. storm to lose force near the coast	.... certain	.... possible	
c. storm to cause little damage to Palm Beach	.... certain	.... possible	
d. hurricane to hit Florida in two days	.... certain	.... possible	

2. Write predictions about one of these weather events. Use *will, be going to, may,* and *might*. Include at least one negative prediction.

1. (will) _____

2. (be going to) _____

3. (may) _____

4. (might) _____

B ▸ Group work.
Talk about the future. Make positive and negative predictions for five of these topics. What do you think will happen soon? What will happen 50 years from now? Explain your reasons. Share your predictions with the class.

education	sports	transportation
entertainment industry	technology	weather

Example: **A:** Pretty soon, students won't be allowed to have cell phones in school.

B: I agree. My teachers get angry when they catch people instant-messaging.

A ▶ Discuss. Look at the photos. What do you think might happen in each situation?

🎧 **B ▶ Listen.** Write what happened at each place and when it happened.

Place	What happened	When
1. Sunset Beach		
2. Payson National Park		
3. Walnut Street		

🎧 **C ▶ Listen again.** What do you predict for each situation? Circle a or b.

1. **Sunrise Beach**
   a. The man will survive.
   b. The man won't survive.
2. **Payson National Park**
   a. They might find the boy.
   b. They will find the boy.
3. **Walnut Street**
   a. The family is not going to return home soon.
   b. The family is going to return home soon.

> **Skill Focus** **Making Predictions Based on Inferences**
> Think about specific information that you hear or read. Is it mostly positive or negative? Then predict: will the outcome of the situation be positive or negative?

D ▶ Pair work.

1. Make a list of some stories in the news right now.

Local news	National news	International news

2. Interview. Find out what your classmates know about current events in the news. What do they predict about them?

    Example: **A:** What's new?
             B: I heard on the news this morning that a volcano is going to erupt in Ecuador soon. They think it might happen this week. . . .

∩ A ▶ **Listen and practice.** Then practice again using the other expressions.

A: Are you OK?

* Is everything OK?
* What's wrong?
* What happened?

B: I just got some bad news. I failed my exam. My parents are going to be disappointed.

* I'm sorry to hear that.
* That's terrible.
* Oh no! How awful / horrifying / terrible / frightening!

A: Oh, that's too bad. Is there anything I can do?

* Can I help?
* How can I help?

B: Not really. I might talk to my teacher about it. And I'm going to study harder, of course.

A: Those are good ideas. I bet you'll do better on the next test.

B ▶ **Pair work.** Continue these conversations with a partner. Use the expressions from Activity A to express sympathy and concern.

1. **A:** Is everything OK?
   B: Not really. I can't find my bag.
   A: . . .

2. **A:** Are you OK? You seem kind of down.
   B: Yes, I'm not so great. My computer crashed. I lost everything.
   A: . . .

3. **A:** _____? You seem upset.
   B: I just got a phone call with some terrible news.
   A: . . .

C ▶ **Group work.** Share some bad news with your classmates. Use the situations below or your own idea. Be sure to use phrases that express sympathy and concern.

• you left your iPod in the library, and it's gone

• you locked yourself out of your apartment

• you were late for class because your bus got in an accident

A ▶ Study it. Study the paragraph.

1. Underline the main prediction. Find three reasons to support the prediction.

Reason 1: _____

Reason 2: _____

Reason 3: _____

2. Circle the words or phrases that introduce each reason.

> There are many great soccer teams in our area. The top teams are the Ravens and the Huskies. These two teams will compete for the "City Cup" trophy at the playoff game this weekend, but only one will win. Who is going to be the champion this year? I predict that the Ravens are going to win, for three reasons. One reason is that the Ravens have an excellent team leader. Their new captain, Karen Wheeler, encourages the team to work together, so this team has a lot of focus and energy. Another reason is that the Ravens have many experienced players. Since many of them started playing soccer when they were very young, they have highly developed skills. But the main reason for my prediction is that the Ravens have a star player: Maria Alvarez. Maria helped her team win every game this season because she scored so many goals. For all these reasons, I'm sure the Ravens will celebrate a big win this weekend and make our city proud.

B ▶ Write it.

1. Choose a topic from the box. Then write four predictions about it. Use *will* in each prediction.

> arts/entertainment   politics/government   technology
> fashion   sports

Topic: _____

Prediction 1: _____

Prediction 2: _____

Prediction 3: _____

Prediction 4: _____

2. Choose and circle one of your predictions. On a separate sheet of paper, draw a mind map. List at least three reasons for that prediction. Write your paragraph.

3. Edit your paragraph.

- Do you have a main prediction and three reasons?
- Do you use expressions such as One reason is that . . . to introduce reasons?
- Do you use the correct verb forms to talk about the future?

PUTTING IT TOGETHER   Great Escapes!

A ▶ Read.

1. Read the article. Why was Houdini famous?

2. Checkpoint. Answer these questions.

   1. What were some situations that Houdini escaped from?

   _____

   _____

   2. How does the writer feel about Houdini? _____

   _____

   _____

   3. What makes escapes like Houdini's difficult? What could go wrong?

   _____

   _____

   _____

> When people think of escape artists, the name Houdini may come to mind. In the 1890s and early 1900s, this great magician was famous for
> 5 escaping from impossible situations.
> He escaped from handcuffs and locked boxes, sometimes underwater. He freed himself from prison cells. He once got out of a paper bag without ripping it at all. He was even buried
> 10 alive: he stayed underground in a coffin for 90 minutes. Audiences thought he might die, but he always survived and escaped. Houdini died of an illness in 1926, but people continue to admire him today because of his creative ideas.
> Other professional escape artists exist today, and I'm sure
> 15 they're going to exist in the future. But none of them will ever be as good as Harry Houdini. By constantly testing his own limits, he expanded our ideas about what is humanly possible.

B ▶ Listen.

1. Why is David Blaine famous? _____

2. Checkpoint. Match Blaine's acts to the years when he did them.

   1. ____ 1999   a. spent 35 hours on a platform on top of a pole

   2. ____ 2000   b. spent seven days submerged in water

   3. ____ 2002   c. spent 61 hours frozen in a block of ice

   4. ____ 2003   d. spent seven days trapped in a box underwater

   5. ____ 2006   e. spent 44 days in a box over a river in London

David Blaine in action

C ▶ Wrap it up.

1. [TOEFL® iBT] Write Houdini and Blaine's similarities and differences in the Venn diagram.

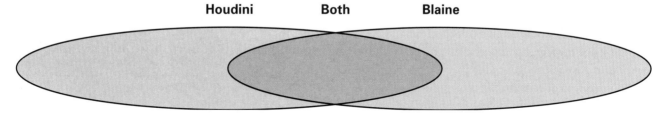

          Houdini   **Both**   **Blaine**

2. Do you think David Blaine is "the new Houdini"? Why or why not?

3. In your opinion, are escape artists like Houdini and Blaine heroes? Why or why not?

READING AND SPEAKING

A ▶ **Warm up.** How often do you buy these items? Frequently, sometimes, rarely, or never? Add your own idea to the last frame.

_____

_____

_____

Your idea:

_____

_____

_____

∩ **B** ▶ **Read.** What are two types of buyers?

Let's Shop!

Julia Choi, 22, loves Hello Kitty. She **shows off** the popular Japanese cartoon character—a white kitten with a pink hair bow—everywhere in her apartment. She has pens and pencils, clothing, towels, a shower curtain, dishes, clocks, a TV/DVD player, a computer, and over 300
5 stuffed animals. She picks up a pink guitar. "I **saved up for** a year to buy this. The store **sold out of** them in two hours. I bought it online." Will she ever quit collecting? "Probably not," she admits. "If I get married, I'll spend less money on Hello Kitty. But I won't **give** her **up**. I can't **do without** her. If someone marries me, he'll marry my collection, too."
10 Matt Anderson, 21, doesn't just collect one thing. He'll buy anything if he likes it. His apartment is filled with his purchases. "If I'm in a store, and I see a cool watch, I'll buy it. Last week, I bought a backpack over the Internet. I know the company **ripped me off**—it was an expensive bag and poor quality. But I liked the color, so I kept it." He worries, though.
15 "I can spend my whole paycheck in a week. I worry I'll **wind up** broke. I'd like to **cut back on** buying things. And my roommate might **kick me out** if I don't **get rid of** some stuff."
Julia and Matt have different spending personalities. "Self-expressive buyers" like Julia, collect things that reflect their personality. "Impulsive buyers" like
20 Matt, don't plan their purchases, and they shop without self-control.

C ▶ Read again. Check (✓) the information that is true about Julia, Matt, or both.

Information	Julia	Matt
1. likes to buy things	-------	-------
2. has a home filled with many purchases	-------	-------
3. plans to buy things	-------	-------
4. does not always plan to buy things	-------	-------
5. sometimes buys things online	-------	-------

Skill Focus Comparing and Contrasting

When we compare, we look for similarities. When we contrast, we look for differences. Usually we compare and contrast at the same time.

D ▶ Discuss. Discuss these questions with your classmates.

1. Do Julia and Matt think their shopping is a problem? How do you know?
2. Could you live with someone like Julia or Matt? Why or why not?
3. Are you a "self-expressive buyer" or an "impulsive buyer"? Describe your shopping habits.

▼ VOCABULARY Phrasal Verbs

A ▶ Identify. Look at these phrasal verbs from the article. Use the contexts in the article to help you match them to their meanings.

1. ____ show off (something) / show (something) off
2. ____ save up for (something)
3. ____ give up (something) / give (something) up
4. ____ do without (something)
5. ____ sell out of (something)
6. ____ rip off (someone) / rip (someone) off
7. ____ cut back on (something)
8. ____ get rid of (something)
9. ____ kick out (someone) / kick (someone) out
10. ____ wind up

a. eliminate
b. live without something you want
c. make someone leave a place
d. reduce the quantity
e. display something you're proud of
f. result in
g. quit, stop doing
h. sell everything in stock
i. make someone pay more than something is worth
j. accumulate money for a reason

B ▶ Pair work. Complete the questions with the correct word. Then discuss them with a partner.

1. What are you saving _____ for right now?
2. What do you like to show _____ in your room?
3. What is one thing you cannot do _____?
4. What do you think you should cut back _____, get rid _____, or give _____? Why?
5. When you're older, do you think you'll wind _____ rich? Why or why not?
6. Did a store or a salesperson ever rip you _____? What happened?
7. Why do managers sometimes kick people _____ of a store or a restaurant?

GETTING INTO GRAMMAR

Future Real Conditional

We use the future real conditional (first conditional) to express future possibilities. We use the simple present in the *if* clause and the future with *will* in the result clause.

> If Julia **gets** married, she**'ll spend** less money on her collection.
> If she **marries**, **will** she **stop** collecting Hello Kitty?
> If she **marries**, she **won't spend** so much money on her collection.

The *if* clause and result clause can change places, but the verb forms don't change.

> Julia **will spend** less money on her collection if she **gets married**.

When we are less certain about the results, we use *may* or *might*.

> Matt's roommate **might kick** him out if he **doesn't get rid of** some stuff.

A ▶ Practice. Find and correct the six errors.

1. If you will join our gym today, we will give you the first month absolutely free!

2. "Renew" face cream will get rid of all your skin problems if you used it every day.

3. If you sign up with our Love.com dating service, you might changed your life forever.

4. What you will do if your computer crashes? Call 1-800-555-HELP!

5. If you bring in your old pair of glasses, Diamond Optical take half off your new pair.

6. If you won't be satisfied with your MP3 player, we'll refund your money.

∩ B ▶ Listen. Listen to the conversations. Decide if each event is certain or possible.

Past	Future	
1. go to the jeans sale on Saturday	certain ☐	possible ☐
2. go to Electronics City	certain ☐	possible ☐
3. not buy a $60.00 concert ticket	certain ☐	possible ☐
4. buy a small bottle of "Attraction" perfume	certain ☐	possible ☐

A ▶ **Read and role-play.**

1. Read about two language schools and then complete the chart.

	GLIB	TALK
1. location		
2. price		
3. class size		
4. teachers		
5. other advantages		

You will be glad at GLIB if you want to . . .

• improve your English
• live in an exciting American city
• meet people from all over the world

The Global Language Institute of Boston is now
5 accepting new students for its summer English
program. Our classrooms are in downtown Boston,
on Newbury Street, which is famous for shopping
and restaurants! Housing is available in dormitories
at nearby Commonwealth College. You'll improve
10 your spoken and written English in classes of 15–20
students. Every week, you'll go on field trips and
explore the city. Our teachers all have certificates
in teaching English. We also offer a resource center
with CD-ROMs, DVDs, and computers.
15 Full-time summer program: $3,000

Do you want to improve your English quickly?

If you do, The Academy of Languages,
Kentucky (TALK) may be for you. We are a
small school located near Lexington, Kentucky.
The school is on an old farm. You may live on
20 campus in the farmhouse, or stay with a host
family in town.

Our teachers all have advanced degrees in
teaching English. Our classes never have more
than 10 students. We have a library and a
25 resource center.

We are now accepting applications for our
summer program. Tuition is $1,800.

2. Role-play. Imagine that you are going to sign up for GLIB or TALK. Convince your friend to go
there. Tell your friend what will, may, or might happen if he or she goes to these schools.

Example: If you go to GLIB, you'll meet a lot of people.
If you go to GLIB, you might not study very much. You'll go out a lot!

B ▶ **Group work.** Design an ad for a new language school. Include location, price, class size,
teachers, and resources. Include a slogan (a short expression to help sell a product) using the future
real conditional. Present your ad to the class. Then answer questions about your school.

A ▶ Discuss. Look at the photos in Activity B. If a salesperson wants to sell these items to someone, what might he or she say about them?

ᑎ B ▶ Listen. Check (✓) the information that the salesperson gives.

Item	Salesperson's Information
Conversation 1	_____ The TV has a 65-inch screen.
	_____ The TV has a DVD player.
	_____ The TV comes with a DVD collection.
	_____ The TV is on sale.
	_____ There is a monthly payment plan option.
Conversation 2	_____ The coat is on sale for $250.
	_____ The coat comes in other colors.
	_____ The lining is removable.
	_____ There are no bigger sizes for this coat.
	_____ The sale ends tomorrow.

ᑎ C ▶ Listen again. According to each customer, what are the pros and cons of each item? Write + by the pros. Write − by the cons.

1. TV: ___ size
         ___ screen quality for DVDs
         ___ price

2. coat: ___ color
         ___ price
         ___ size

> **Skill Focus** Evaluating Advantages and Disadvantages
>
> *Advantages* (pros) focus on the positive. *Disadvantages* (cons) focus on the negative. People may have different ideas about pros and cons. Listening for tone of voice and specific details can help you identify pros and cons.

D ▶ Interview.

1. What's useful to you? Rank these items from 1 (the most useful) to 6 (the least useful).

   ___ fashionable shoes   ___ a digital camera

   ___ magazines   ___ a cell phone

   ___ a backpack   ___ an MP3 player

2. Interview your classmates. Discuss which items you think are the most and the least useful.

   Example: A: The most useful is a digital camera. If I get a camera, I'll be able to email photos to all my friends.

   B: Really? I ranked that as least useful. My cell phone has a camera. I do everything with my phone. That's why I ranked it most useful.

> **TIP** *Enough, very,* and *too*
>
> *Enough* means a satisfactory amount. *Very* and *too* make adjectives and adverbs stronger: they both mean "more than enough," but *too* sometimes indicates a negative feeling or a problem. Compare:
>
> A: That bag is *very* expensive. But I should have *enough* money for it – I just got paid.
>
> B: I think it's *too* expensive. I can find a cheaper bag.

CONVERSATION STRATEGY Hesitating and Refusing Politely

🎧 **A ▶ Listen and practice.** Then practice again using the other expressions.

A: Would you like to open a charge account today? If you do, you'll save ten percent on your purchase.

A: You'll save five percent on all your future purchases if you pay with our charge card.

B: I'm not sure.

* I don't know.
* I doubt it.
* Probably not.

B: Hmm. That sounds great, but it's not what I need right now.

* I'll keep that in mind.
* Maybe some other time.
* Not today, thanks.
* I'll pass on that for now.

B ▶ Pair work. Continue these conversations with a partner. Use the phrases from Activity A to hesitate or refuse politely.

1. **Salesperson:** May I have your phone number and email address? We'd like to let you know about our upcoming specials and store events.
   Customer: . . .

2. **Co-worker 1:** Would you like to buy a book of coupons? I'm selling them to raise money for my soccer team. You'll save money at restaurants and shops if you use these coupons.
   Co-worker 2: . . .

3. **Gym Director:** Would you like to sign up for a two-year gym membership instead of one? If you sign up for two years, you'll save five percent on your monthly membership fees.
   Customer: . . .

C ▶ Role-play. For each photo, work with a partner and role-play a conversation between a salesperson and a customer. The salesperson should try to sell the product. The customer should hesitate or refuse politely.

A hat

A pet snake

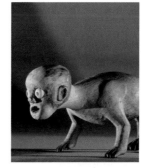

A work of art

A lamp

A ▶ Study it. Study the interviews and the paragraph.

1. Find sentences from the interviews in the paragraph. Underline the sentences in both the interview and the paragraph.

2. Circle the quotation marks before and after each direct quotation in the paragraph.

3. Circle the verb and punctuation mark that introduce each quotation.

Interview with Alison Chang:

Q: What do you spend your extra money on?

A: Downloading music off the Internet.

Q: Do you think you spend too much money

5   on music?

A: Probably. The songs on the Internet only cost
     $1.00 each. But if I sit at my computer for
     one hour, I might buy 20 songs.
     That's $20.00!

10 Interview with Chris Emmet:

Q: What do you spend most
     of your extra money on?

A: I buy a lot of DVDs online.
     I collect martial arts movies.

15 Q: Do you think you spend too much money?

A: I think so. If I keep buying DVDs, I won't have
     enough money to go out with my friends.

Ten of my classmates spend their extra money
on entertainment. All of them regularly down

20 load music and buy DVDs, CDs, and video games.
They buy most of these things online. Almost
everyone I interviewed thinks they spend too
much money on entertainment. Alison Chang
said, "The songs on the Internet only cost
$1.00 each. But if I sit at my computer for

25 one hour, I might buy 20 songs. That's $20.00!"
Similarly, Chris Emmet complained, "If I keep
buying DVDs, I won't have enough money to go
out with my friends." I think people might save

30 money on entertainment if they didn't buy
things online. The Internet makes it easy to
spend a lot of money.

B ▶ Write it.

1. Interview classmates to find out what they spend money on. Write down their exact words. Then read their answers and complete this topic sentence:

> Some of my classmates spend money on _____.

In your notes, underline two direct quotations that support this topic sentence.

> **TIP** You can use a variety of words in place of "said": *argued, asked, mentioned, noted, complained, pointed out.*

2. Write a paragraph. Use the topic sentence above. Include the two quotations that support it. Include your opinion about the spending habits of your classmates.

3. Edit your paragraph.
   - Do you conditional statements correctly?
   - Do you use quotation marks around direct quotes?
   - Do you introduce quotes correctly?

A ▶ Read.

1. What deal did Judith Levine make with her husband?

2. Checkpoint. Answer these questions.

1. What things did the Levines stop buying? _____

_____

_____

2. What did Judith miss the most?

_____

_____

3. What were the pros and cons of their year of doing without?

_____

_____

_____

Judith Levine Is Not Buying It

   In her new book, *Not Buying It*, Judith Levine describes what it was like to live for one year without shopping. Levine, 53, and her husband made a deal with each other. They would buy only basic necessities. They cut out all
5 luxury items and activities: no movie theaters, no restaurants, no Starbucks coffee, no new clothes. "At first it was difficult," says Levine. She missed eating out. She missed talking about the latest movies with her friends. She missed buying fresh flowers at the market. Most of all, she missed ice
10 cream. But all of the sacrifices were worth it. She and her husband felt more creative. They found inexpensive ways to entertain themselves at home, including just getting together with friends. "I ended up feeling like a citizen, not just a consumer," said Levine. "And I'm now no longer an
15 impulse buyer. I think before I buy." There was one more pro, or advantage, to their year of doing without: the Levines paid off their $8,000 credit card debt.

B ▶ Listen.

1. Listen to the news report about a holiday. What is it called? _____

2. Checkpoint. Answer these questions.

1. What are some things people can do on Buy Nothing Day?

_____

2. Why did Buy Nothing Day start? What is the message of this holiday?

_____

_____

3. What are some ways in which people could advertise Buy Nothing Day?

_____

C ▶ Wrap it up.

1. (TOEFL® iBT) How does the news report about Buy Nothing Day relate to the article about Judith Levine? Circle a, b, c, or d.

a. The listening gives examples that support the theory in the article.
b. The listening gives examples of shoppers that reject the theory in the article.
c. The listening describes an alternative way to promote the idea of not shopping.
d. The listening provides a solution to the problem presented in the article.

2. Could you give up shopping for one day? For one year? Why or why not?

3. What things could you do without? What would be hardest to do without?

Expansion Units 4–6

A ▶ Warm up. In your opinion, which of these items might bring good luck? Which might bring bad luck? Write your answers in the chart. Then compare your answers with a partner.

Shamrock	Black cat	Handprint in blood
Japanese cat (*maneki neko*)	Smile with gapped teeth	Broken mirror

Good luck	Bad luck

🎧 **B ▶ Listen.** Listen to two conversations. Why is each person worried? What should they do for good luck? Complete the chart.

Person	Cause of worry	Good luck idea that is being discussed
Sally		
Rick		

C ▶ Discuss. Discuss these questions with your classmates.

1. Do you think the ideas really would bring them good luck? Explain your answer.
2. What other good luck customs have you heard about? Do you think they work?

D ▶ Listen again. Check who probably will or won't follow the ideas for bringing good luck. Then write the reasons for your choice and explain them to a partner.

Person	Probably will or won't follow?	Why?
Sally	_____ will follow _____ won't follow	
Rick	_____ will follow _____ won't follow	
Elle	_____ will follow _____ won't follow	

E ▶ Interview. Interview four classmates. Find out what they do for good luck and why. Is it a family tradition? Is it based on actual experience? Complete the chart.

Person	What to do for good luck	Reason
1.		
2.		
3.		
4.		

A ▶ Vocabulary boost! Read the sentences. From the context, check the correct definition for the phrases in bold.

1. "I'm going home! Gambling is no fun if you don't **hit the jackpot!**"

   Hit the jackpot means: ____ win a large amount   ____ run out of money

2. Jen had to wait over an hour at the doctor's office, but she **put** her time **to good use** by studying for the exam.

   Put to good use means: ____ use all of (something)   ____ use (something) wisely and effectively

3. Philip got his first paycheck today, so he's going to the bank to **set up** a savings account.

   Set up means: ____ start (something)   ____ buy (something)

4. "I'm reading a suspenseful mystery. I can't wait to find out how the story **turns out**."

   Turns out means: ____ results in or ends   ____ begins

5. My brother used to be wealthy, but he nearly **went broke** when the stock market fell.

   Went broke means: ____ injured himself   ____ ran out of money

6. We expected Alex to attend the meeting today, but he never **showed up**.

   Showed up means: ____ spoke   ____ arrived

B ▶ Read. Circle the main idea in each paragraph and the concluding sentence in the article. Underline the supporting details throughout.

Unlucky Winners

Everyone who buys a lottery ticket imagines how different life will be after they **hit the jackpot**. And in fact, many lottery winners say it has helped them to buy a new home, take a dream vacation, or send their children to the best schools. Often, winners **put** the money **to good use** by starting a charity or
5 **setting up** a business. For them, sudden wealth brings happiness and stability.

Yet, in some cases, winning a jackpot **turns out** to be more of a curse than a blessing. Winners who have no experience with money often lose it as quickly as they won it and end up **going broke**. One common problem among lottery winners is unwise investment. New winners often invest large
10 amounts of money in businesses that they know little about. If the business does poorly, they put more and more money into it, trying to keep from losing their initial investment.

Another pitfall for jackpot winners is needy friends and family. Winners are often surprised at how many relatives and acquaintances **show up** asking
15 for help in the form of loans, new houses, or new cars. Because they won the money rather than earned it, they find it hard to say no to these requests.

In some cases, lottery winners have problems with alcohol, drugs, or gambling. They may think that sudden wealth will solve these problems, but they quickly learn that money might only make things worse. After winning
20 a lot, they watch their fortunes disappear at bars or into slot machines. So, while some people gain financial security when they win the lottery, others experience disappointment or even ruin because they are not ready for financial success.

C ▶ Discuss. Discuss these questions with your classmates.

1. What are some of the factors that cause lottery winners to lose their fortunes?
2. If a friend suddenly becomes rich, what advice can you offer to help him or her avoid the problems mentioned in the article?
3. Because of the problems related to lotteries and similar types of gambling, some people want to ban them or make them illegal. Do you agree with this opinion? Why or why not?

D ▶ Read again. For each of the examples, list the cause or effect related to it in the article.

	Cause	Effect
1	Some lottery winners set up successful charities or businesses.	
2	Some lottery winners invest in businesses that are not familiar to them.	
3		Some lottery winners can't say "no" when friends or family ask them for money.
4		Some lottery winners waste their money on drinking, drugs, or gambling.
5	Some lottery winners are not ready for financial success.	

E ▶ Write about it. Write about what will happen if you or someone close to you wins the lottery.

1. List some ideas about yourself or someone else. Use the future real conditional. <u>If I win the lottery, I</u>
   <u>will. . .</u>

   _____

   Choose one idea to write about. List reasons for your choice.
   Choice: _____
   Reasons: _____
   _____
   _____
   _____

2. Write your paragraph.

3. Edit your paragraph.
   • Do you use connecting words to introduce your reasons?
   • Do you use correct verb forms to talk about the future?

Make Up Your Mind!

READING AND SPEAKING

A ▶ **Warm up.** How do you make decisions? Check (✓) the things that you do.

___ ask other people for advice

___ write lists of all your options

___ write lists of pros (+) and cons (-)

___ look for more information

___ pay attention to how you feel

___ try not to think about it

___ go to a quiet place and think

___ other: _____

🎧 **B** ▶ **Read.** Why did Rachel Safier want to cancel her wedding?

There Goes the Bride!

Several months before her wedding, Rachel Safier was sending out invitations and choosing flowers. She was also feeling very nervous. She **was on the fence** about getting married. What if her fiancé wasn't really "the one"? One day, while she was standing in the church, she realized that she could not walk down the aisle. She didn't know what to do. Then two weeks before the big day, her fiancé canceled the wedding.

Later, Safier learned that many brides (and grooms) change their minds. Some **call off** their wedding weeks in advance. Others decide **at the last minute** and don't show up for the ceremony. Others put off their wedding while they try to **make up their minds**. Some couples have doubts but marry anyway. In some cases, brides and grooms **get cold feet** because of stress.

Safier has some advice for worried couples. For example, they should try to take one evening a week to spend time together and not talk about the wedding. If this doesn't work, the couple may need to discuss serious issues, such as having children and managing money. Counseling may help. If the couple cannot **see eye-to-eye**, they may decide not to **tie the knot**.

Canceling a wedding can be embarrassing and expensive. Specifically, Safier had to notify her guests, return gifts, and cancel the musicians, flowers, and food. Yet she was sure all this was better than getting divorced **down the road**.

Safier wanted to help others who might have second thoughts. She wrote a book called *There Goes the Bride: Making Up Your Mind, Calling it Off, and Moving On*. She also has a website. There, people can share their stories or ask for advice.

C ▸ Read again. Check (✓) the things that Rachel did after her wedding was canceled.

1. ___ notified her guests
2. ___ asked other brides for advice
3. ___ returned gifts
4. ___ practiced walking down the aisle
5. ___ canceled her musicians, flowers, and food
6. ___ wrote a book
7. ___ got divorced
8. ___ started a website

> **Skill Focus** — Identifying Examples
> Examples give more specific information about a general idea. In a paragraph, they usually follow the topic sentence. They sometimes follow words like *for example, specifically,* and *such as.*

D ▸ Discuss. Discuss these questions with your classmates.

1. Do you think Rachel Safier made a good decision? Why or why not?
2. According to the article, what are three things that couples can do if they're not sure about getting married? Name three other things they can do.
3. Name at least five reasons that people get married. Rank them in order of importance to your group.

VOCABULARY Idioms

A ▸ Identify. Match each idiom from the article with its meaning.

1. ___ be on the fence (about something)
2. ___ call off (something)/call (something) off
3. ___ at the last minute
4. ___ make up your mind
5. ___ get cold feet
6. ___ see eye-to-eye
7. ___ tie the knot
8. ___ down the road

a. get married
b. feel too nervous to do something
c. not know what to do
d. in the future
e. cancel (something)
f. come to a decision
g. the time just before an action
h. come to an agreement

B ▸ Pair work. Complete the items with a partner.

1. Match two idioms from Activity A with the two pictures.

a. _____   b. _____

2. Individually, draw four pictures to illustrate four more idioms from Activity A.

3. Show your drawings to your partner and have him or her guess the idioms.

The Past Continuous and the Simple Past

We use the past continuous to describe an action in progress at a specific time in the past.

> What **was** Rachel Safier **doing** several months before her wedding?
> She **was sending out** invitations and **choosing** flowers.

We also use the past continuous to describe a past action that was interrupted by a second past action. The second action that interrupts the first action is in the simple past.

> What **did** Rachel **realize** while she **was standing** in the church?
> While she **was standing** in the church, she **realized** she didn't want to get married.

We use the simple past to talk about completed actions.

> What did Rachel do? → She **canceled** the wedding. Then she **wrote** a book about it.

A ▶ Practice. Complete the questions and answers using the past continuous or the simple past.

1. **A:** (What / do) _____ last night?
   B: I went out to dinner with my family.

2. **A:** Where were you going yesterday at noon when I (see) _____ you?
   B: I (go) _____ to my dentist appointment.

3. **A:** (When / finish) _____ the homework last night?
   B: I (finish) _____ it at midnight.

4. **A:** Who was the teacher talking about a few minutes ago?
   B: She (talk) _____ about a famous writer.

5. **A:** (What / do) _____ when I (call) _____ you last night? You didn't answer the phone.
   B: I (fix) _____ my computer.

B ▶ Read. Complete the article using the past continuous or simple past of the verbs in parentheses.

Runaway Bride!

Last night, 400 wedding guests at the Sorrento Hotel in Seattle (wait) <u>were waiting</u>
                                                                              1
for a wedding to begin when the maid of honor suddenly (run) _____
                                                                              2
up to the mother of the bride. The bride, Jessica Winters, was gone! "The last time

I (see) _____ her, she (fix) _____ her hair," said the
             3   4
5   bridesmaid. "We (help) _____ her with her dress." The wedding
                                    5
party (start) _____ looking for the bride.
                       6
     Finally, at 7:30, Jessica (call) _____ her father on his cell phone.
                                                7
"I (take) _____ a bus to Los Angeles," she explained. "I
                   8
(want) _____ to call off the wedding weeks ago. I just
              9
10 (know, not) _____ how." No one was more confused than the
                           10
groom. "I (think) _____ she loved me," he said. "I don't understand."
                            11

A ▶ Listen.

1. Listen and sequence the pictures. Number them from 1 (what happened first) to 6 (what happened last).

a. ____

b. ____

c. ____

d. ____

e. ____

f. ____

What happened next?

2. Pair work. Tell the story to a partner, but complete the story in any way you wish. Use the past continuous and simple past.

B ▶ Interview.

1. Write what you were doing at the following times. Use the past continuous.

   1. Yesterday evening at 7:00: _____

   2. This morning at 7:00: _____

   3. An hour ago: _____

   4. Yesterday at noon: _____

   5. Last night at 10:00: _____

2. Interview a partner about his or her activities at a specific time. Ask at least four questions to get more information. Use these question words: *who, what, where, when, why,* or *how.* Use the past continuous and simple past.

   Example: **A:** What were you doing yesterday evening at 7:00?
               B: I was watching TV.
               A: Really? What were you watching?
               B: A movie called "Office Space."
               A: I never saw that, but I heard it's really funny. Who's in it?

A ▶ Discuss. Look at the three photos. What decision do you think each person made recently?

🎧 **B ▶ Listen.** Write the decision each person made. Circle the letter of the reason for the decision.

Person	Decision	Reason
1. Monica		a. She has a job interview tomorrow. b. She wanted to be different. c. She wanted to look like a girl she saw.
2. Nathan		a. He wanted to make his neighbor happy. b. The car was cheap, in his opinion. c. He likes to fix old cars.
3. Sammy		a. He wanted to be closer to work. b. He wanted to be closer to the coffee shop. c. He wanted to see his friends easily.

🎧 **C ▶ Listen again.** Choose the best word to describe how each person feels.

angry	confused	happy	sad	worried

Skill Focus Listening to Infer Speaker's Attitude

A speaker's tone can tell us about his or her feelings or attitude. If a speaker's voice goes up at the end, the person is probably happy. If a speaker's voice goes down, he or she might be sad. If the speaker says something that sounds like a question, he or she might feel confused, frustrated, or worried.

1. How does Monica's friend feel about her decision?

_____

2. How does the woman feel about Nathan's decision?

_____

3. How does the woman feel about Sammy's decision?

_____

D ▶ Group work. What kinds of decisions do people make?

1. In groups, write more ideas for the mind map.

get married
_____
Relationships
buy a car
_____
Purchases

DECISIONS

quit my job
_____
Work / Education
move/get a haircut
_____
Lifestyle/Appearance

2. Talk about a time when you made one of these decisions. Was it the right decision? Explain.

∩ A ▸ **Listen and practice.** Then practice again using the other phrases.

A: I don't know whether to adopt a dog or not. On the one hand, dogs are so friendly. On the other hand, they need a lot of attention.

* I don't know if I should . . .
* I can't decide if I should . . .

B: That's true. Have you thought about what kind of dog you might get?

* Have you considered . . . ?

A: Well, I love big dogs. They're lots of fun.

B: Don't you think you should get a small dog? Your apartment is really small.

* Wouldn't it be better to . . . ?
* Doesn't it make more sense to . . . ?
* What if you . . . ?

B ▸ **Pair work.** Continue these conversations with a partner. Use the phrases from Activity A to help your partner make a decision. Then switch roles.

1. **A:** I was thinking about getting a car, but I don't know if I should get a new car or a used one. On the one hand . . .
   B: Have you considered . . .
   A: . . .

2. **A:** I was considering moving to . . .
   B: . . .

3. **A:** I want to take a night class, but there are so many to choose from.
   B: . . .

C ▸ **Role-play.** Work with a partner. Choose three topics from this list and role-play three conversations about decisions that you are trying to make. Use phrases for helping people make decisions. Switch roles.

- which classes to take
- whether or not to attend an event
- whether or not to take / quit a job
- whether or not to buy something
- whether or not to get married
- whether or not to start / end a relationship
- what to wear to an event
- your idea: _____

_____

A ▶ Study it. Study the paragraph.

1. Underline the topic sentence.

2. Circle the words or phrases that show the sequence of steps in the process.

3. Highlight words or phrases that introduce specific examples.

> **TIP** ▶ Words that show sequence include: *first, second, third, then, next, after that, finally.*

Where Should I Study English?

Last year, I had to make a difficult decision: should I study English in the United States for one month, or should I go to a language school near my home? My first step in making this decision was to ask my friends and family for advice. However, my friends all had very different opinions, and my family wanted me to stay at home. My next step was to get more information. For example, I researched American language schools online and visited some language schools near me. After that, I made lists. Specifically, I wrote down the pros and cons of studying in the U.S. Next, I reviewed the two lists. While I was reading them, I realized there were more pros than cons. Finally, I showed the lists to my family and talked about my feelings. I decided to go to the U.S. Fortunately, they agreed with my decision. I'm now studying English in the U.S. I'm learning a lot and I'm very happy. So is my family!

B ▶ Write it. Write a paragraph about the process of making a decision.

1. Choose an important decision from your life. For example: deciding to study in another country, starting a new job, ending a relationship. Make notes about this event in the chart.

What decision did you have to make?	
What choices did you have?	
Was it easy or difficult to make this decision? Why?	
What was your decision-making process? List at least three steps.	1. 2. 3.
What decision did you make? Why?	
Do you think it was a good decision? Why or why not?	

2. Write your paragraph.

3. Edit your paragraph.
   - Do you have a topic sentence that states where and when you made this decision?
   - Do you use words or phrases that show sequence?

PUTTING IT TOGETHER Calling It Quits

A ▶ Read.

1. Why don't most family businesses survive more than 25 years in the United States?

The End of an Era

Over 90 percent of American companies are owned and managed by families. Yet most family businesses don't survive more than 25 years or beyond the second generation. These days, young people have less interest in carrying on the family business because there are many more job options for them. As a result, most family businesses either sell the company to someone outside the family, or they call it quits.

Matt Gottman, 69, is experiencing this trend first-hand. Next week, he will close down his company, Gottman Enterprises. "It's the end of an era," he says, looking at the factory and showroom that his family has owned for three generations. "Young people today don't want to continue a family business. My father was in this business. So were my grandfather and great-grandfather. Now I'm retiring, and I have no one to pass the business on to. I was hoping my son or daughter would take over, but they aren't interested. They wanted to choose their own careers. My son is a lawyer, and my daughter is studying dance."

2. Checkpoint. Answer these questions.

    1. What are some reasons people decide not to go into their family business?

    _____

    2. What options do business owners have when their children don't take over?

    _____

    3. How do you think Gottman feels about closing his business? How do you know?

    _____

B ▶ Listen.

1. What kind of competition did Ashley Jones win? _____

2. Checkpoint. Answer these questions.

    1. What will Jones study in college? _____

    What job will she pursue? _____ Who made this decision? _____

    2. What will Jones do with the $10,000? _____

    Who made this decision? _____

    3. How do you think Jones feels about her future? _____

    How do you know? _____

C ▶ Wrap it up.

1. (TOEFL® iBT) The relationship between Ashley Jones and her parents _____.

    a. supports Gottman's opinion   **c.** provides an example of Gottman's opinion

    b. challenges Gottman's opinion   **d.** shows a theory related to Gottman's opinion

2. Does Ashley Jones have other options? What else could she do?

3. What kinds of decisions should people be able to make on their own? Which decisions should be made by other people such as parents, the government, or schools?

READING AND SPEAKING

A ▶ Warm up. Check (✓) the things that you are afraid of.

____ heights   ____ being alone at night   ____ big dogs

____ flying   ____ getting lost in a strange city   ____ black cats

____ speaking in public   ____ spiders   ____ other: _____

B ▶ Read. Scan the reading to find answers to these questions.

1. What does Alain Robert do for a living? _____

2. What would psychologists call Alain Robert? _____

Reaching New Heights

On June 11, 2005, thousands stood below Hong Kong's 62-story Cheung Kong building to watch the "Amazing Spiderman" climb up the side. Without using complex tools or ropes, he reached the top in one hour.

Frenchman Alain Robert is an "urban free-climber." He climbs the world's
5   tallest buildings with his bare hands and feet and doesn't worry about falling. He has climbed the Petronas Towers in Kuala Lumpur, the Eiffel Tower in Paris, the Empire State Building in New York, and more than 70 others.

Robert started climbing when he was 12. One day, he forgot to take the key to his family's eighth-floor apartment, so he climbed through a window.
10   After that, he practiced climbing rocks and mountains, then buildings. "Taking risks is my way of life," he says. "Modern people are only willing to believe in their computers, but I believe in myself." He plans on climbing a building in South Korea next.

Psychologists would classify Robert as a **thrill-seeker**: someone who looks
15   forward to taking risks. Thrill-seekers may have a higher **risk tolerance** than most people. High in energy and confidence, they need excitement. Instead of avoiding their fears, they face them.

Many **risk-takers** do **extreme sports** like bungee jumping or skydiving. Going to an **amusement park** and riding a roller coaster are less dangerous
20   **leisure-time activities** that also provide a sense of freedom. So are **adventure tours**, whitewater rafting, or mountain climbing when experienced guides and **safety equipment** make the experience less risky. In addition, thrill-seekers don't have to be athletes. Businesspeople, artists, and scientists often take risks, finding excitement in ideas.

C ▶ Read again. Check (✓) the qualities or attitudes of the thrill-seekers that are mentioned in . article.

1. ___ look forward to taking risks
2. ___ have a higher risk tolerance than most people
3. ___ have a lot of energy and confidence
4. ___ need to have excitement in their lives
5. ___ always do extreme sports
6. ___ face their fears
7. ___ see a psychologist
8. ___ don't have to be athletes

Skill Focus Categorizing
When we categorize information, we look for a general topic or class, that contains smaller examples, or types.

D ▶ Discuss. Discuss these questions.

1. Alain Robert says, "Modern people are only willing to believe in their computers, but I believe in myself." What do you think he means?
2. Are amusement parks and adventure tours safe places for thrill-seeking? Explain.
3. Name a risk-taker who isn't an athlete. What kind of risks does he or she take?

▼ VOCABULARY Compound Words

A ▶ Identify. Match each compound word with its meaning.

1. ___ thrill-seeker   a. the ability to take risks and not be afraid
2. ___ risk tolerance   b. tools, ropes, or other things to protect you
3. ___ risk-takers   c. places to go on rides like roller coasters
4. ___ extreme sports   d. a personality type that likes risky behavior
5. ___ amusement parks   e. people who do dangerous things
6. ___ leisure-time activities f. traveling to unusual or dangerous places, with guides
7. ___ adventure tour   g. athletic events involving some danger or risk
8. ___ safety equipment   h. things you do for fun when you aren't working

B ▶ Practice. Choose the best compound word to complete each sentence.

1. At the X-Games, athletes compete in _____ like skateboarding and inline skating. These events can be dangerous, so these athletes are _____. Fortunately, they wear _____ for protection.

2. Many _____ like Roller Coaster Island appeal to both children and adults.

3. My _____ include playing video games and reading. I'm definitely not a _____!

4. My friend wants to go on a whitewater rafting _____ where guides lead us down a river. But I have a low _____ and worry about danger.

Using Gerunds and Infinitives to Talk about Activities

Gerunds (verb + *ing*) and infinitives (*to* + verb) are verb forms used as nouns.
Gerunds can be used as subjects and can begin a sentence.

> "**Taking risks** is my way of life," says Alain Robert.

Gerunds can also be used as objects after certain verbs: *discuss, enjoy, practice, quit.*

> Alain Robert **practiced climbing** rocks and mountains.

Gerunds can also come after a verb + preposition: *apologize for, argue about, believe in, insist on, look forward to, plan on, talk about, think about, worry about.*

> Alain Robert doesn't **worry about falling**.

Infinitives are usually used as objects of certain verbs: *agree, appear, can't wait, decide, expect, forget, hope, intend, learn, love, need, offer, plan, refuse, want, would like / love.*

> One day, he **forgot to take** the key to his family's eighth-floor apartment.

Some verbs can be followed by either a gerund or an infinitive: *begin, can't stand, continue, hate, like, love, prefer, start, try.*

> "I **like taking** risks," says Robert.   "I **like to take** risks," says Robert.

A ▶ Practice. Eight of the ten underlined words and phrases are in the wrong form. Correct them.

If you decide <u>try</u> skateboarding, here is some advice. You need <u>to buy</u> some
₁   ₂
safety equipment. You should definitely get a helmet. <u>Protect</u> your head is the
                                                                          ₃
most important thing. <u>Taking</u> a few lessons can also help. If you learn <u>using</u> your
                              ₄   ₅
skateboard correctly, you can avoid <u>to have</u> painful falls. If you want <u>learning</u>
                                              ₆   ₇
5 turns and jumps, an instructor or coach can help. Then you must think about
<u>to buy</u> the right skateboard. Some people buy inexpensive boards; they plan on
₈
<u>use</u> them only on sidewalks and streets. Above all, practice <u>ride</u> every day,
₉   ₁₀
and you will see improvements in no time!

◠ B ▶ Listen. Complete the questions and answers using the gerund form of the words in the box.

1. What does the man love doing? He loves _____.

2. Why does the woman hate _____? She doesn't
   like _____.

3. What does the man look forward to _____ the next
   time he goes to Seven Hills?

4. When does the man plan on _____ there? He'll
   return next weekend.

5. Why does the man think the woman should try the Death Drop ride?

   _____ is the first step toward overcoming them.

get dizzy
go back
face one's fears
ride roller coasters
spin around
try again

A ▶ Read and role-play.

1. Read the obituary of a mountain climber. Underline the gerunds and infinitives.

Ulrich Inderbinen

December 3, 1900 – June 14, 2004

On June 14, 2004, the Swiss mountain climber Ulrich Inderbinen died at the age of 103. Inderbinen rarely left his small mountain village of Zermatt, except to climb in the Swiss Alps. He did that until
5 he was 95. He worked as a mountain guide for 70 years. He always looked forward to taking tourists up the Matterhorn, one of the world's most dangerous and challenging mountain peaks. He climbed the 14,700-foot tall mountain more than 370 times. He
10 never got bored leading tourists up the mountain, except, he said, "when they walked too slowly."

Inderbinen started to climb at an early age. He ascended the Matterhorn for the first time at age 20 and began working as a mountain guide soon after.
15 Climbing was Inderbinen's passion, but he also enjoyed going down. He started ski-racing at the age of 82. He was the only competitor in his age group, so he won every race. Three years ago, on his 100th birthday, Inderbinen told the news media that he
20 lived a full and happy life and didn't worry about dying. Perhaps Inderbinen continues to serve as a guide. He reminds us that anything is possible.

2. Role-play. Role-play the last interview with Inderbinen. One of you is a news reporter. The other person is Inderbinen. Ask and answer questions about his life using gerunds and infinitives. Use information from the article and your own ideas.

> **Example:** Reporter: Do you think you'll ever quit mountain climbing?
> Inderbinen: I hope not. I'll keep on climbing as long as I can. I don't plan to stop anytime soon.

B ▶ Group work.

1. Think of an inspirational person that you know about. You can choose a famous person or someone you know. Write notes about his or her activities and accomplishments.

> **Example:** Joanna:
> • bad knee, but ice skates every day
> • hopes to compete in the Olympics

2. Tell your classmates about this person using gerunds and infinitives. Then answer any questions and give more information.

> **Example:** My friend Joanna is an ice skater. She has a bad knee, but she practices skating every day. She needs to practice because she hopes to compete in the Olympics.

A ▶ Discuss. Look at the photos. What do you think these people are doing? Which of these activities look risky to you? Which look like fun?

B ▶ Listen. Write the activities or events that are discussed next to the correct names.

Category	Activity/Event	Thrill-seeker?	Clues
1. Vivian Wegrath			
2. The Yasutoko Brothers			
3. Noha Fahmy			
4. Sam Garland			

C ▶ Listen again. Make inferences about each person. Check (✓) the thrill-seekers in the chart above. Write the clues that helped you make the inference.

D ▶ Pair work.

1. What's your risk tolerance? Rate the activities from 1 (low risk) to 4 (high risk).

1. skydiving	1	2	3	4
2. confronting your boss	1	2	3	4
3. eating fatty foods	1	2	3	4
4. starting a new business	1	2	3	4
5. opening a restaurant	1	2	3	4
6. driving fast	1	2	3	4
7. disagreeing with your family's views	1	2	3	4
8. riding a roller coaster	1	2	3	4
9. visiting a foreign country alone	1	2	3	4
10. not sleeping enough	1	2	3	4

2. Interview a classmate about his or her answers. Does he or she have a low or high risk tolerance?

> **Example: A:** Do you think it's dangerous to skydive?
> **B:** Not really. I rated it a 2. Skydiving isn't very dangerous if you have safety equipment and if you go with a guide. What about you?
> **A:** I rated it a 4. I think it's very dangerous.

∩ **A** ▶ **Listen and practice.** Then practice again using the other expressions.

A: I have a great idea for my 25th birthday. I plan to bungee-jump off a bridge!

B: Cool! Bungee-jumping sounds like a fun way to celebrate an important birthday!

* Good for you!
* Sweet!
* Awesome!
* That's amazing / exciting / great / wonderful / fantastic!
* What a/an _____ idea!

C: Are you out of your mind? You can't trust that safety equipment they give you.

* Have you lost your mind?
* You're kidding!
* You're joking!
* Are you serious?
* I can't believe it!
* That's (How) dangerous / risky / terrifying!

B ▶ **Pair work.** Continue these conversations with a partner. First react positively. Then switch roles and react negatively. Give information to explain your opinion.

1. **A:** What are you cooking?
   B: I'm making up a new recipe. It's a soup made of everything that was in my refrigerator.
   A: . . .

2. **A:** I sent out applications for 15 jobs. How many are you applying for?
   B: Just one.
   A: . . .

3. **A:** Did you know that Maria is starting her own business?
   B: You're kidding! What kind of business?
   A: A restaurant. Unfortunately, she doesn't know much about running a business . . . or about cooking!
   B: . . .

C ▶ **Group work.** Discuss a risky activity that you or someone you know participated in. Use exclamations to show your opinion about the activities people describe. Explain your opinion.

Example: A: Last weekend, I rode my motorcycle without a helmet.
   B: Are you serious? It's against the law here.
   C: That's risky! I'm glad you didn't get hurt!

A ▶ **Study it.** The beginning of a piece of writing is sometimes called a *hook*. Read about three types of hooks. Then read the beginnings of three paragraphs. Which type of hook does each one use? Write a, b, or c in the blanks.

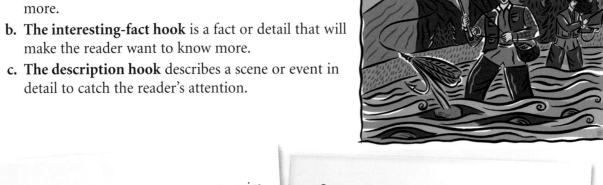

a. **The question hook** is an interesting question. If the reader wants to know the answer, he/she will read more.

b. **The interesting-fact hook** is a fact or detail that will make the reader want to know more.

c. **The description hook** describes a scene or event in detail to catch the reader's attention.

1. ____ Lynne Cox was the first person to swim to Antarctica. Her love of swimming outside began at a young age. When she was three, Lynne learned to swim in a lake called "Snow Pond." She loved to swim in cold, open water.

2. ____ Danica Patrick was ahead of all the men in the biggest racecar event of the year, the Indianapolis 500. She was going to reach her goal. She would be the first woman to win the race. Then she realized she was low on gas.

3. ____ Do you know which Japanese athlete won the first World Cup for snowboarding? The answer may surprise you.

B ▶ **Write it.**

1. List your favorite activities on a separate piece of paper. Circle one to write about. Then list interesting facts about this activity. Choose at least four facts to include in your paragraph.

2. Write a paragraph about a leisure-time activity for a magazine or website. Explain the activity and try to make readers interested in the topic from the beginning.

3. Edit your paragraph. Share your hook first with a partner. Ask your partner if your hook is interesting and makes the reader want to know more.

> **TIP** Sometimes it's easier to write the body of the paragraph first. After you know what you want to say about your topic, go back to the beginning and write the hook.

A ▶ Read.

1. What is the key to success for Olympic athletes?

How do Olympic athletes handle the pressure of competing when the whole world is watching? The key to their success is called being "in the zone." Their mind and body are working perfectly together, and they are at their best level of performance. They are totally focused on being in
5 the present moment. They feel confident and fearless.

How do they get "into the zone"? It's a matter of training both body and mind. Athletes train their muscles to remember specific movements and skills. They take care of their bodies: they eat right and get rest. Similarly, they train their minds. They learn to concentrate and to
10 control their emotions. Instead of worrying about failing, they practice being calm, thinking positive thoughts, and imagining success. They also learn to relax. They hope to see their physical and mental training pay off in a competition.

2. Checkpoint. Answer these questions.

  1. How do athletes feel when they are in the zone? _____

  2. Name five things that athletes do to get into the zone. _____
  _____

  3. Have you ever been "in the zone" or do you know someone who has? Talk about it. _____
  _____

B ▶ Listen.

1. When will Brad find out if he gets the job? _____

2. Checkpoint. Answer these questions.

  1. What risk did Brad take? Was he nervous? Why or why not? _____
  _____

  2. Do you think Brad will get this job? Explain your answer. _____
  _____

  3. Describe an interview that you've had. What happened? Did you feel like Brad?

C ▶ Wrap it up.

1. List at least five things that Brad did to prepare for the interview.

_____
_____

2. (TOEFL® iBT) Based on Brad's experiences, do you think that people not involved in sports can get "into the zone"? Give examples to support your opinion.

Makeovers

READING AND SPEAKING

A ▶ **Warm up.** Check (✓) the things you might want to change about your life.

- ☐ find a new job
- ☐ get a new boyfriend or girlfriend
- ☐ change your appearance
- ☐ go to a new school
- ☐ learn to play a musical instrument
- ☐ move to a new country
- ☐ make new friends
- ☐ other: _____

B ▶ **Read.** Skim the article. What is *MADE*? Why do some people want to be on it?

Seventeen-year-old Alyssa Hart dreams of dancing in a Broadway show. There is one problem. Alyssa can't dance.

David Barsky, 16, has an **ambition** to be a rock star, but there is also an **obstacle** in his way. "I can't sing or play an instrument," he admits. "If I could, I'd be in a band now."

Ethan Miller, 17, has an aspiration, too. He hates his **appearance** and wants a complete change. "If I liked my looks, I'd have more self-confidence," he says. "And if I were more confident, I'd ask a girl out. I need a **makeover**."

Alyssa, David, and Ethan are among 300 teenagers who **auditioned** today for the television show *MADE*. The television network MTV is looking for "dreamers" to try out for the show. *MADE* helps people pursue difficult goals. Each episode focuses on someone who wants to be "made" into something different. For example, a shy person runs for class president, or an unathletic person tries out for the football team.

A **mentor**—a coach or a tutor—works with the people for a month, providing training and **motivation**. That encouragement can make a big difference. A TV crew films the process. "I'd feel terrible if someone spent all that time with me, and I didn't reach my goal. And I'd be so embarrassed if I failed on national TV," David says. While *MADE* provides opportunities, it doesn't promise success. Many people on the show don't **achieve** their goals or realize their dreams. But according to *MADE*, it's better to try and fail than never to try at all.

C ▶ Read again. Choose the better summary of the article. Why is it better?

a. ___   Summary 1

Alyssa, David, and Ethan all want to change their lives on the popular MTV show, *MADE*. Alyssa can't dance, but dreams of dancing in a Broadway show; David has an ambition to be a rock star; and Ethan wants to change his appearance. They were among 300 teenagers who auditioned for the TV show. *MADE* helps people reach difficult goals. A mentor works with the people for a month. That extra encouragement really works. This is a good TV show. I'd like to try out for it.

b. ___   Summary 2

Alyssa, David, and Ethan all want to be on the popular MTV show, *MADE*. They and 300 other teenagers all tried out for the show. The TV show *MADE* changes lives. Everyone selected for it has a challenging goal. With the help of a mentor, they spend one month working to achieve that goal while a TV crew films them. *MADE*'s producers feel it is important for people to try to pursue their goals even if they don't succeed.

D ▶ Discuss.

1. The article says, "*MADE* emphasizes that it's better to try something and to fail than never to try at all." What does this mean? Do you agree?
2. Is it possible for Alyssa, David, and Ethan to reach their goals in one month? Why or why not?
3. Would you try out for *MADE*? Why or why not?

VOCABULARY Synonyms

A ▶ Identify. Find synonyms for these words from the article. The synonyms are in the article.

1. ambition: _____
   _____
   _____

TIP Synonyms are often found very close to each other. You can also use context clues to help you find the meaning.

2. obstacle: _____
3. appearance: _____
4. makeover: _____
5. audition: _____
6. mentor: _____
   _____
7. motivation: _____
8. achieve: _____

B ▶ Pair work. Discuss these questions with a partner. Use vocabulary from Activity A.

1. What is one of your ambitions? Circle some of the obstacles that you face.

   appearance   education   money   motivation   talent   time   other: _____

2. Name one of your mentors. How does he or she motivate you?

GETTING INTO GRAMMAR

Present Unreal Conditional

We use the present unreal conditional (second conditional) to discuss future results of imagined, or unreal, conditions in the present. The results are unlikely to happen.

We use the past tense in the *if* clause. (We use *were* with all subjects for the verb *be*.) We use *would* + verb in the result clause. We use *could* or *might* in the result clause if we are even more doubtful about the results.

If Ethan **liked** his appearance, he **would feel** more confident.

> Present real situation: He does not like his looks.

If he **were** more confident, he**'d ask** a girl out.

> Present real situation: He is not confident.

If he **asked** a girl out, she **might say** yes!

> Present real situation: He has not asked a girl out.

Compare with the future real conditional (first conditional) in Unit 6, page 48. In the future real conditional, the results are possible.

If *MADE* **chooses** Alyssa, she **will learn** to dance.

> Present real situation: She is trying out for MADE. They may choose her.

A ▶ Practice. Underline the result clause in each sentence and decide if the sentence should be a future real conditional or a present unreal conditional. Complete each sentence with the correct form of the verb in parentheses.

1. If David _____ on national TV, he would be really embarrassed. (fail)

2. Alyssa will audition for a Broadway show if *MADE* _____ her to dance. (teach)

3. Many people might be more motivated if they _____ a mentor. (have)

4. If I _____ on *MADE*, I'd pursue my dream of becoming an ice skater. (be)

5. Some people wouldn't be happy if cameras _____ them around. (follow)

6. If you _____ for *MADE*, what goal will you pursue? (try out)

B ▶ Read. Decide where real or unreal conditionals are needed. Circle the best verb forms.

What (will / would) you do if you (have / had) a friend who didn't like
his or her looks? This is my problem. If I (hear / heard) my friend Stephanie
complain one more time about her appearance, I (will / would) scream!
First, Stephanie hates her hair. I guess if she (likes / liked) it, she
5 (won't / wouldn't) wear a hat all the time. She also says she doesn't know
how to wear makeup. She says if she (knows / knew) how to wear it, she
(may / might) talk to more guys. Finally, she thinks her clothes are out of
style. She says she (will / would) go out more often if they (are / were) more
fashionable. I don't get it. If I (am / were) Stephanie, I (won't / wouldn't)
10 change anything. I think she looks great the way she is!

▼ ACTIVATING GRAMMAR

🎧 A ▶ **Listen.**

1. Listen to two roommates discussing ideas for redecorating their apartment. Check (✓) if each plan is possible or unlikely. Write the clue from the conversation.

Plan	Possible	Unlikely	Clue
1. buy a bigger couch			
2. get a big-screen TV			
3. paint the kitchen walls yellow			
4. hang new shower curtains			
5. buy a new shower curtain and rug			
6. clean the bathroom			

2. Pair work. Predict future results of the changes the roommates discussed. Use the present unreal conditional and the future real conditional depending on whether their plans are unlikely or possible. Use verbs and phrases from the box and your own ideas.

be more pleasant	look bigger / smaller
let in more light	provide a space to relax in
like the room more	save money

Example: If they paint the kitchen walls yellow, the kitchen will look more cheerful.

B ▶ Group work. Answer these questions individually. Then discuss them with your classmates. Come to a group decision for number 6 and present your opinion to the class.

1. If I had enough money to redecorate my home, _____

_____.

2. If I could change one thing in my bedroom, _____.

3. If I paint my walls, _____.

4. If I had just one more room in my home, _____.

5. If I move, _____.

6. If I could give my classroom or school a makeover, I would _____

_____.

A ▶ Discuss. Look at the photos. What would someone have to do to be successful on a basketball team? in Hollywood?

B ▶ Listen. Listen to the interviews with people trying out for *MADE*. Write each person's ambition and his or her reasons for the ambition. Check (✓) the obstacles that they face.

	Ambition	Reason	Obstacles
Eric			_____ is not good at basketball _____ has no friends on the team _____ is short _____ never wins anything _____ can't run fast
Amber			_____ is not self-confident _____ doesn't have much money _____ has no acting experience _____ is nervous about public speaking _____ doesn't know anyone in Hollywood

C ▶ Listen again. Compare and contrast the two candidates. Check (✓) Eric, Amber, or both.

Which candidate….	Eric	Amber
1. wants to be noticed by other people?	☐	☐
2. needs a coach?	☐	☐
3. wants a makeover?	☐	☐
4. is motivated?	☐	☐
5. is most likely to be chosen by *MADE*?	☐	☐

D ▶ Group work.

1. Think of a secret ambition you have or make one up. Write ideas in the chart.

> What's one of your secret ambitions?
>
> What are some of the obstacles in your way?
>
> What would happen if you were on *MADE*?
> How might *MADE* help you?
>
> What would happen if you achieved your goal?
> How would your life change?

2. Role-play. With a partner, role-play an interview between someone from *MADE* and a candidate trying out for the show. Decide if the candidate should be on the show.

> **Example: A:** What's your secret ambition?
> **B:** I want to be a champion snowboarder.
> **A:** That's interesting. What are some of the obstacles in your way?
> **B:** Well, I don't live near a mountain. Also, I don't own a snowboard . . .

A ▶ **Listen and practice.** Then practice again using the other expressions.

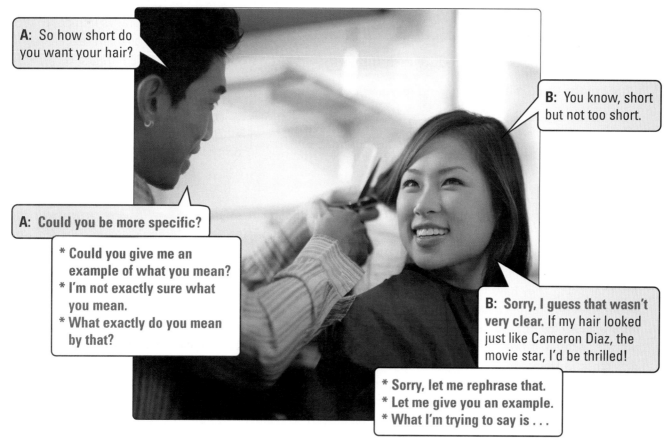

A: So how short do you want your hair?

B: You know, short but not too short.

A: Could you be more specific?

* Could you give me an example of what you mean?
* I'm not exactly sure what you mean.
* What exactly do you mean by that?

B: Sorry, I guess that wasn't very clear. If my hair looked just like Cameron Diaz, the movie star, I'd be thrilled!

* Sorry, let me rephrase that.
* Let me give you an example.
* What I'm trying to say is . . .

B ▶ **Pair work.** Continue these conversations with a partner. Use the expressions from Activity A to ask for clarification and to clarify ideas.

1. **A:** I just bought a new outfit for the party tonight.
   B: . . .

2. **A:** I hate the way my room looks.
   B: . . .

3. **A:** I'm completely exhausted.
   B: . . .

C ▶ **Group work.** Tell each other about a big change you are thinking of making. Give reasons. Be sure to ask each other for clarification and clarify your ideas.

Example: A: I'm thinking of getting a rose on my shoulder.
B: I'm not exactly sure what you mean.
A: I'm sorry, let me rephrase that. I'm thinking of getting a *tattoo* of a rose on my shoulder.

A ▸ **Study it.** Read the paragraph comparing two laptops and answer these questions.

1. What are the three similarities? _____,
_____, and _____

2. Underline the phrases that introduce each similarity.

3. What are the three differences? _____,
_____, and _____

4. Highlight the phrases that introduce each difference.

> **TIP** ▸ Transition phrases introduce similarities and differences:
> * *One similarity / difference is . . .*
> * *Another similarity / difference is . . .*
> * *Another thing they have in common is . . .*
> * *The biggest difference is . . .*

Which Laptop Should I Buy?

I can't decide between two laptop computers. They are both the same brand, but one is used and one is new. They have some similarities. One similarity is weight. They both weigh about nine pounds. Another similarity is software. They each come with the basic programs. Another thing they have in common is memory. If I bought either one, I would have no trouble storing all my papers, photos, and music. However, there are some differences. One difference is screen size. The used computer has a small screen. The new one has a bigger screen. If I wrote my papers on the new one, they would be easier to see. Another difference is keyboard size. The used keyboard might be hard to use because it's small. The keyboard on the new computer is more comfortable. The biggest difference is cost. The new computer costs $1,100. The used one costs $800. Which would you choose if you were me?

B ▸ **Write it.** Write a paragraph comparing two items.

1. Choose one of these items. Think of two types or brands of these items. Then complete the Venn diagram with information about each item.

> a car   a computer   your idea: _____
> a cell phone   an MP3 player

Item 1: _____   **Similarities**   **Item 2:** _____

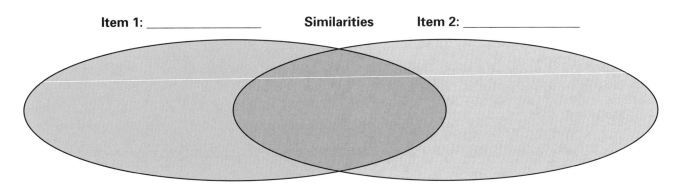

2. Write your paragraph. Use ideas from the Venn diagram. In the last sentence, state which item you prefer, or ask for advice about which item to buy.

3. Edit your paragraph.
   * Do you discuss both similarities and differences?
   * Do you use transition phrases to introduce them?

PUTTING IT TOGETHER   Trash or Treasure?

A ▶ Read.

1. Where do these artists create their artwork?

2. Checkpoint. Answer these questions.

   1. What must artists do if they are chosen for this program?

   _____

   _____

   2. What are the advantages of working there?

   _____

   _____

   _____

   3. Can you think of any disadvantages of working there?

   _____

   _____

> If you were an artist, where would you dream of working? At a studio in New York? At an apartment in Paris? How about at a garbage dump in San Francisco? San Francisco Recycling and Disposal, Inc., sponsors a unique artist-in-residence
> 5 program. Artists work on projects there for three to six months. They receive 24-hour access to a studio, a small amount of money for expenses, and a public exhibit.
>
> In exchange, artists must create art out of the city's garbage. They must also talk to tour groups about what it is
> 10 like to transform trash into art. "If I were working at home, I wouldn't get anything done," says one artist-in-residence, Kara Allen. "But what I really love is all the great material I can use. I made this sculpture of a woman from old coat hangers and broken TV sets."
>
> 15 The program started in 1990, when an artist asked to look around for materials. The company saw an opportunity to educate people about recycling, and they opened their doors to more artists. They hoped that the public exhibits would inspire people to think about recycling.

B ▶ Listen.

1. What is going on right now at the San Francisco dump? _____

2. Checkpoint. Discuss these questions.

   1. What did the artist Gabriel Moura create?

   2. Is the public response to the exhibit mostly positive or negative? Why?

   3. If you saw this art exhibit, do you think it would change you? Why or why not?

C ▶ Wrap it up.

1. **TOEFL® iBT** Write the effects of the program and exhibition on each person in the chart. Which two people show the effects that the company hoped for? Circle their names.

Gabriel Moura	Woman at the exhibit	Man at the exhibit

2. Can you think of other examples of "transformed trash" in society?

3. Think of other ways to educate people about the importance of recycling. Present one idea to the class. Vote on the best idea.

Expansion Units 7–9

LISTENING AND CONVERSATION Twins

A ▶ Warm up. Which two members of your family are the most alike? Check (✓) the ways in which they are similar. Describe them to a partner.

___ eye color	___ blood type	___ height
___ hair color	___ interests	___ other: _____
___ intelligence	___ personality	

⌒ **B ▶ Listen.** Read the incomplete sentences below. As you listen, use words and phrases from the box to complete the sentences. Use each word or phrase only once.

friends	taking classes
graduated	taking risks
rock-climbing	to become
studied	to have
studying	twins

1. Lisa and Laura are _____.

2. Gary and Laura are _____.

3. Gary and Laura took a _____ class together.

4. Lisa avoids _____, but Laura needs _____ excitement in her life.

5. In school, Laura was still _____ when Lisa _____.

6. When Lisa was a student, she _____ hard.

7. Instead of _____, Laura used to go surfing or skiing on the weekends.

8. Laura decided _____ a singer.

C ▶ Pair work. Work with a partner to answer these questions.

1. How did Gary and Laura meet each other? When did they meet? What was Laura doing when they met? What is she doing now? _____

   _____

2. How does Lisa feel about Laura? Do you agree? Why or why not? _____

   _____

3. What kinds of activities do you or did you participate in as a student? Do you prefer to concentrate on your studies, or do you think it's important to have other interests? _____

   _____

∩ D ▶ Listen again. In what ways are Lisa and Laura similar? How are they different? Use the Venr diagram to show Lisa's and Laura's characteristics, and the ones they have in common.

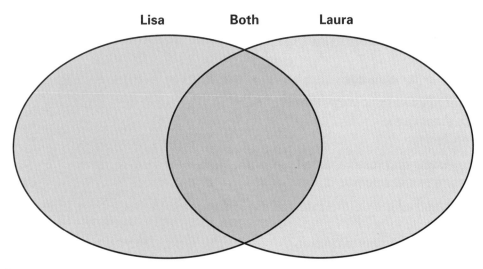

Lisa   Both   Laura

E ▶ Interview.

1. With your classmates, discuss the advantages and disadvantages of being a twin. Write your answers in the first two columns of the chart.

Advantages of Being a Twin	Disdvantages of Being a Twin		Preference	Reasons for Preference
		Student 1		
		Student 1		
		Student 1		
		Student 1		

2. Interview four classmates and write their answers in the last two columns of the chart. Ask this question:

If you had a choice, would you prefer to be a twin? Why or why not?

A ▸ Vocabulary boost! Read the sentences. Circle the correct definition for the words in bold.

1. I need a quiet **environment** when I'm trying to study. Any noise or activity nearby really bothers me.
   - a. setting or surroundings
   - b. trees, fresh air, and clean water

2. The Summer Festival is a **long-standing** tradition. This town has been doing it every summer for hundreds of years.
   - a. very famous
   - b. existing for a long time

3. You always know that Justin will tell the truth. Honesty is his best **trait**.
   - a. feature or characteristic
   - b. rule or law

4. Janine is tall, and all her children are, too. Even her grandchildren are tall. It must be something **genetic**.
   - a. passed from parents to children
   - b. lucky or fortunate

5. There were many **factors** contributing to the failure of the company—bad management, high labor costs, an untrained sales staff, and tough competition from other companies.
   - a. places where products are made
   - b. conditions that contribute to a result

6. Mary was unable to make her father change his mind. She pleaded, she reasoned, she gave him presents, but she just couldn't **influence** his decision.
   - a. agree with
   - b. have an effect on

7. I thought the dance performance was excellent! Each dancer was good alone, and their **interaction** on stage together was even better.
   - a. effect of two or more things on each other
   - b. costumes and lighting

◯ B ▸ Read. What is the main idea of the article?

Twins

Studies of twins who are raised separately show that they often remain very similar. In one case, male twins who had never met not only looked alike, but also drove the same kind of car, smoked the same brand of cigarettes, and had wives named Betty. Some scientists conclude from this that our personalities and preferences are "natural," something we are
5   born with. Other scientists challenge this view, arguing that personality is largely shaped by the social **environment**—school, culture, religion, and family. These two positions represent a **long-standing** scientific debate, "nature versus nurture."

   Many **traits** such as eye color and blood type are clearly **genetic** ("nature"). But are other qualities, such as intelligence and personality, also caused by genes or by environmental
10 **factors** ("nurture")? We all know people with traits that "run in the family"—parents and children who all draw well or excel at sports. Is this the result of natural ability, or is it because the family members **influence** each other in their common interests and activities? We aren't sure, but the question becomes important when considering issues like criminal behavior, mental illness, and poverty. For example, if criminal behavior is learned, then
15 perhaps it can be reduced through training and education. If it is genetic, training and education will probably be insufficient.

   While some scientists stand on the side of "nature" and others defend "nurture," many argue that human behavior results from a complex **interaction** between the two. Someone may be born with a talent for playing music, but whether that person prefers to play classical
20 music, jazz, or rock is probably determined by education and other social influences. Still, the debate over "nature" versus "nurture" continues and has a large impact on policies and practices in such critical areas as education, criminal justice, and mental health.

C ▶ Discuss. Discuss these questions with a partner.

1. Why are twins important to the debate over "nature" versus "nurture"? Which side of the debate does their case support?
2. How does the debate over "nature" versus "nurture" affect the criminal justice system? Which side of the debate do you think is right? Why?
3. Think of a family with a particular trait that "runs in the family." This can be either a family you know or a famous family. Describe the trait.

D ▶ Read again. According to the article, which of the items below could be categorized as "nature" and which as "nurture"? Write the items in the chart. Some items belong in the "can't tell" column.

ability to draw	eye color	musical talent
blood type	good at sports	preference for jazz
criminal behavior	intelligence	religion

Nature	Nurture	Can't tell

E ▶ Write about it. Write a profile comparing two siblings.

1. Think of two siblings you know well from your own family or another family. Use the Venn diagram to show how they are similar and different.

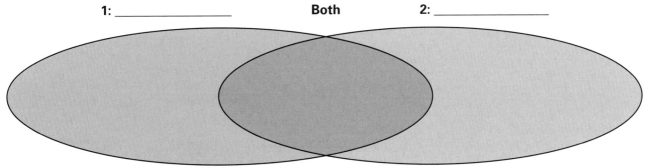

1: _____   **Both**   2: _____

2. Write a paragraph comparing and contrasting the siblings. Use at least three points of comparison.

3. Edit your paragraph.
   - Do you discuss both similarities and differences?
   - Do you use transition phrases to introduce them?

10 Staying in Touch

READING AND VOCABULARY

A ▶ Warm up. Check (✔) the reasons why you use (or would use) the Internet. Discuss with a group.

___ to read the news   ___ to shop   ___ to do research for school or for work

___ to use email   ___ to take a class   ___ other: _____

⌒ **B ▶ Read.** Preview the article. Look at the title, photos, and headings to answer these questions:

1. What is this article about?
2. What part of the world do you think this is?

> **Skill Focus — Previewing a Reading**
>
> Reading an article or any reading passage for the first time is easier if you have a general idea of what the text is about and how it is organized. This is why previewing is important. Before reading, look at clues such as the title, photos, and headings. You can then predict the topic and general ideas.

Emails on Motorcycles

Like 3,000 other tiny villages in Cambodia, O Siengle has no electricity. Residents don't have cell phones, and they've never seen a **text message**. But with the help of one red motorcycle, O Siengle was transformed by the Internet.

Free Wireless, Free Computers

5　Every day, a man on a red motorcycle drives through the village for one hour. His bike holds a wireless (Wi-Fi) box. This box lets the residents **browse** the Internet using solar-powered computers in the village. The box also downloads and uploads emails. At the end of each day, it is driven to the closest big city and connected to a **server**. Through this server, the
10　village's emails are sent to people around the world. This is all made possible through the Internet Village Motoman Project. This charity organization distributes free computers to villages like O Siengle.

How the Internet Is Changing Lives

After the Internet came to O Siengle, the residents' lives were changed in many ways. Now, the schoolchildren
15　can learn how to use a computer. They can communicate with one another by sending emails and by **posting** messages on a website. This site has **links** to other schools in the area, which have their own webpages. There are message **boards**, and in the future, there might be **chat rooms**, too. Every month, the number of **hits** to the site increases. In addition, crafts made in O Siengle are sold through the village's website. The profits will pay for more computers and teachers.

20　### What's Next?

The founders of the Internet Village Motoman Project hope to connect many more villages to the Internet in the next five years.

C ▶ **Read again.** Check (✓) the three statements below that can be inferred from the article.

1. ____ People in O Siengle can only connect to the Internet for one hour a day.
2. ____ There are 3,000 red motorcycles in Cambodia.
3. ____ The man on the red motorcycle drives the Wi-Fi box to the closest big city.
4. ____ The Internet Village Motoman Project has brought a lot of tourism to villages in Cambodia.
5. ____ The residents of O Siengle are going to buy more computers and hire more teachers.

D ▶ **Discuss.**

1. What benefits has the Internet given the residents of O Siengle? What are some other useful ways that the residents could use the Internet in the future?
2. How do you think the Internet is changing other parts of the world? Name five effects it has had on the world and/or on your hometown.

VOCABULARY Internet Terminology

A ▶ **Identify.** Match each word or phrase with its definition.

1. ____ board	a. (*noun*) visit to a website	
2. ____ browse	b. (*noun*) message; (*verb*) to put a message online	
3. ____ chat room	c. (*noun*) place to post a message	
4. ____ hit	d. (*noun*) main computer that provides special services	
5. ____ link	e. (*noun*) place to discuss things online in real time	
6. ____ post	f. (*noun*) typed message sent by cell phone	
7. ____ server	g. (*verb*) look at different websites without specific purpose	
8. ____ text message	h. (*noun*) highlighted Internet address that connects to another website; (*verb*) connect one website to another	

> **TIP** Note that many of these words and phrases also have meanings that are not related to technology.

B ▶ **Practice.** Complete these sentences with the correct form of the words from Activity A.

1. Angie is in a _____ with her sister, and Frank is sending a _____ to his professor.

2. I'm making my own website, but I don't know how to _____ to other sites.

3. She's finished working, so she wants to _____ the Internet. But her company's _____ is down, so she can't get online.

4. He _____ something new on his blog every day. Yesterday he included _____ to all his favorite videos on the Internet.

5. When I first started that message _____, I only got about 20 _____ a day. Now I get about 1,200!

The Passive Verb Form in the Present, Past, and Future

A verb can be active or passive. A sentence with an active verb form focuses on the subject—**who** or **what** does something. A sentence with a passive verb form focuses on the **action**. We form the passive with the verb *be* plus a past participle. In a passive sentence, the person or thing doing the action can be pointed out in a phrase beginning with *by*, or it can be left out.

Active: The server **sends** messages to people around the world.
Passive: Messages **are sent** by the server to people around the world. OR
Messages **are sent** to people around the world.

We can use the passive form in any verb tense. In passive questions, we do not use *do, does,* or *did*—unlike in active questions, which often use *do, does,* or *did.*

Present: Where **are** the boxes **taken**? → The boxes **are taken** (by someone) to a big city.
Past: **Were** the residents' lives **changed** by the Internet? →
Yes, their lives **were changed** (by the Internet) in many ways.
Future: **Will** more villages **be connected** to the Internet in the future? →
Yes, many more villages **will be connected** (by a server) in the next five years.

A ▶ **Practice.** Underline the verbs in these sentences. Are the verbs active or passive? Write *active* or *passive* after each sentence. Rewrite the active sentences in the passive form.

> **TIP** ▶ **Verbs Without a Passive Form**
> Only transitive verbs (verbs that can take an object) can be put in the passive form. Intransitive verbs (verbs that can't take an object) cannot be put in the passive form. These verbs include: *come, die, fall, run, sleep,* and *swim.*

1. Students wrote an angry email about the new policy. _____

_____

2. Our school's policy about using chat rooms was changed. _____

_____

3. Starting next week, the lab instructor won't allow video chatting.

_____

_____

4. Will the new policy affect students' attitudes? _____

_____

🎧 B ▶ **Listen.** Listen to the woman. Then write the missing verb in the correct form (active or passive) and the correct tense.

1. The program iChat _____ (install) on Sima's computer yesterday.

2. She is happy about how much money she _____ (save) by using iChat.

3. This morning she _____ (call) her uncle to tell him about iChat.

4. A laptop _____ (give) to Deepak as a present a couple of years ago.

5. Deepak asked, "Where _____ iChats _____?" (sell)

▼ ACTIVATING GRAMMAR

A ▶ Read and write.

1. Circle the verbs that are in the passive form.

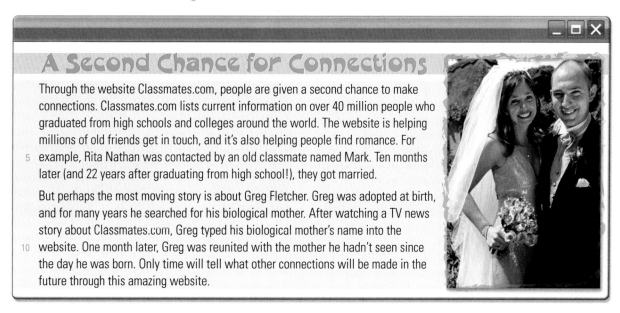

A Second Chance for Connections

Through the website Classmates.com, people are given a second chance to make connections. Classmates.com lists current information on over 40 million people who graduated from high schools and colleges around the world. The website is helping millions of old friends get in touch, and it's also helping people find romance. For
5 example, Rita Nathan was contacted by an old classmate named Mark. Ten months later (and 22 years after graduating from high school!), they got married.

But perhaps the most moving story is about Greg Fletcher. Greg was adopted at birth, and for many years he searched for his biological mother. After watching a TV news story about Classmates.com, Greg typed his biological mother's name into the
10 website. One month later, Greg was reunited with the mother he hadn't seen since the day he was born. Only time will tell what other connections will be made in the future through this amazing website.

2. Look at the passive structures you circled in Activity 1. Choose three and write questions about Classmates.com. Use the passive voice. Ask a partner your questions and write down his or her answers.

Example: Q: *What is given to people by Classmates.com?*

A: *A second chance is given to people by Classmates.com.*

1. Q: _____

A: _____

2. Q: _____

A: _____

3. Q: _____

A: _____

B ▶ Group work.
Imagine that your group is going to post its own webpage on a site like Classmates.com. Discuss your webpage. Answer the questions below as a group.

Questions	Answers
1. Who will your webpage be used by?	
2. What information about your group members will be given on your webpage?	
3. Will music or graphics be used on the webpage? What kind?	

A ▶ Discuss. Look at the people and guess their relationship. How do they know each other, and why do you think they communicate by computer?

⌒ B ▶ Listen. Check (✓) the correct problem and solution.

Problem

____ a. Lili didn't have enough money to start her own business.

____ b. Lili was given money when she graduated college, but she spent it all.

____ c. Lili just started her own business a few months ago.

Solution

____ a. Lili was given free surfing supplies.

____ b. Lili met Erica online, and Erica invested in Lili's company.

____ c. Lili closed her business.

⌒ C ▶ Listen again. For each person, put the events in the order that they happened. Number them from 1 to 4. (Number 1 is what happened first.)

_____ Lili saw that all the surfing supplies websites were aimed at men.

_____ Erica offered to invest in Lili's company.

_____ Lili saw a post on a message board.

_____ Lili chatted with Erica online and became her friend.

D ▶ Pair work.

1. Complete the sentences about advice you were given when you were younger.

      Example: When I was a child, I was told by ___my father___ to always _sit up straight_.

      1. When I was a child, I was told by _____ to always _____.

      2. When I was in high school, I was told by _____ to _____.

      3. When I started studying English, I was _____.

2. Share your answers with your partner. Say who gave you the advice. Make a list of good advice and bad advice that you were given.

∩ **A** ▶ **Listen and practice.** Then practice again using the other expressions.

A: Richard? Is that you?

A: Wow! I think the last time I saw you was at graduation!

B: Jim? No way!

B: That's right! It's been so long. I have to run to a meeting now, but let's catch up. **What's your number?**

* **I don't have your number.**
* **Why don't you give me your number?**
* **What's your email address?**

A: Here's my card. **Shoot me an email** and tell me how to reach you.

* **Send me an email.**
* **Write me an email.**
* **Give me a call.**
* **Call me.**

B: I will. It's really good to see you. **Let's keep in touch.**

* **Let's talk soon.**
* **Let's stay in touch.**

A: Definitely.

B ▶ **Pair work.** Continue these conversations with a partner. Use the expressions from Activity A for keeping in touch.

1. A: Alex, could you help me with my project?
    B: Sure. But I'm busy right now, so . . .

2. A: It was great to see you again. Let's catch up.
    B: Definitely . . .

3. A: Ms. Farmington? I'm Jeff Barnes. You were my teacher in tenth grade.
    B: Jeff? Oh, of course! The last time I saw you was . . .

C ▶ **Role-play.** Tell your partner about an old friend, teacher, or relative with whom you want to get back in touch. Then have your partner role-play that person. Imagine running into each other on the street. Have a conversation. Be sure to use expressions for keeping in touch.

Examples: What are you doing these days?
              How is your family?
              When was the last time we saw each other?
              What did you do after we last saw each other?

A ► Study it. Study the article and the summary.

1. Compare the original article to the summary. Underline all the information in the original article that is included in the summary. Notice that the writer of the summary uses his own words.

2. Look at the information that isn't included in the summary. Why was it left out?

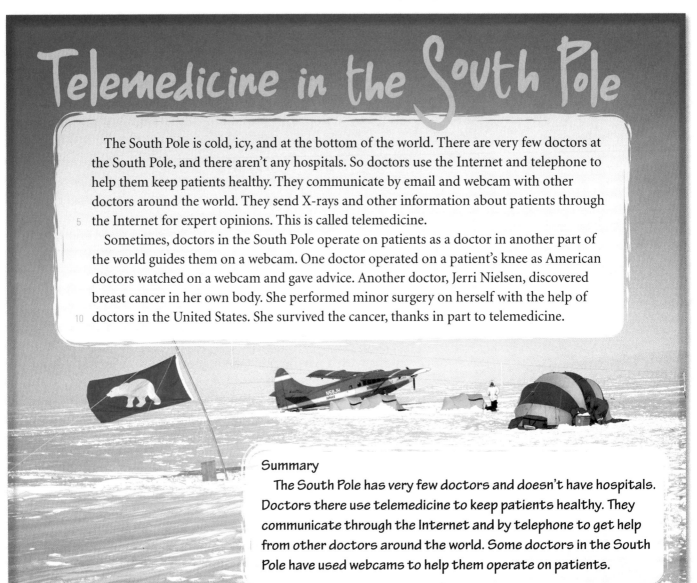

Telemedicine in the South Pole

The South Pole is cold, icy, and at the bottom of the world. There are very few doctors at the South Pole, and there aren't any hospitals. So doctors use the Internet and telephone to help them keep patients healthy. They communicate by email and webcam with other doctors around the world. They send X-rays and other information about patients through
5 the Internet for expert opinions. This is called telemedicine.

Sometimes, doctors in the South Pole operate on patients as a doctor in another part of the world guides them on a webcam. One doctor operated on a patient's knee as American doctors watched on a webcam and gave advice. Another doctor, Jerri Nielsen, discovered breast cancer in her own body. She performed minor surgery on herself with the help of
10 doctors in the United States. She survived the cancer, thanks in part to telemedicine.

Summary

The South Pole has very few doctors and doesn't have hospitals. Doctors there use telemedicine to keep patients healthy. They communicate through the Internet and by telephone to get help from other doctors around the world. Some doctors in the South Pole have used webcams to help them operate on patients.

B ► Write it. Write a one-paragraph summary of an article.

1. Reread "A Second Chance for Connections" on page 89. Underline the main idea. Then highlight the details that should be included in your summary.

2. Write your paragraph.

3. Edit your paragraph.
- Do you explain clearly what Classmates.com is and what it is used for?
- Do you include the items that you highlighted? Do you use your own words?
- Is your summary brief?

A ▶ Read.

1. Underline the information that supports the sociologist's theory about how the Internet affects human relationships.

Is Technology Making Us Mean?

Dr. Sara Kiesler studies how people communicate. After many studies, Dr. Kiesler believes that email, text messaging, and web postings are making communication more difficult in some ways. She also believes it is making people meaner and more aggressive.

Dr. Kiesler's studies show that electronic communication often leads to misunderstandings between people.
5 This is because email and text messages can't show important communication cues or signs, such as the writer's tone of voice, loudness and speed of speech, and facial expressions. As a result, a person might read an email and misunderstand it. For example, a reader might think that the writer is upset, when in fact the writer is just trying to be funny. On the other hand, some people write things in messages that they never would say to someone in person. They feel safe even when they are rude because they do not have to look the other person in the eye at the moment
10 of communication. Often, people don't have to give their real name when they communicate electronically. For all of these reasons, Dr. Kiesler thinks electronic communication is making us meaner and more aggressive.

2. Checkpoint. Answer these questions.

1. According to Dr. Kiesler, how is electronic communication affecting people? _____

_____

2. Why does Dr. Kiesler think that people often misunderstand each other when communicating

electronically? _____

3. Do you agree with her theory? Why or why not?

_____

B ▶ Listen.

1. Listen to people talk about how they communicate. Write where they work or study.

Speaker 1: _____

Speaker 2: _____

2. Checkpoint. Answer these questions.

1. What communication cues does the dean of the Arizona college list?

_____

2. What was the misunderstanding between the freshman and her professor?

_____

C ▶ Wrap it up.

1. TOEFL® iBT Which of the people you listened to have had experiences that support what Dr. Kiesler found in her study? Explain. Who has had experiences that challenge her theory? Explain.

2. Describe your own experiences with communicating by computer. Do your experiences support or challenge Kiesler's theory? In what ways?

Making a Difference

READING AND SPEAKING

A ▶ Warm up. On a scale of 1–10, rate how interested you are in deforestation (cutting down trees to clear land and make wood and paper products). Tell a partner two other issues you care about. Rate those on the scale and discuss your ratings.

1	2	3	4	5	6	7	8	9	10

don't care at all   *care very much*

⌒ B ▶ Read.

1. Read the first two paragraphs about Julia Hill. Then make two predictions about what happened to Julia and the tree.

Predictions: 1. _____

2. _____

Julia "Butterfly" Hill has a passion for helping the environment. On December 10, 1995, the 25-year-old climbed up a 180-foot (55 meters), 1,000-year-old redwood tree. She named the tree "Luna" and made it her home for the next two years. Hill lived there to **protest** the logging
5 of giant redwood trees. She **believed** these trees should be saved because they were very old and were part of the natural environment. Hill **refused** to come down until the Pacific Lumber Company agreed to stop cutting down these very old redwoods.

Hill lived on two wooden platforms in the tree. Twice a week, friends
10 brought her food, mail, and fuel for her stove. For exercise, she climbed up and down part of the tree trunk.

The Tree-Sitter

2. Continue reading. Were your predictions correct?

Soon, Julia became a **controversial** person. Some people **opposed** her protest. They **argued** that the lumber company provided jobs and useful wood products. These people said these jobs were more important than trees. However, many people **supported** Hill. They wrote letters to the lumber company, **urging** it to
15 save the redwoods. Finally, on December 10, 1997, the Pacific Lumber Company agreed to protect "Luna" and some of the forest around it. Hill came down from the tree.

Hill has been recognized as a hero. Since she left the tree in 1997, she has written about her experience in many publications. Hill has never stopped working for environmental issues. "I wake up in the morning asking myself what can I do today, how can I help the world today," Hill says.

C ▶ Read again. Choose the best paraphrase for each sentence. Circle a or b.

1. She believed the trees should be saved because they were very old and were part of the natural environment.
   a. She thought the trees should be saved.
   b. Because these trees were old and part of the natural environment, she wanted to save them.

2. Hill refused to come down until the Pacific Lumber Company agreed to stop cutting down the very old redwoods.
   a. Until the Pacific Lumber Company said it would stop cutting down the redwoods, Hill wouldn't come down.
   b. Hill wouldn't come down until the lumber company agreed to stop.

3. Some people argued that the lumber company provided jobs and useful wood products.
   a. People said the lumber company offered important wood products and jobs.
   b. The company provided wood products and jobs.

D ▶ Discuss. Discuss these questions with a partner.

1. Imagine you're going to live in a tree for 30 days. What would you take with you? What things would you miss the most?
2. Talk about two things you feel passionate about changing in your community or in the world. What could people do to make this change?

▼ VOCABULARY Persuasive Language

A ▶ Identify. Use a dictionary to find other forms of these words from the article.

	Verb	Noun	Adjective
1.	protest	protest; protester	(none)
2.		belief	believable
3.		refusal	(none)
4.	(none)		conroversial
5.	oppose		opposite; opposed
6.		argument	argumentative
7.	support	support; supporter	
8.		urge	urgent

B ▶ Practice. Complete the sentences with words from the chart in Activity A. Make sure you change the form of the verbs if necessary.

1. I hear she _____ the new law against smoking, but her husband opposes it.

2. He _____ with the teacher, but the teacher still _____ to change his mind.

3. He is _____ to cars that use gas, so he _____ his friend to buy an electric car.

4. They don't _____ that the government should support controversial art.

5. Last year, students marched in front of the dean's office to _____ the school's decision to require uniforms.

GETTING INTO GRAMMAR

The Present Perfect versus the Simple Past

We use the present perfect (*has/have* + past participle) for actions that started in the past and continue to the present. We can use *for* with amounts of time and *since* with specific dates or events.

> She **has tried** to raise awareness about deforestation for many years.
>> She began to raise awareness in the past and continues to do that today.
> Since she was a teenager, Julia **has helped** environmental groups.
>> She began helping groups when she was a teenager and continues to do so today.

We also use the present perfect for actions that occurred and were completed at an unspecified time in the past. When we know the specific time that an action was completed, we use the simple past instead.

> **Present perfect:** The lumber company **has argued** that it provides jobs.
>> The lumber company argued this in the past, but we do not know when.
> **Simple past:** Last year, the lumber company **argued** that it provides jobs.
>> The lumber company argued this at a specific time in the past—*last year.*

We use *ever* and *never* for emphasis. *Ever* is used in questions. *Never* is used in statements.

> **Have** you **ever worked** for a lumber company?
> No, I **have never worked** for a lumber company. / No, I **have not worked** for a lumber company.

A ▶ Practice. Complete the paragraph with the present perfect form of the verbs in parentheses.

Fast Facts about Julia "Butterfly" Hill

Julia (have) _____ the nickname "Butterfly" since she was a child. One day, while she
1
was hiking with her family, a butterfly landed on her and stayed there. Since then, everyone
(call) _____ her "Butterfly." At age 16, Julia went to college to study business.
2
But business and the environment aren't her only interests. Julia (be) _____
3
interested in cooking since she was a young girl. When she was just 18, she started her own
vegetarian café. She (eat, not) _____ meat for a long time.
4

B ▶ Listen. Read each sentence about John and Denise Davis. Write the correct form of the verb and check (✓) the correct column.

	Past	Present Perfect
1. Since they got married, John and Denise Davis (spend) _____ every day following their passion.	☐	☐
2. John and Denise (start) _____ Greyhound Rescue in 1989.	☐	☐
3. Greyhound Rescue (save) _____ over 2,000 dogs to date.	☐	☐
4. Last month they (begin) _____ selling dog products online.	☐	☐

ACTIVATING GRAMMAR

A ▶ Read and role-play.

1. Read the article. Then use the words provided to write paraphrased sentences about the article. Use the present perfect or simple past.

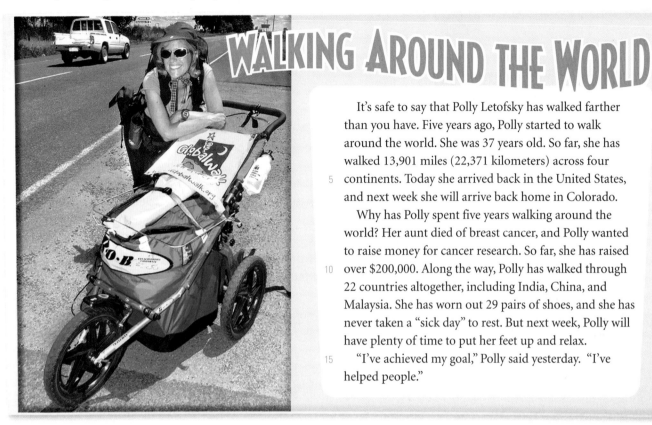

WALKING AROUND THE WORLD

It's safe to say that Polly Letofsky has walked farther than you have. Five years ago, Polly started to walk around the world. She was 37 years old. So far, she has walked 13,901 miles (22,371 kilometers) across four
5 continents. Today she arrived back in the United States, and next week she will arrive back home in Colorado.

Why has Polly spent five years walking around the world? Her aunt died of breast cancer, and Polly wanted to raise money for cancer research. So far, she has raised
10 over $200,000. Along the way, Polly has walked through 22 countries altogether, including India, China, and Malaysia. She has worn out 29 pairs of shoes, and she has never taken a "sick day" to rest. But next week, Polly will have plenty of time to put her feet up and relax.
15 "I've achieved my goal," Polly said yesterday. "I've helped people."

1. return / Polly / today / to the United States

   Today Polly returned to the United States. (OR) Polly returned to the United States today.

2. for cancer research / she / five years / raising money / spend

   _____

3. she / as of today / India, China, and 20 other countries / walk through

   _____

4. use / she / 29 pairs / of shoes

   _____

2. Role-play. Work with a partner. Role-play Polly (or someone like her) and a TV reporter. The reporter interviews Polly. Talk about these topics. The reporter checks the boxes as you talk about the topics. Then switch roles.

Example: Reporter: When did you start walking around the world?
Polly: I started five years ago.

☐ when Polly started
☐ why she walked around the world
☐ how many countries she has walked through
☐ how much money she has raised

B ▶ Discuss.
Think of someone (famous or not) who is passionate about an issue. Tell your classmates at least three things this person has done to make other people aware of the issue.

A ▶ Discuss. Look at the pictures in Activity B below. What are the people talking about?

∩ B ▶ Listen. For each conversation, check (✓) the person's paraphrased response.

1. ____ a. He has already signed the petition.
____ b. He hasn't signed the petition yet.

2. ____ a. She has never signed a petition.
____ b. She has signed many petitions.

∩ C ▶ Listen again. Fill in the missing words in the volunteers' statements. Then check whether each statement is a fact or an opinion.

Conversation 1:	Fact	Opinion
a. It's a _____ practice that too many people ignore.	☐	☐
b. About _____ racing greyhounds are born every year.	☐	☐

Conversation 2:	Fact	Opinion
a. The amount of money earned from dog racing has declined over _____ percent in the past _____ years.	☐	☐
b. The only way to stop dog racing is for everyone to start _____.	☐	☐

Skill Focus **Fact or Opinion?**
A fact is something that can be proven. Often, facts include specific information, such as numbers and dates. An opinion is someone's judgment or belief about something or someone; it may or may not be true. Most opinions do not include numbers or dates, but they often contain emotional words.

D ▶ Pair work.

1. Work with a partner. Think of an issue that is important to the people in your school or class. Find and list at least four facts about the issue that will convince people to support it.

_____

_____

_____

_____

2. Now make a petition with lines for people to sign their names. With your partner, talk to students in your class about your petition. Try to get every classmate to sign it.

🎧 **A** ▶ **Listen and practice.** Then practice again using the other phrases.

A: Did you hear about the tuition increase? I heard that over 10,000 students will be protesting it.

B: Yeah, I heard. But, **in my opinion**, protesting is a really bad idea.

* I believe that . . .
* I feel that . . .
* my feeling is that . . .
* if you ask me . . .

A: I respect your opinion, **but** how can you be against the protest? The tuition increase is too high.

* I hear what you're saying, but . . .
* I understand what you're saying, but . . .
* I understand where you're coming from, but . . .

B: I disagree. **I've thought about this a lot.** If we protest, people will just get angry at us.

* I've read a lot about this . . .
* I've talked to a lot of people about this.

B ▶ **Pair work.** Work with a partner. Continue these conversations. Use the phrases from Activity A to express and discuss opinions.

1. A: I think that money is more important than love.
   B: . . .

2. A: My feeling is that smoking should be illegal everywhere.
   B: . . .

3. A: I heard that public schools are making all students wear uniforms.
   B: . . .

C ▶ **Role-play.** Role-play these situations with your partner. Express your opinions using the phrases above.

• One of you is Julia "Butterfly" Hill (or someone like her) and you are meeting the owner of the Pacific Lumber Company for the first time.
• You both work at a news magazine and have to decide on the "most important leader" of the decade.

A ▶ Study it. Read the email.

1. Circle the three sentences that state Peter Tanaka's opinion about the highway construction. Then underline the details he uses to support his opinion.

2. What is the main purpose of the first paragraph? Circle a, b, or c.
   a. to explain why he's writing and to give the mayor specific examples of why the highway is a bad idea
   b. to describe the issue in general terms, to state his opinion, and to make a request
   c. to explain why he's writing, to state his opinion, and to give specific examples of why the highway is a bad idea

3. What is the main purpose of the second paragraph? Circle a, b, or c.
   a. to give specific reasons why the highway is a bad idea and repeat his request
   b. to tell the main reason why the highway is a bad idea and to ask the mayor to find a different solution
   c. to give specific reasons why the highway is a bad idea and suggest a better solution

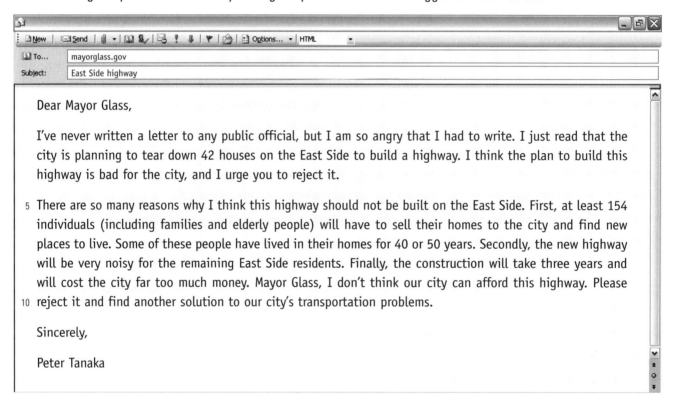

To... mayorglass.gov
Subject: East Side highway

Dear Mayor Glass,

I've never written a letter to any public official, but I am so angry that I had to write. I just read that the city is planning to tear down 42 houses on the East Side to build a highway. I think the plan to build this highway is bad for the city, and I urge you to reject it.

5 There are so many reasons why I think this highway should not be built on the East Side. First, at least 154 individuals (including families and elderly people) will have to sell their homes to the city and find new places to live. Some of these people have lived in their homes for 40 or 50 years. Secondly, the new highway will be very noisy for the remaining East Side residents. Finally, the construction will take three years and will cost the city far too much money. Mayor Glass, I don't think our city can afford this highway. Please
10 reject it and find another solution to our city's transportation problems.

Sincerely,

Peter Tanaka

B ▶ Write it. Write a two-paragraph email that expresses your opinion about an issue.

1. Choose an issue that you feel strongly about. The issue could be related to your school, your community, or your government. Who will you send your email to? What actions will you ask this person to take?

2. Use Peter's email as a model to write your paragraphs. In the first paragraph, explain why you are writing and present your opinion. In the second paragraph, give details to support your opinion.

3. Edit your paragraphs.
   • Does the first paragraph describe the issue, state your opinion, and make a request?
   • Does the second paragraph give details and/or examples to support your opinion?

A ▶ Read.

1. Scan the article and underline the three leadership styles.

2. Checkpoint. Answer these questions.

1. What type of leader does Bass think is the least effective? Most effective? Why?

_____

_____

_____

_____

2. How do transactional leaders motivate people? _____

_____

_____

3. Which type of leader is more likely to focus on everyday details?

_____

Three Types of Leaders

Dr. Bernard Bass believes there are many types of leaders, but that they all fall under three main types: *laissez-faire* ("hands-off"), transactional, and transformational.

Bass believes the worst kind of leader is the *laissez-faire*
5 one. This type of leader trusts that followers or employees can do their jobs without help. As a result, the *laissez-faire* leader doesn't actually lead. Instead, he or she spends time working independently.

Transactional leaders are more effective. They focus on
10 getting the job done. They motivate people by promising a reward for good work—for example, a higher salary or a job promotion. But transactional leaders can spend too much time dealing with daily issues and workplace politics.

Bass says that transformational leaders are the best leaders.
15 They motivate their followers or employees and inspire them to achieve more. Transformational leaders emphasize honesty, loyalty, and fairness. They spend most of their time looking at the "big picture" rather than the small details of daily life.

B ▶ Listen.

1. Match the leaders to the places they work.

1. _____ Al Sparkes   a. Whales of the World

2. _____ Lyn Naylor   b. City Medical Center

3. _____ Vincent Cappelli   c. Forests Forever

4. _____ Erin Reed   d. recycling program

2. Checkpoint. Answer these questions.

1. What did Al Sparkes tell his employees to make them work harder? _____

2. How did Vincent Cappelli make his employees fix the server? _____

3. What is most important to Lyn Naylor? _____

4. What does Erin Reed think her employees need? _____

C ▶ Wrap it up.

1. (TOEFL® iBT) Write each person's leadership type. Explain your answers.

a. Al Sparkes: _____   c. Vincent Cappelli: _____

b. Lyn Naylor: _____   d. Erin Reed: _____

2. What types of leaders have you worked with? What type of leader are you?

12 Memories

▼ READING AND SPEAKING

A ▶ **Warm up.** Make a list of 15 cities or countries. Show it to a partner for one minute, then ask the partner to write down the list from memory. Switch roles. How many places could you and your partner remember?

🎧 **B** ▶ **Read.** Circle the three internal definitions in the article. Then write the terms and their definitions below.

Term 1: _____

Definition: _____

Term 2: _____

Definition: _____

Term 3: _____

Definition: _____

> **Skill Focus** **Internal Definitions**
> Words and phrases can be defined within a sentence or paragraph by using punctuation (commas, dashes, and parentheses) and special terms (*or, that is*) to present the definition. **Example:** Most of my childhood *recollections,* or memories, are happy. (recollections = memories)

Why Can't Clive Wearing Remember Anything?

In 1985, Clive Wearing got a disease that attacked his brain. Suddenly, this former musician and radio announcer couldn't **recall** anything except his name.

Clive has been living with amnesia, or memory loss, ever since. He has forgotten most of the details of his life that occurred before 1985, and he forgets new information after about 30 seconds. When his adult children visit him, he doesn't **recognize** them. The only person he recognizes is his wife, Deborah Wearing, but each time he sees her, he thinks he has not seen her in 20 years.

Deborah has written about her family's experiences in her book, *Forever Today: A Memoir of Love and Amnesia.* It tells how she and her family have **dealt with** Clive's amnesia and how they've gotten through

(survived) the hard times. For example, soon after losing his memory, Clive became very paranoid– excessively distrustful–of other people. He thought that people were trying to hurt him. Deborah couldn't care for him by herself, so she had to move him into a hospital.

Doctors have been trying to help Clive, but they don't know how to **cure** him. Dr. Barbara Wilson has **examined** him many times in recent years. "Clive's memory, unfortunately, has improved only a bit," said Dr. Wilson. She believes his **condition** is **permanent**. But Deborah thinks her husband is getting better. He seems calmer, she believes, and more accepting of his situation. Only time will tell whether Clive Wearing will get his memory back.

C ▶ Read again. Match each cause to its correct effect.

Cause	Effect
1. ___ Clive Wearing got a disease that attacked his brain.	a. Deborah believes her husband is getting better.
2. ___ Clive grew paranoid and his wife couldn't care for him.	b. He has been living with amnesia.
3. ___ Examinations have shown that Clive's memory hasn't improved very much.	c. Dr. Wilson thinks Clive's amnesia is permanent.
4. ___ Clive seems calmer and more accepting of his situation.	d. Deborah moved Clive to a hospital.

D ▶ Discuss. Discuss these questions with a partner.

1. What do you think daily life is like for Clive and Deborah? What are some things that would be hard for each of them to do because of Clive's amnesia?
2. What is one of your first memories as a child?

▼ VOCABULARY

A ▶ Identify. Match each word with its meaning. Use the contexts in the article to help you.

1. ___ condition		a. cope; find a way to accept something
2. ___ cure		b. a book about one's own life
3. ___ deal with		c. a person's health or state of being
4. ___ examine		d. remember
5. ___ memoir		e. make a sick person or animal better
6. ___ permanent		f. identify after seeing something before
7. ___ recall		g. continuing forever
8. ___ recognize		h. look at closely, often for medical reasons

B ▶ Practice. Complete the story with words from Activity A. Change the verb forms as needed.

Anna Frye was having trouble remembering things. When she went shopping, she sometimes couldn't _____ where her car was parked. And when

1
people said hello to her on the street, she didn't always _____ them. Her

2
memory loss scared her, so she went to her doctor, and he _____ her

3
very carefully. After asking a lot of questions and running some tests, the doctor said, "Anna, I don't think
your _____ is very serious. You don't have _____ memory loss; in fact, I think you'll be

4   5
fine." The doctor explained that Anna was having a bad reaction, or response, to the medicine she was
taking to help her sleep at night. The medicine made her forget things. "As soon as you stop taking that
medicine, your memory loss will stop. You'll be _____. You can go write a _____ about

               6   7
your experience!" The doctor smiled and added, "But of course, we'll have to _____ your

                            8
sleeping problem!"

GETTING INTO GRAMMAR

The Present Perfect Continuous vs. the Present Perfect

We use the present perfect continuous to talk about an action that began in the past and is still happening in the present. We can use it to show or emphasize the duration of an event. When an action at an unspecified time in the past was *completed*, we do not use the present perfect continuous. Instead, we use the present perfect.

Present perfect continuous:

His wife **has been writing** about her experiences.

She began writing in the past and is still writing in the present.

Present perfect:

His wife **has written** about her experiences.

She wrote about her experiences in the past, but is not writing about them now.

When used with *for* or *since*, the present perfect continuous and present perfect have the same meaning. Use *for* with amounts of times and *since* with specific dates or events.

Since 1985, Clive **has lived** with amnesia.

Since 1985, Clive **has been living** with amnesia.

A ▶ Practice. A 30-year-old man, Louis, has amnesia. Help him remember the important events in his life by completing his biography. Use the present perfect or the present perfect continuous for each verb in parentheses. In some sentences, either choice is correct.

Louis is an American man who (live) _____
                                                    1

in Mexico City since he was 27. He (write) _____
                                                    2

soap operas in the past, but since last year, he (act) _____
                                                    3

in a soap opera. For the past year, he (date) _____
                                                    4

5 a woman named Rosa, who is a famous writer. He (save) _____
                                                    5

money to buy her an engagement ring for the past five months. But he

(tell, not) _____ many people that he wants to marry her.
                6

B ▶ Pair work. Think about events in your life. Complete the sentences by writing about the things you have done or have been doing for many years. Discuss them with a partner.

1. Ever since I was a young child, I _____.

2. I have traveled _____.

3. I have _____ for over ten years.

4. My family has _____.

5. My _____ has _____ every day for _____ years.

104   Unit 12   Memories

ACTIVATING GRAMMAR

A ▶ Listen and write.

1. Listen to the information about a special painter. Check (✓) True or False.

	True	False
1. Franco Magnani has been painting scenes of Pontito since he was a boy.	☐	☐
2. He has been living in San Francisco for the past 60 years.	☐	☐
3. A famous scientist has written about Magnani's amazing memory.	☐	☐
4. Magnani has been considering moving back to Pontito.	☐	☐
5. His paintings are becoming more and more popular.	☐	☐

2. Imagine that you have to write an article about Magnani's story. First write three sentences about what he and others have done in the past. Then write three sentences about what he has been doing and continues to do.

What Magnani and others have done:

_____

_____

_____

What Magnani has been doing:

_____

_____

_____

B ▶ Pair work. Think about someone who has lived in your hometown for most of his or her life.

1. Write five things that this person has done in the past or has been doing.

_____

_____

_____

_____

_____

2. Now describe this person to a partner.

A ▶ Discuss. Try to remember what you did on these dates:

June 21, 1999   January 1, 2001   February 14, 2004   October 29, 2003

How much were you able to recall? What did you think about to help you remember?

B ▶ Listen. Check (✓) the sentence that gives the gist of the news report. Then explain your answer to a partner. Why are the other sentences incorrect?

a. ____ AJ is a 40-year-old woman with an amazing memory who has been thinking about writing a book.

b. ____ Researchers at University of California Irvine have been studying AJ.

c. ____ Researchers have been studying a 40-year-old woman who can remember almost every detail of her life, but they haven't been able to figure out why.

d. ____ AJ's memory has been tested many times, and the results are always incredible.

> **Skill Focus Listening for Gist**
> Remember, the gist of a listening is similar to the main idea of a reading. The gist is the most important idea in a conversation or speech. To determine the gist, listen to the details and identify their common idea.

C ▶ Listen again. Fill in the missing information.

1. For the past _____ years, scientists have been studying an extraordinary woman named AJ.

2. Researchers _____ AJ's memory many times.

3. AJ isn't good at memorizing _____ dates.

4. Even after years of study, researchers have _____ _____ to figure out how AJ has such an amazing memory.

5. Lately, AJ has been thinking about _____ a memoir about her _____.

D ▶ Pair work. Test your memory and your partner's memory.

1. Complete the sentences with your personal information. Don't let your partner see it.

1. I have been studying English for _____. I started when I was _____ years old.

2. In the past year, I have read _____ books, seen about _____ movies, gone to _____ parties, and made _____ new friends.

3. One of the most memorable events of my childhood: _____ _____

2. Tell your partner all the information you wrote. Say it in any order you wish. Don't let your partner take notes or read your sentences.

3. Ask your partner to tell you the information about you. Circle the items your partner remembered.

4. Next, show your partner your sentences for one minute, then take them away. How much additional information can your partner remember?

∩ **A** ▶ **Listen and practice.** Then practice again using the other expressions.

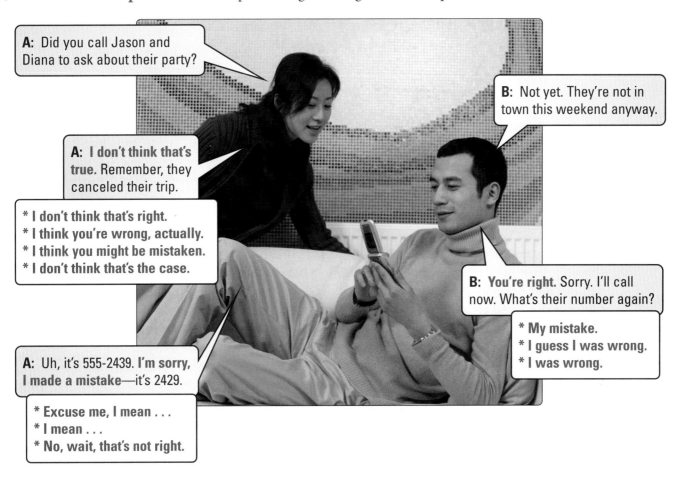

A: Did you call Jason and Diana to ask about their party?

B: Not yet. They're not in town this weekend anyway.

A: I don't think that's true. Remember, they canceled their trip.

* I don't think that's right.
* I think you're wrong, actually.
* I think you might be mistaken.
* I don't think that's the case.

B: You're right. Sorry. I'll call now. What's their number again?

* My mistake.
* I guess I was wrong.
* I was wrong.

A: Uh, it's 555-2439. **I'm sorry, I made a mistake**—it's 2429.

* Excuse me, I mean . . .
* I mean . . .
* No, wait, that's not right.

B ▶ **Pair work.** Continue these conversations with a partner. Use the expressions from Activity A to correct yourself and others, and to admit your mistakes. Then switch roles.

1. **A:** We should probably cancel the picnic. It's supposed to rain tomorrow.
   B: . . .

2. **A:** Tomorrow's exam is only going to cover vocabulary, not grammar.
   B: . . .

3. **A:** What time do we have to be at the party?
   B: . . .

C ▶ **Role-play.** With your partner, use your imagination to complete these three situations. Then role-play each of them with your partner. Be sure to correct yourself and your partner in your conversations.

1. A teacher asks a student if _____. The student admits that he/she

   hasn't _____. The teacher says, "_____."

2. Friend A asks friend B if he/she has bought a present for _____.

   Friend B says, "To be honest, I haven't. But _____."

3. A mother asks her son or daughter _____.

A ▶ Study it. Read the description.

1. What are the two main topics in the essay? (Hint: Identify the topic of each paragraph.)

2. Circle the adjectives the author uses to describe his experiences and his world.

3. Underline the information about the emotions the author has had in the past year.

Skill Focus

Descriptive Writing about Personal Experiences

Good descriptive writing about personal experiences includes these elements:

1. details about a person's accomplishments and experiences
2. information or adjectives that tell how something looks, sounds, smells, tastes, or feels
3. information about emotions (how a person feels)

A Memorable Year

This past year has been very memorable. There were many moments that were challenging and difficult. First, all of my college courses have been really hard to get through. Then right before my midterm exams, I broke my left leg. I was in a lot of pain so I couldn't concentrate on studying. And because I had to wear a big, heavy cast for two months, I had to quit my job as a waiter at a small Italian restaurant. I was a little depressed. Then there was a huge fire in my apartment building, and all my furniture and clothes have smelled like smoke ever since. It made me so sad. Finally, a new neighbor moved in about six months ago, and she's been playing her rock music so loudly, that I can barely sleep at night. It's been so frustrating for me.

But many good things have happened in the past year, too. I've made a lot of interesting friends at college, like Becky. She's a really tall basketball player with a great sense of humor. And my friend Todd has been teaching me how to cook, so now I can make delicious food, like French onion soup. I've also learned to drive, so I've been taking weekend trips to the mountains with my friends. I like to go hiking and smell the pine trees. Last time we went hiking, I sat on a big rock and thought about all the amazing things that I've done in the past year. It made me really happy.

B ▶ Write it. Write two paragraphs describing your past year. In paragraph 1, describe difficulties and challenges. In paragraph 2, describe positive experiences.

1. First, generate ideas. For each paragraph, make notes about the experiences in the chart.

	Experiences and accomplishments	Feelings	Looks, sounds, smells, tastes, textures
Paragraph 1 (difficulties/challenges)			
Paragraph 2 (positive experiences)			

2. Write your paragraphs. Write about your experiences and accomplishments in the past year. Tell how you felt about them.

3. Edit your paragraphs.
   - Do you use adjectives to describe your experiences, accomplishments, and feelings?
   - Do you provide details about your experiences?

PUTTING IT TOGETHER Do you remember?

A ▶ Read.

1. What kind of job does Tracy Baird want to get at Ratcliff Pharmaceuticals?

> Dear Sir or Madam:
>
> I recently graduated from Ohio State University with a master's degree in neuroscience. I have always wanted to work in Ratcliff Pharmaceuticals' Memory Research Lab, and if you have any job openings, I would like to be considered.
>
> 5   I have been studying human memory for six years, and I would like to find a research position in this field. I am very interested in researching drugs that improve people's memory. I strongly believe that even our worst memories can help us learn from our past and become better people. Bad memories often teach us crucial lessons and help us to appreciate the good things in our lives. This belief in the importance of memory is what makes me want to work in your Memory Research Lab. Recently, I read that you are developing a memory drug called Memora. I do not yet
> 10 know a lot about it, but I feel that I would be a fine addition to the Memora research team.
>
> Enclosed please find my résumé. I look forward to speaking with you about opportunities with your company.
>
> Sincerely yours,
> *Tracy Baird*
> Tracy Baird

2. Checkpoint. Answer these questions.

    1. What has Tracy Baird been studying for six years? _____

    2. What does Tracy Baird think our worst memories can do? _____

    3. What job does Tracy Baird think she would be good for? _____

B ▶ Listen.

1. Listen to learn about Ratcliff Pharmaceuticals' new drug. Who is talking about the drug? Circle a, b, c, d, or e.

    a. a professor   b. a news reporter   c. a police officer   d. a scientist   e. a student

2. Checkpoint. Answer these questions.

    1. What drug have the scientists at Ratcliff Pharmaceuticals' Memory Research Lab just announced? _____ What can the drug do? _____

    2. Who does Ratcliff Pharmaceuticals think this drug can help? _____

    _____

    3. What does Ratcliff Pharmaceuticals plan on doing within the next week?

    _____

C ▶ Wrap it up.

1. (TOEFL® iBT) Based on what Tracy Baird wrote in her letter, you can infer what she will think of Memora. Will she think it's a good idea or a bad idea? Tell why.

2. Do you think a drug like Memora could be useful? Explain why.

3. What are some things people do to try to forget bad memories? What are some things people do to try to remember good memories?

Expansion Units 10–12

A ▶ **Warm up.** Read the descriptions of types of university classes. Label the photos according to the descriptions. With a partner, ask and answer questions about the descriptions and the photos.

Example: A: Have you ever attended a lecture class? **B:** No, I haven't. What about you?

  a. **Lecture class:** In a lecture class, the professor gives an instructional speech in a large classroom or auditorium. There can be 50–200 students in a lecture class.
  b. **Seminar:** A seminar is a small class, often with fewer than 20 students. It usually focuses on a very specific topic.
  c. **Lab class:** A lab (short for laboratory) class is usually held in a laboratory. Students set up and study experiments in courses such as biology, chemistry, or psychology.
  d. **Online course:** In an online course, a student studies independently. The course materials, worksheets, and tests are all online.
  e. **Webcast:** A webcast is a video of a lecture that was given by a professor. Students use the Internet to watch the lecture on a computer.
  f. **Tutorial:** A type of study session, often led by a graduate student.

1. _____

2. _____

3. _____

4. _____

B ▶ **Listen.** Which sentence gives the clearest gist, or main idea? Circle a, b, or c. Discuss your answer with a partner and say why the other sentences are incorrect.

  a. Crystal hasn't attended a lecture since the first week of class because the lecture hall was too crowded, but Nick usually goes to the lectures.
  b. Nick has gotten behind in Econ 101, and Crystal says that he should watch a webcast of the lectures or go to the tutorial.
  c. Nick has missed two lectures because he was sick with the flu, so Crystal offers to help him download the webcast and says he should go to the tutorial on Wednesday nights.

C ▶ **Discuss.** Read the phrases and their definitions in the box. Then discuss the questions with classmates or a partner.

> **get behind:** be late in completing assignments or commitments
> **catch up:** complete assignments or work that was due in the past
> **miss a class:** not attend a class

1. Have you ever gotten behind in a class? What did you do to catch up?

2. How often do you miss a class because of sickness? How often do you miss a class for other reasons? What do you do when you miss a class?

3. Have you ever been in a class with too many or too few students? Describe it.

D ▶ **Listen again.** Look at the problems and solutions in the box. Write them in the correct column in the chart.

> could go to the tutorial   doesn't know how to download the webcast
> could learn how to download the webcast   is behind in class
> could never find a seat   watches the webcast

Person	Problem(s)	Solution(s) / Possible solution(s)
Crystal	1.	a.
Nick	1.	a.
	2.	b.

E ▶ **Interview.** Interview three classmates and complete the chart. Then discuss what you learned from your classmates. Did anything surprise you?

	Student 1: _____	Student 2: _____	Student 3: _____
1. What is the best class you have taken?			
2. What type of class was it?			
3. How many people were in the class?			
4. Why did you like the class?			

A ▶ Vocabulary boost! For each bold word below, choose the best definition. If you are not sure, make a decision based on the context.

1. The new students will **equip** their dorm room with a refrigerator and microwave.
    a. to buy on sale   b.   provide with needed things   c.   rent for a semester

2. The politician was very skilled at **getting** his points **across** to the audience. They always understood what his opinion was.
    a. convincing   b.   communicating c.   listening

3. Student drinking is a **grave** problem on college campuses. The administration is holding meetings with students and campus police to find solutions.
    a. very serious   b.   deadly c.   very common

4. I am **considering** studying in Spain next year, but I haven't decided yet.
    a. planning b.   worried about c.   thinking about

5. The number of students majoring in English literature is expected to **drop** in the coming years because more students are majoring in information technology.
    a. decrease b.   withdraw   c.   increase

6. Given the choice, I would **opt** to attend an early morning class. I like to get up early.
    a. prefer   b.   decline c.   not like

7. Usually, **undergraduates** are required to live in dormitories on the college campus.
    a. students taking online courses
    b. high school students
    c. students studying for a college degree

B ▶ Read. Read the opinion letter written to a college newspaper by a professor. Then read it again and underline the vocabulary from Activity A.

Dear Campus Beat:

    The administration is currently considering spending $800,000 to equip all of our lecture halls with new technology. This new technology will allow the university to film all lectures and then put them online as webcasts. In my
5 opinion, based on 20 years of teaching undergraduates, this plan would be a grave mistake.

    Having all lectures available as webcasts will result in many problems. First of all, I know that lecture attendance will drop. Students will opt to watch a lecture on their computers in the dorm rather than come to class. As a student,
10 how would you feel if you walked into a nearly empty lecture hall, knowing that most of your classmates were sleeping rather than attending class? Secondly, I believe that attending class and taking notes during a lecture are the best ways to truly learn the material. Finally, as a professor, I depend on students' questions and comments after a lecture to help me see how well
15 I am getting my points across.

    I prefer to be a real teacher, not a video star who must spend precious time on the production of a webcast.

                 Professor Rachel Evans, Math Department

C ▶ Discuss. Answer these questions. Then discusss them with a partner.

1. What are the three reasons Professor Evans gives for not wanting lectures to be filmed?

_____

2. Do you agree or disagree with the opinions stated in the letter? Explain your answers.

_____

3. Would you prefer to attend a lecture in a classroom or see it on a webcast? Why?

_____

D ▶ Read again. Write the answers to these questions.

1. In this opinion letter, what facts does Professor Evans provide? _____

_____

2. Underline the verbs she uses for expressing her opinion.

3. What kinds of facts could she include to make her letter stronger? _____

_____

E ▶ Write about it. Write a letter to the newspaper. Respond to Professor Evans' letter.

1. Organize your ideas. Use the model below to make a mind map on a separate sheet of paper.
   - Start with a brief summary of the professor's letter (one or two sentences).
   - Include your own opinion: Do you agree or disagree with the professor?
   - Give reasons for your opinion. You may agree or disagree with her points.
   - Support each of your reasons with examples and facts. Your facts can be based on personal experience (for example, *I learn best if I am by myself.*).

   Summary: _____

   _____

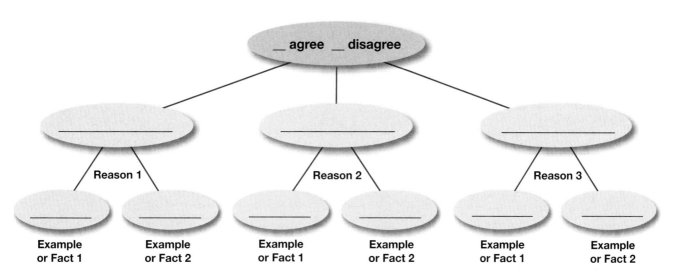

2. Write a first draft and share it with a classmate. Discuss how you can improve your letter.

3. Edit your paragraph.
   - Do you start with a summary of the professor's letter and your opinion?
   - Do you give reasons for your opinion?
   - Do you support your reasons with examples and facts?

VOCABULARY EXPANSION ACTIVITIES

UNIT 1 Identifying Word Forms

A ▶ Multiple choice. Circle the letter of the correct form of the word to complete the sentence.

1. People think that John isn't intelligent, but that's a _____.
   a. misconception
   b. misconceived
   c. misconceive

2. Harry _____ that Martin was a doctor because he was wearing a white coat.
   a. presumption
   b. presumed
   c. presume

3. People who make judgments of other people in two seconds are _____.
   a. superficiality
   b. superficial
   c. superficially

4. First impressions of people are often very _____.
   a. accuracy
   b. accurate
   c. accurately

5. When I met her, I _____ that she was an athlete because of her powerful handshake.
   a. assumption
   b. assume
   c. assumed

6. You should never _____ a person too quickly.
   a. judgment
   b. judge
   c. judgmental

7. His presentation about environmental problems was very _____.
   a. impression
   b. impressed
   c. impressive

8. His _____ made a bad first impression because his clothes were dirty.
   a. appearance
   b. appeared
   c. apparent

A ▶ Practice. Write as many synonyms as you can for each word below. Use a dictionary if necessary.

1. unique _____ _____ _____

2. journey _____ _____ _____

3. fan _____ _____ _____

4. donation _____ _____ _____

B ▶ Adjectives ending in -*ing* and -*ed*. Circle the correct word in parentheses.

1. The professor's lecture was (boring / bored). The students felt (boring / bored).

2. My friends were (exciting / excited) because the movie was (exciting / excited).

3. The story had a (surprising / surprised) ending, so my son was very (surprising / surprised).

4. Our vacation was very (relaxing / relaxed). We all felt very (relaxing / relaxed).

5. I was (annoying / annoyed) because I received an (annoying / annoyed) phone call.

C ▶ Pair work. Write answers to these questions. Then discuss them with a partner.

1. Describe a voyage that you made. _____

_____

_____

2. Are you a fan of any sports teams? Which ones? _____

_____

_____

3. What city do you think is unique? Why? _____

_____

_____

4. What contributions have you made in your life? _____

_____

_____

A ▶ Phrasal verbs. Complete the sentences with an appropriate preposition or adverb.

1. My friend Harry never calls me anymore. I'm ready to give up _____ him!

2. Don't let your friend bully you. When you have something to say, speak _____.

3. She is so insulting. She is always putting me _____.

4. I made plans with Mary, but she didn't show up. She really let me _____.

5. We used to really like each other, but now we don't get _____.

6. My old friend Martin drank too much and lost his job. I hate to see him mess _____ like that.

7. I used to hang _____ with Sherry, but after she got married, she stopped calling.

8. Sometimes friends grow _____ after major life events.

B ▶ Pair work. Write answers to these questions. Then discuss them with a partner.

1. Give an example of a time when you gave up on a friend. _____
_____
_____

2. Do you ever need to speak up more? _____
_____
_____

3. Do any of your friends put you down? Give an example. _____
_____
_____

4. Who do you get along with very well? _____
_____
_____

5. When did you last mess up? _____
_____
_____

6. Have you and any of your friends grown apart? _____
_____
_____

EXPANSION UNITS 1–3 Reality Shows

A ▶ Practice. Complete the letter with words from the word box. Then compare your answers with a partner.

alter	come up with	redecorated
catch on	instant	script

Dear Aunt Agnes,

I hope that you're doing well. Mom said that you had a cold, but that you were better now. She also said that you _____ your house. How is your new kitchen?
₁

Now that I'm out of college, life is a little complex. I'm still trying to decide what to do. I'm very impatient in my job search. I want _____ results! I need to _____ some creative ideas for interesting jobs.
₂ ₃

I'm still acting part time. I just read a really good _____ for a TV show. It's a new show, so it's not popular yet. I hope that it will _____. I'm going to try for the role of a waitress. I would have to _____ my appearance a little bit. The waitress has blond hair, but mine is brown. My friends want me to go on a reality show instead, but I'm not sure.

Well, I'll talk to you soon!

Love, Tammy

B ▶ Write. Write a letter to a friend or relative. Use at least four of the six words from Activity A. Read your letter to a partner. Your partner should circle the word in the box when they hear it in your letter.

_____
_____
_____
_____
_____
_____
_____
_____
_____
_____
_____

UNIT 4   Identifying Positive and Negative Connotations

A ▶ **Practice.** Read each statement. Then check (✓) whether the sentence is true or false for you.

	True	False
1. People in my country are often **pressed for time**.	☐	☐
2. Studying English is **refreshing**.	☐	☐
3. I don't have many schedule **conflicts** in my life.	☐	☐
4. I am often **running behind**.	☐	☐
5. People in this school are always **rushing around**.	☐	☐
6. I sometimes feel **overwhelmed**.	☐	☐
7. I have a good **balance** of work and fun in my life.	☐	☐
8. I am able to **take time off** several times a year.	☐	☐

B ▶ **Pair work.** Compare your answers from Activity A with a partner. Then identify which bold phrases have a positive connotation and which have a negative connotation. Write the phrases in the correct place in the T-chart below.

Positive Connotation	Negative Connotation

A ▶ **Crossword puzzle.** Complete the crossword. It includes vocabulary words from Unit 5 and from other units.

ACROSS

1. far from cities or people
3. equipment or food
6. improved the appearance of a room or house because of painting, buying new furniture, etc.
8. a large rock
10. not die; continue to live
11. made by humans; not natural
13. a written text that tells people what to say

DOWN

2. unable to move
4. change
5. fight against something or someone
7. become popular
9. free yourself from a trap or problem
12. immediate; very quick

A ▶ Rewrite. Rewrite the sentences so that the phrasal verbs in bold are separated.

  1. I love to **show off** my doll collection.

    _____

  2. I **gave up** smoking.

    _____

  3. That store **ripped off** my brother!

    _____

  4. I had to **kick out** my roommate because he didn't pay the rent.

    _____

B ▶ Multiple choice. Circle the letter of the expression that has the same meaning as the underlined words.

  1. Sam is <u>not buying</u> luxury items.
    a. showing off
    b. doing without
    c. saving up for

  2. The store <u>doesn't have any more TVs in stock</u>.
    a. is sold out of TVs
    b. saved up for TVs
    c. rips off the TVs

  3. I'm <u>not</u> eating in restaurants <u>as much as I used to</u>.
    a. giving up
    b. getting rid of
    c. cutting back on

  4. I'm either <u>throwing out or giving away</u> a lot of my stuff.
    a. getting rid of
    b. kicking out
    c. saving up for

A ▶ Practice. Complete the story with expressions from the box. Then compare your answers with a partner.

hit the jackpot	set up	turns out
put it to good use	showed up	went broke

Last month, at the Grand Bonanza Casino in Las Vegas, there was an amazing story of good luck. Martin Lewis, of San Jose, California, won $100,000 in three days. He really _____! He

_____ at the casino at noon on Tuesday and kept playing through Thursday night.

Martin's luck changed from good, to bad, to good again. At one point, he almost _____. He

only had $100 left, but he continued to gamble. His luck changed and he started to win again.

Talking about the money, Martin says that he will _____. He intends to

_____ a charity for sick children. We will continue to follow this story. We'll tell you

how it _____ .

B ▶ Group discussion. Write answers to these questions. Then discuss them in small groups.

1. Name three ways that people can hit the jackpot. _____

_____

_____

_____

2. How can your school or city improve? What is something you think your school or city should set up? Why?

_____

_____

_____

3. What are some things that people could put to better use? _____

_____

_____

_____

4. Name at least five things that might cause people to go broke. _____

_____

_____

_____

A ▶ Practice. Complete the sentences with phrases from the word box. Then check (✓) whether the sentence is true or false for you.

the fence	call off	last minute	my mind
cold feet	eye-to-eye	the knot	the road

	True	False
1. I have tied _____.	☐	☐
2. My parents and I usually see _____.	☐	☐
3. When my friends are making a decision, I am usually on _____.	☐	☐
4. When my friends want to do something dangerous, like skydiving, I always get _____.	☐	☐
5. I often make decisions at the _____.	☐	☐
6. When I was choosing a language school, it was difficult for me to make up _____.	☐	☐
7. I know someone who had to _____ a wedding and return all of the gifts.	☐	☐
8. In my opinion, canceling a wedding is better than getting a divorce down _____.	☐	☐

B ▶ Pair work. Write about each of your answers in Activity A. Then discuss them with a partner. If a statement is true for you, offer more information.

Example: I often make decisions at the last minute. I don't like to make decisions.

If a statement is false for you, change it to a true statement and give more information.

Example: I haven't tied the knot. I'm too young to get married!

1. _____
2. _____
3. _____
4. _____
5. _____
6. _____
7. _____
8. _____

A ▸ Compound words. For each compound word, put a check (✓) next to the correct form.

1. _____ adventure-tour   _____ adventure tour
2. _____ amusement-parks   _____ amusement parks
3. _____ extreme-sports   _____ extreme sports
4. _____ leisure-time activities   _____ leisuretime activities
5. _____ risk-takers   _____ risk takers
6. _____ risk-tolerance   _____ risk tolerance
7. _____ safety-equipment   _____ safety equipment
8. _____ thrill-seeker   _____ thrillseeker

B ▸ Group discussion. Complete the statements with a word from Activity A. Then check (✓) whether you agree or disagree with each statement. Write an example to support your opinion. Discuss your opinions in small groups.

1. I enjoy taking risks. I am a _____.

   _____ I agree

   _____ I disagree

   _____

2. Carrying _____, like ropes and tools, makes hiking less enjoyable.

   _____ I agree

   _____ I disagree

   Example: _____

3. I would really love to take an _____. I love visiting unusual places.

   _____ I agree

   _____ I disagree

   Example: _____

4. I enjoy watching _____. I think danger and risk in sports are exciting!

   _____ I agree

   _____ I disagree

   Example: _____

5. Roller coasters are great! I love going to _____.

   _____ I agree

   _____ I disagree

   Example: _____

A ▶ Practice. Find the words in the box that are synonyms. Write each group of synonyms in a circle. Some circles will have more words than others.

achieve	barrier	goal	obstacle
ambition	coach	looks	problem
appearance	complete change	makeover	realize
aspiration	desire	mentor	try out for
audition	dream	motivation	tutor

1.

5.

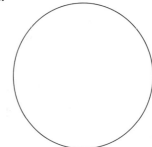

2.

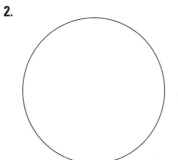

6.

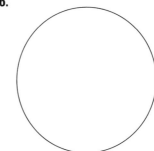

3.

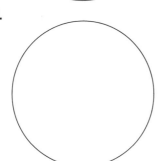

7.

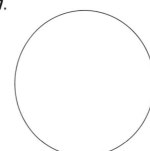

4.

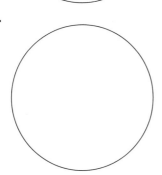

8.

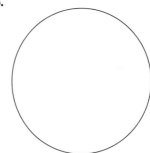

A ▶ Practice. Complete the paragraph with words from the box.

environment	interaction	factors	long-standing
genetic	traits	influences	

The "nature versus nurture" argument is very old. It is part of a _____ scientific

debate. Scientists generally agree that physical _____, such as hair color and eye color,

are clearly _____ (nature), that is, they are inherited from the mother and the father.

Other qualities, such as personality and intelligence are more difficult to explain. There are two possibilities

discussed in the debate. The first is that a person's _____ (nurture), school, culture,

family, and religion, has a very strong or even controlling influence. Others believe that nature

_____ these qualities more strongly. It may be that both _____, nature

and nurture, are important in understanding intelligence and personality. Many scientists now believe that it

is the _____ between the two of them that controls human behavior.

B ▶ Pair work. Compare your answers with a partner.

A ▸ Multiple choice.   Circle the letter of the correct form of the word to complete each sentence.

1. Mary wrote a long answer to his question on that message _____.
   a. server   b. chat room   c. board

2. Harry sent me a _____ on his cell phone.
   a. text message   b. link   c. server

3. The website gets over 10,000 _____ every day! It's really popular.
   a. post   b. hits   c. text message

4. Our website has 15 _____ to other sites.
   a. links   b. servers   c. posts

5. You should go to that blog. The writer _____ a new article about an hour ago.
   a. browsed   b. linked   c. posted

6. I spend about two hours a day _____ the Internet.
   a. browsing   b. posting   c. linking

7. My sister loves _____. She just goes in and talks to different people.
   a. servers   b. hits   c. chat rooms

8. You can't get to my company's website today. The _____ is down.
   a. text message   b. link   c. server

B ▸ Pair work. Ask your partner the questions. Write his or her answers.

1. How many hours per week do you spend browsing the Internet? _____
   _____
   _____

2. Have you ever posted a message on a message board? What happened? _____
   _____
   _____

3. What are some advantages to joining a chat room? _____
   _____
   _____

4. What are some advantages to sending text messages? What are some disadvantages? _____
   _____
   _____

5. Do you read any blogs? If so, what are they? If not, why not? _____
   _____
   _____

A ▶ Practice. Circle the correct word in parentheses to complete each sentence. Then check (✓) whether the statement is true or false for you. Write an example to support your opinion.

1. I try to avoid discussing (controversy / controversial) topics because they just cause bad feelings.
   _____ true
   _____ false

   Example: _____

2. I am very unhappy if I have an (argue / argument / argumentative) with my friends.
   _____ true
   _____ false

   Example: _____

3. I (believe / belief / believable) that logging companies are cutting down too many trees.
   _____ true
   _____ false

   Example: _____

4. I agree with (protest / protesters / protests) against increasing tuition.
   _____ true
   _____ false

   Example: _____

5. I often (oppose / opposition / opposite) the actions of my government.
   _____ true
   _____ false

   Example: _____

6. I (refuse / refusal) to get involved in politics.
   _____ true
   _____ false

   Example: _____

7. I am a (support / supporter / supportive) of increased government money for cancer research.
   _____ true
   _____ false

   Example: _____

8. I feel that there are many (urge / urgent) problems in the world.
   _____ true
   _____ false

   Example: _____

B ▶ Pair work. Discuss your answers from Activity A with a partner.

A ▶ Crossword puzzle. Complete the crossword. It includes vocabulary words from Unit 12 and from other units.

ACROSS

1. object to something that you think is wrong
2. heal; stop a disease or sickness
6. feel that something is true
7. the state of someone's health
9. look at carefully
10. reject; say no to something
11. use logic to formally oppose an idea
12. a book about a person's life
13. remember

DOWN

1. not temporary; continuing forever
3. causing argument or disagreement
4. identify something or someone that you have seen before
5. typed words sent from one cell phone to another: text _____
6. visit many websites
8. (two words) find a way to manage or accept something; cope

A ▶ Practice. Complete the sentences with words from the box.

consider	grave	drop	opt
equip	undergraduates	get across	

1. The college is going to _____ the classrooms with the newest technology.

2. That teacher has an excellent ability to _____ his points.

3. The rise in tuition is a _____ problem for our students.

4. There has been a _____ in enrollment at our college. We really need more students!

5. The college administration should _____ spending more money on sports facilities. For example, we need a new gym.

6. I have been teaching _____ at a college near my home for 20 years.

7. We have two choices: borrowing money or closing the school. If we _____ to borrow money, the students can continue their studies.

B ▶ Pair work. Write answers to these questions. Then discuss them with a partner.

1. Should your school consider reducing its tuition? _____

_____

2. In your country, do undergraduate students sometimes have to live in dormitories? _____

_____

3. Has college enrollment dropped in your country in the last few years? _____

_____

4. Given the choice, would you opt to avoid an early morning class? _____

_____

5. Are you able to get your points across when you are speaking to a group? _____

_____

6. Has your school equipped its classrooms with new technology? _____

_____

7. What is a grave problem at your school or in your city? _____

_____

GRAMMAR REFERENCE

UNIT 1

A ▶ The Simple Present

Affirmative Statements

I	play	
You	play	
He	plays	
She	plays	music.
It	plays	
We	play	
You	play	
They	play	

Negative Statements

I	don't play	
You	don't play	
He	doesn't play	
She	doesn't play	music.
It	doesn't play	
We	don't play	
You	don't play	
They	don't play	

Yes-No Questions

Do	I		
Do	you		
Does	he		
Does	she	play	music?
Does	it		
Do	we		
Do	you		
Do	they		

Wh-Questions

What does he study?
Where do you go on Saturday?
What kind of movies do you like?
Why do you watch horror movies?
Who teaches you English?
When do we leave?
What time does the bus come?

B ▶ The Present Continuous

Affirmative Statements

I	am working.
You	are working.
He	is working.
She	is working.
It	is working.
We	are working.
You	are working.
They	are working.

Negative Statements

I	am not working.
You	aren't working.
He	isn't working.
She	isn't working.
It	isn't working.
We	aren't working.
You	aren't working.
They	aren't working.

Yes-No Questions		
Am	I	
Are	you	
Is	he	
Is	she	working?
Is	it	
Are	we	
Are	you	
Are	they	

Wh-Questions		
When	am I	
Where	are you	
Why	is he	
How	is she	working?
What time	are we	
How much	are you	
How often	are they	

A ▶ The Simple Past

Affirmative Statements		
I		
You		
He		
She	worked	yesterday.
It		
We		
You		
They		

Negative Statements		
I		
You		
He		
She	didn't work	yesterday.
It		
We		
You		
They		

Yes-No Questions			
	I		
	you		
	he		
Did	she	work	yesterday?
	it		
	we		
	you		
	they		

Wh-Questions			
What		I	do yesterday?
Where		you	work?
When		he	work?
How	did	she	work yesterday?
Why		we	work yesterday?
What time		you	work yesterday?
How much		they	work yesterday?

B ▶ Irregular Verbs—Simple Past Forms and Past Participles

Base Form	Simple Past	Past Participle	Base Form	Simple Past	Past Participle
be	was/were	been	keep	kept	kept
become	became	become	know	knew	known
begin	began	begun	leave	left	left
bleed	bled	bled	lend	lent	lent
break	broke	broken	lose	lost	lost
bring	brought	brought	make	made	made
buy	bought	bought	meet	met	met
choose	chose	chosen	pay	paid	paid
come	came	come	put	put	put
cost	cost	cost	read	read	read
cut	cut	cut	ring	rang	rung
do	did	done	run	ran	run
drink	drank	drunk	see	saw	seen
drive	drove	driven	sell	sold	sold
eat	ate	eaten	send	sent	sent
fall	fell	fallen	set	set	set
feel	felt	felt	shake	shook	shaken
fight	fought	fought	shut	shut	shut
find	found	found	sleep	slept	slept
forget	forgot	forgot	speak	spoke	spoken
fry	fried	fried	speed	sped	sped
get	got	gotten	spend	spent	spent
give	gave	given	take	took	taken
go	went	gone	teach	taught	taught
grow	grew	grown	tell	told	told
have/has	had	had	think	thought	thought
hear	heard	heard	wear	wore	worn
hold	held	held	write	wrote	written
hurt	hurt	hurt			

UNIT 4

A ▶ *Be Going to*

I	am going to			I	am not going to	
You	are going to			You	aren't going to	
He	is going to			He	isn't going to	
She	is going to	leave tomorrow.		She	isn't going to	be here tomorrow.
It	is going to			It	isn't going to	
We	are going to			We	aren't going to	
You	are going to			You	aren't going to	
They	are going to			They	aren't going to	

B ▶ *Will*

I				I		
You				You		
He				He		
She	will	go now.		She	won't	go now.
It				It		
We				We		
You				You		
They				They		

UNIT 6

A ▶ The Future Real Conditional (1st Conditional)

	I	arrive early,		I	
	you	arrive early,		you	
	he	arrives early,		he	
	she	arrives early,		she	
If	it	arrives early,		it	will send a message.
	we	arrive early,		we	
	you	arrive early,		you	
	they	arrive early,		they	

I			I arrive early.
You			you arrive early.
He			he arrives early.
She			she arrives early.
It	will send a message	if	it arrives early.
We			we arrive early.
You			you arrive early.
They			they arrive early.

UNIT 7

A ▸ The Past Continuous

Affirmative Statements

I	was working.
You	were working.
He	was working.
She	was working.
It	was working.
We	were working.
You	were working.
They	were working.

Negative Statements

I	was not working.
You	weren't working.
He	wasn't working.
She	wasn't working.
It	wasn't working.
We	weren't working.
You	weren't working.
They	weren't working.

Yes-No Questions

Was	I	
Were	you	
Was	he	
Was	she	working?
Was	it	
Were	we	
Were	you	
Were	they	

Wh-Questions

When	was I	
Where	were you	
Why	was he	
How	was she	working?
What time		
How much		
How often		

UNIT 9

A ▶ The Present Unreal Conditional (2nd Conditional)

If	I you he she it we you they	arrived early,	I you he she it we you they	would send a message.

I You He She It We You They	would send a message	if	I you he she it we you they	arrived early.

UNIT 10

A ▶ Passive Verb Forms in the Present, Past, and Future

Affirmative Statements				Negative Statements		
The message The messages	is are	written.		The message The messages	isn't aren't	written.
The message The messages	was were	read.		The message The messages	wasn't weren't	read.
The reply The replies	will	be sent.		The reply The replies	won't	be sent.

The Present Perfect

Affirmative Statements		
I	have	
You	have	
He	has	
She	has	studied here for 3 hours.
It	has	studied here since 2007.
We	have	
You	have	
They	have	

Negative Statements		
I	have not	
You	have not	
He	has not	
She	has not	left yet.
It	has not	
We	have not	
You	have not	
They	have not	

Yes-No Questions		
Have	I	
Have	you	
Has	he	
Has	she	finished the test yet?
Has	it	
Have	we	
Have	you	
Have	they	

Wh-Questions			
Who	has		accepted the invitation?
What	have	I	done?
Where	have	you	worked?
When	has	he	called?
Why	have	we	come to this party?
How much	have	you	studied this week?
How much	have	they	paid?

The Present Perfect Continuous

Affirmative Statements			
I	have		
You	have		
He	has		
She	has		
It	has	been	living here since 2005.
We	have		
You	have		
They	have		

Negative Statements

I	have not		
You	have not		
He	has not		
She	has not	been	living here very long.
It	has not		
We	have not		
You	have not		
They	have not		

Yes-No Questions

Have	I		
Have	you		
Has	he		
Has	she	been	studying English for ten years?
Has	it		
Have	we		
Have	you		
Have	they		

Wh-Questions

What	have	I		doing?
Where	have	you		working?
Who	have	you		working with?
When	has	he	been	calling?
How	has	she		sleeping?
How much	have	you		studying?
How much	have	they		paying?

VOCABULARY SUMMARY

Unit 1

accurate *(adj)*
appear *(v)*
assumption *(n)*
impression *(n)*
judgment *(n)*
misconception *(n)*
presume *(v)*
superficial *(adj)*

Unit 2

contribution *(n)*
donation *(n)*
fan *(n)*
journey *(n)*
original *(adj)*
supporter *(n)*
travels *(n)*
trip *(n)*
unique *(adj)*
voyage *(n)*

Unit 3

get along *(phrasal verb)*
give up on (someone/something) *(phrasal verb)*
grow apart *(phrasal verb)*
hang out *(phrasal verb)*
let (someone) down *(phrasal verb)*
mess up *(phrasal verb)*
put (someone) down *(phrasal verb)*
speak up *(phrasal verb)*

Expansion Units 1–3

alter *(v)*
catch on *(phrasal verb)*
come up with *(phrasal verb)*
instant *(adj)*
redecorate *(v)*
script *(n)*

Unit 4

balance *(v)*
conflict *(n)*
overwhelmed *(adj)*
pressed for time *(adj phrase)*
refreshing *(adj)*
running behind *(v phrase)*
rushing *(v)*
take time off *(v phrase)*

Unit 5

artificial *(adj)*
boulder *(n)*
escape *(v)*
remote *(adj)*
struggle *(v)*
supplies *(n)*
survive *(v)*
trapped *(adj)*

Unit 6

cut back on *(phrasal verb)*
do without *(phrasal verb)*
get rid of *(phrasal verb)*
give up *(phrasal verb)*
kick out *(phrasal verb)*
rip off *(phrasal verb)*
save up for *(phrasal verb)*
sell out of *(phrasal verb)*
show off *(phrasal verb)*
wind up *(phrasal verb)*

Expansion Units 4–6

go broke *(expression)*
hit the jackpot *(expression)*
put to good use *(expression)*
set up *(phrasal verb)*
show up *(phrasal verb)*
turn out *(phrasal verb)*

Unit 7

at the last minute *(expression)*
be on the fence *(expression)*
call off *(phrasal verb)*
down the road *(expression)*
get cold feet *(expression)*
make up your mind *(expression)*
see eye-to-eye *(expression)*
tie the knot *(expression)*

Unit 8

adventure tour *(n phrase)*
amusement park *(n phrase)*
extreme sport *(n phrase)*
leisure-time activity *(n phrase)*
risk tolerance *(n phrase)*
risk-taker *(n phrase)*
safety equipment *(n phrase)*
thrill-seeker *(n phrase)*

Unit 9

achieve *(v)*
ambition *(n)*
appearance *(n)*
audition *(v)*
makeover *(n)*
mentor *(n)*
motivation *(n)*
obstacle *(n)*

Expansion Units 7–9

environment *(n)*
factor *(n)*
genetic *(adj)*
influence *(v)*
interaction *(n)*
long-standing *(adj)*
trait *(n)*

Unit 10

board *(n)*
browse *(v)*
chat room *(n phrase)*
hit (on a Web site) *(n)*
link *(n)*
post (a message) *(v)*
server *(n)*
text message *(n phrase)*

Unit 11

argue *(v)*
believe *(v)*
controversial *(adj)*
oppose *(v)*
protest *(v)*
refuse *(v)*
support *(v)*
urge *(v)*

Unit 12

condition *(n)*
cure *(v)*
deal with *(phrasal verb)*
examine *(v)*
memoir *(n)*
permanent *(adj)*
recall *(v)*
recognize *(v)*

Expansion Units 10–12

consider *(v)*
drop *(v)*
equip *(v)*
get across (a point) *(phrasal verb)*
grave *(adj)*
opt *(v)*
undergraduate *(n)*

SKILLS INDEX

Page 2 (left): © Aura/Getty Images; 2 (middle): © Patrik Giardino/CORBIS; 2 (right): © PhotoDisc/Getty Images; 3: © Bluemoon Stock/photolibrary; 4: © Tim Kiusalaas/ CORBIS; 5 (top left): © Image Source/CORBIS; 5 (top right & bottom left): © Brand X Pictures/Jupiter Images; 5 (bottom right): © Image Source/SuperStock; 6 (left): © Renaud Visage/age footstock; 6 (right): © Elton McFall/age fotostock; 7: © image100/PunchStock; 8: © Peter Miller/Getty Images; 9: © Bryn Lennon/Getty Images; 10: © Winter; 12: © A. Ramey/PhotoEdit; 13 (top): © Hugh Lansdown/Alamy; 13 (bottom): © Emmanuel Faure/Getty Images; 14 (from left to right): © Alden Pellett/The Image Works, © Brand X Pictures/PunchStock, © Relax Image/JupiterImages, © Rex Butcher/Getty Images; 15: © Stewart Cohen/Blend Images/CORBIS; 16: © José Fuste Raga/zefa/CORBIS; 17: © Pedro Coll/age fotostock; 18: © ColorBlind Images/Blend Images/CORBIS; 19: © Comstock Images/age fotostock; 20: © Bob Daemmrich/The Image Works; 21: © Image Source/CORBIS; 22 (left): © Directphoto.org/Alamy; 22 (middle): © Jose Luis Pelaez Inc/Robertstock.com; 22 (right): © Masterfile Royalty Free; 23: © Digital Vision/ SuperStock; 24: © James Marshall/The Image Works; 25: © Roger Bamber/Alamy; 26 (top left): © It Stock Free/age fotostock; 26 (top middle): © Flint/CORBIS; 26 (top right): © Chase Jarvis/age fotostock; 26 (bottom left): © Uli Wiesmeier/zefa/CORBIS; 26 (bottom middle): © Francis Dean/Dean Pictures/The Image Works; 26 (bottom right): © Thomas Michael Corcoran/PhotoEdit; 28: © Kevin Winter/Getty Images; 30: © Tom Mareschal/Getty Images; 31: © Javier Pierini/Getty Images; 32: © Dynamic Graphics/ JupiterImages; 33: © Stoneimages/age fotostock; 34 (left): © Rick Rusing/Getty Images; 34 (right): © Stephen Matera/Alamy35: © George Shelley/age fotostock; 36 (top): © Photolibrary/Alamy; 36 (bottom left): © Tongro Image Stock/age footstock; 36 (bottom right): © Royalty-Free/CORBIS; 37: © Glenn Sapadin; 38 (from left to right): © The McGraw-Hill Companies, Inc./Jacques Cornell photographer, © David Young-Wolff/ PhotoEdit, © Hemera Technologies/Alamy, © Brand X Pictures/PunchStock, © Ryan McVay/Getty Images; 39: © Gretel Daugherty/Getty Images; 40: © Bettmann/CORBIS; 41 (left): © Alan Schein/Alamyl 41 (right): AP Photo/David J. Phillip; 42 (left): © Royalty-Free/CORBIS; 42 (middle): © Dave LaBelle/The Image Works; 42 (right): © Rhoda Sidney/PhotoEdit; 43: © altrendo images/Getty Images; 45 (top): © Bettmann /CORBIS; 45 (bottom): © Scott Wintrow/Getty Images; 46 (top left): © Rick Friedman/

CORBIS; 46 (top middle): © Michael Newman/PhotoEdit; 46 (top right): © Maya Barnes Johansen/The Image Works; 46 (middle top left): © David J. Green/Alamy; 46 (middle top right): © Catherine Karnow/CORBIS; 46 (middle bottom): © Yuriko Nakao/Reuters /CORBIS; 46 (bottom): © age fotostock/SuperStock; 47: © Blend Images/Jupiter Images; 48 (left): © Corbis RF/Jupiter Images; 48 (right): © Photononstop/photolibrary; 49 (top left): © Marty Heitner/The Image Works; 49 (bottom right): © Briljans Image/ Jupiter Images; 50 (top): © Lee Jae-Won/Reuters/CORBIS; 50 (bottom): © Virgo Productions/zefa/CORBIS; 51 (top): © Eileen Bach/Getty Images; 51 (bottom, from left to right): © Masterfile Royalty Free, © Jessica Rinaldi/Reuters/CORBIS, © Werner Forman/Topham/The Image Works, © Retrofile RF/Getty Images; 52: © Kayte M. Deioma/PhotoEdit; 53: AP Photo/Rick Bowmer; 54 (top left): © Burazin/Masterfile; 54 (top middle): © Purestock/photolibrary; 54 (top right): © David H. Wells/CORBIS; 54 (bottom left): © Robert Holmes/CORBIS; 54 (bottom middle): © PhotoDisc/ photolibrary; 54 (bottom right): © Lew Lause/SuperStock; 55 (top): © Masterfile Royalty Free; 55 (bottom): © Brand X Pictures/SuperStock; 56: Brand X Pictures/Jupiter Images; 58: © Thinkstock/CORBIS; 60: © Nicholas Prior/ Getty Images; 62 (left): © Coneyl Jay/CORBIS; 62 (middle): © Image Source/CORBIS; 62 (right): © Dan Lim/Masterfile; 63: © Mary Kate Denny/PhotoEdit; 65: Jeff Greenberg/PhotoEdit; 66: © Beawiharta/Reuters/CORBIS; 67: © Blaine Harrington III/CORBIS; 68: © Royalty-Free/CORBIS; 69: © Bettmann/CORBIS; 70 (from left to right): © Ken Fisher/Getty Images, © Stanley Chou/Getty Images, © Kelly-Mooney Photography/CORBIS, © David Harry Stewart/Getty Images; 71: © Bruce Laurance/Getty Images; 72: © Images.com/CORBIS; 73 (top): © Tony Avelar/Animals Animals Earth Scenes; 73 (bottom): © Stockbyte/Getty Images; 74: © Rainer Holz/zefa/CORBIS; 75: © Paul Hawthorne/Getty Images; 76: © Eastcott-Momatiuk/The Image Works; 77: © Eric McNatt/Getty Images; 78 (left): © Journal-Courier/Steve Warmowski/The Image Works; 78 (right): © Grant Taylor/Getty Images; 79: © Simon Marcus/CORBIS; 80: © Dibyangshu Sarkar/AFP/Getty Images; 81: © Digital Vision/PunchStock; 82: © Matilda Hartman/zefa/CORBIS; 83: © Royalty-Free/CORBIS; 84: © Ed Freeman/Getty Images; 85 (top): © Barbara Penoyar/Getty Images; 85 (bottom): © Daniel Morovan; 86 (both): courtesy of American Assistance for Cambodia; 88: © Ron Krisel/Getty Images; 89: